SEEDS OF NONVIOLENCE

John Dear, S.J.

FORTKAMP PUBLISHING COMPANY
BALTIMORE, MARYLAND

ISBN: 1-879175-11-8

LCCN: 92-071043

Cover artwork, "the Sower," by Susan MacMurdy.

Author photo by Jay Solmonson, Tri-Valley News Photos, Hayward, California.

Laser typography by Elizabeth McHale, Williamsburg, Massachusetts.

FORTKAMP PUBLISHING COMPANY
202 Edgevale Road
Baltimore, Maryland 21210
1-800-43-PEACE
1-800-437-3223

Also by John Dear, S.J.

Disarming the Heart: Toward a Vow of Nonviolence

*Our God Is Nonviolent: Witnesses in the Struggle for Peace and
    Justice*

Jean Donovan: The Call to Discipleship

Oscar Romero and the Nonviolent Struggle for Justice

*Christ Is with the Poor: Stories and Sayings of Horace
    McKenna, S.J. (Co-editor with Joe Hines)*

*Words of Peace: Selected Writings of Daniel Berrigan, S.J.
    (Editor)*

*It's a Sin to Build a Nuclear Weapon: The Collected Works on
    War and Christian Peacemaking of Richard McSorley, S.J.
    (Editor)*

We are constantly being astonished these days at the amazing discoveries in the field of violence. But I maintain that far more undreamt of and seemingly impossible discoveries will be made in the field of nonviolence.

—*Mohandas Gandhi*

CONTENTS

FOREWORD

Bishop Thomas Gumbleton
Detroit, Michigan

One of the difficulties of trying to be a peacemaker is maintaining a balance between the struggle against structured social injustice and the need to be always "on call" for the poor who are all around us. It is so easy to be "involved" with major social issues, to do all the advocacy work that is so *important*—lobbying the Congress, mobilizing big peace rallies, organizing carefully planned acts of resistance and civil disobedience—all of the things that someone who keeps a diary about peacemaking will obviously be doing.

The special thing about John Dear is that he "acts for justice and participates in the transformation of the world" from within the shared experience of the poor and oppressed. This diary and journal of reflections was born in Washington, D.C., where John has lived and worked with the poor in their struggle for justice. For those who have never sensed or entered into the "third world" that is present a few blocks from the Capitol building of the world's richest and most militarily powerful nation, this sensitively written diary and collection of reflections will provide an experience of our nation's slums which will not easily be forgotten.

Amazingly, John is able to mix these two ways of life into one and come up on his feet. He shows how it is possible to walk boldly into the Pentagon—sometimes by invitation from the Secretary of the Army—sometimes uninvited and even resisted by the "powers that be"—and confront this power with the truth of Jesus who rejected violence, who taught us how to die, not how to kill. As important as these efforts are in trying to "act for justice," John also spends himself in long hours of responding to the immediate needs of the poor. There is no schedule for this work. The poor don't plan when they will run out of food or milk or when violence will occur and when someone needs to be rushed to the hospital. Running a shelter for the homeless, doing the referrals for welfare applicants, driving someone for a job interview, parenting a five-year-old over a period of days in an emergency, organizing a party in the heat of a Washington summer for inner-city kids—all of these things take long hours. The temptation for the activist is to leave those things to others so that one can do the really important things that will change the structures that force people to be poor.

John resists the temptation. He does both. And he jots down his reactions and reflections along the way. We come to know through him some of the extraordinary people from the streets who come to the neighborhood church where John is called to serve. We also begin to feel his frustrations and anger at the oppression that is destroying so many lives. We also reflect and pray with John in his conversations with God about all that is happening around him. It's not hard to join in these prayerful reflections with him.

But clearly prayer and direct service are no escape from action for justice. John's journal records the many times he has confronted the evil system: whether it is the race to nuclear annihilation or imperialist intervention in Central America and the Philippines or the corruption in local housing programs for the poor that cheat them of a chance for decent shelter or on death row. The collection concludes with his theological and scriptural reflections written while attending theology school in Oakland, California, and a final testimony of his Christian response to the US war in the Persian Gulf. The underlying theme throughout is the Gospel call to nonviolence.

The whole list of issues is John's. He lives out the opening words of the document on "The Church in the Modern World" from the Second Vatican Council of the 1960s:

> The joys and the hopes, the griefs and the anxieties of people everywhere, especially the poor and the oppressed, these are the joys and the hopes, the griefs and the anxieties of the Church.

Anyone who reads this journal collection of experiences, shares in these reflections, and joins in the prayers John writes down from his own ever deeper union with God, will begin to value every person—especially the poorest—as a uniquely beautiful and sacred image of God. This will be perhaps the greatest blessing of entering into John's intimate thoughts and reflections. But there will also be no escape from the call to "act for justice."

Bishop Thomas Gumbleton

INTRODUCTION

When I professed a vow of nonviolence years ago with a small group of friends on a hillside in rural Pennsylvania, I had no idea what the consequences would be. Sure, there would be various works and projects, but I did not know that the life of biblical peacemaking could be such an adventure or such a joy. More important, I could never have imagined how the power of nonviolence could spiritually explode in the depths of my own heart with such immediate and real ramifications. I am still just beginning to imagine, much less realize, the possibilities of nonviolence.

With much study, prayer, and conversation with others, I prepared for two years before professing the vow. I remember reading Gandhi's *Autobiography* for the first time, the writings of Dr. King, the newspaper columns of Dorothy Day. I remember my first participation in a demonstration at the Pentagon, my first arrest for nonviolent civil disobedience, my first foray into public speaking as a way to speak out against the nuclear arms race and on behalf of faith and nonviolence.

I remember praying, in effect, the request of James and John and their mother, to Jesus (Mt. 20:23): "Christ, I want to follow you in your nonviolent love, even to prison, even to death. I want to follow you into your reign of nonviolence, the risen life of peace."

The answer I heard was familiar: "You do not know what you are asking.... Can you drink of the cup I am to drink of? The cup of nonviolent suffering love? Can you be a servant for all, a ransom for the many, a sign to the nations?"

When I professed my vow of nonviolence, I was trying to say, "I can. I will!"

I did not know what I was asking. I still do not, but perhaps I am beginning to trust more in our nonviolent God to transform me and our world. I still choose to walk the Way of nonviolence.

These years have taken me across the country to keep vigil and to protest and speak out at places of violence. They have taken me to El Salvador, Guatemala, Nicaragua, and the Philippines to live and work with the victims of US-sponsored violence and injustice. They have taken me onto the streets of New York City and Washington, D.C., San Francisco and Los Angeles, into the world of the homeless, the poor, the addicted. They have taken me to death row to visit friends and into various jail cells after arrests for demonstrations against the nuclear arms race, on behalf of the homeless, on behalf of the Central American and Filipino peoples, indeed, all the suffering, oppressed peoples of the world.

Since I professed my vow of nonviolence, life has been one miracle after another.

Along the way, as I ponder and pray over the vow and the meaning of nonviolence, I find myself on the verge of deeper and deeper levels of nonviolence. I have discovered in practice that nonviolence is not something that is ever fully attained; rather it is a way of life which one struggles to live for the rest of one's life.

Sometimes in sinful pride, I think, "Look at me: I'm nonviolent," and then, I do something, say something, don't do something, or don't say something that invariably brings pain to others. My brother David jokes that I go around saying, "Be nonviolent or I'll beat you up." I am ashamed to admit that, unfortunately, there is more truth in his statement than I know. I am a sinner; a participant in the original sin of systemic violence; a violent person; a victim of the culture of violence and a victimizer who would be, to paraphrase Camus, "neither victim nor victimizer." I fail constantly at nonviolence, as my family and friends will attest. I break my vow day after day, only to begin humbly again at the beginning, asking God to give me the Spirit and the strength to live out the Gospel call to nonviolence. I pray to move beyond my own violence to one day realize the full, human potential of nonviolence—in my own heart and life—just as that potential is open and available to every human being in history. I would someday be transformed by the Spirit of nonviolence so that I can be an instrument of that transforming Spirit of nonviolence in our world. I would, by the grace of God, be a saint—in other words, a complete human being.

But I still do not know what I am asking.

I feel I have not even begun to enter into the depths of nonviolence, to put nonviolence into practice for peace in the world and for justice for the poor. I have only begun to resist death and abolish war and the causes of war in my own heart and on the planet. I know I have yet to plumb the depths of this great life of love and peacemaking to which we are all called.

And yet, I know too that my struggle to be faithful has been a blessing, every step of the way; my vow of nonviolence has opened up a new world to me: new friends, new life, new possibilities, new peace.

Jesus' response to James and John is a response I hear addressed to myself: "You will drink the cup of nonviolent, suffering love." Nonviolence is possible.

These days, I find myself with an even greater desire to be faithful to Jesus' Way of life: loving enemies, practicing nonviolence, accompanying the poor and the oppressed peoples of the earth, praying, being compassionate, resisting the powers of death, entering into suffering for the sake of justice, creating community with friends as a sign of the beloved community in our midst. I long more than ever to see God face to face; to set my heart, disarmed at last, in God; to do God's will; to act within God's reign of nonviolence for justice and peace; to risk my life in the nonviolent struggle for all humanity.

Indeed, my prayer is always the same, "Jesus, my disarmed God, the Image of nonviolence, make me an instrument of Your peace."

The notes that follow are reflections that I set down in the late night hours of my journey in Gospel peacemaking. They are not meant to be definitive truths, nor pious platitudes; simply, thoughts of wonder about the wisdom of nonviolence from a seeker of truth. They are a mixture of diary writings from my work with the homeless poor; reflections on my acts of nonviolent civil disobedience for peace and other experiments in nonviolence; prayers from my heart; accounts of my travels into Central America, the Philippines, and death row, and the realities I learned in such places; essays that ponder the theological and biblical roots of nonviolence; a closing journal of peacemaking kept during the Persian Gulf War. They begin in Washington, D.C., where I lived in a small Jesuit community and worked among the homeless, and conclude in Oakland, California, where I attended the Graduate Theological Union in Berkeley as part of my Jesuit training. There I became actively involved in the campaign to stop US military aid to El Salvador after the brutal killing of my six Jesuit brothers, their cook and her daughter on November 16, 1989. I was also active in the movement to oppose the US war with Iraq. The Spirit of nonviolence led me on a coast-to-coast journey and continues to lead me, like the movement of the sections of this book, from the witness of nonviolence to prayer and the practice of nonviolence—finally, I hope, into the Wisdom, the Christ, of nonviolence.

These writings are offered in a spirit of peace as a sharing of the peace that has been granted this pilgrim over the years. May they be seeds of nonviolence.

John Dear, S.J.

Part One:
The Road to Nonviolence

I choose to identify with the underprivileged. I choose to identify with the poor. I choose to give my life for the hungry. I choose to give my life for those who have been left out of the sunlight of opportunity. I choose to live for and with those who find themselves seeing life as a long and desolate corridor with no exit sign. This is the way I'm going. If it means suffering a little bit, I'm going that way. If it means sacrificing, I'm going that way. If it means dying for them, I'm going that way, because I heard a voice saying, "Do something for others."

Martin Luther King, Jr.

If the church does not care for the poor, they will be neglected. That is the test of our faithfulness to Christ: how we relate to the poor.

Horace McKenna, S.J.

Christ came to make the rich poor and the poor holy.

Eric Gill

1.
Walking the Streets of Violence
with the Homeless:
A Washington, D.C., Journal

*Summer, 1988**

Throughout the late 1960s and 1970s and into the 1980s, I lived with my family in one of the wealthiest suburbs in the United States, in the Bethesda-Potomac area of Maryland, just outside of Washington, D.C. Everything was perfect: each house had a driveway, a mail box, a finely manicured front lawn, and a few expensive cars. Our neighbors were numbered among the rich and famous. It was the elite world of white, upper-class "America."

Now, after years of searching and traveling and journeying, after years of training and prayer and study and work, I have returned to Washington. But this time I live across town in a devastated, African-American neighborhood, working among the homeless and the poor. I have come to the other side of Washington, and I am just a few blocks from the US Capitol. The most powerful places on earth—some would say the most lethal—are within walking distance; yet they are situated among some of the poorest people in the country, perhaps the world. The neighborhood is not at all tidy; it is a

---

* These sections in Part I are all from 1988–1989, as the subheads indicate, but are not in chronological order.

mess. The streets are dirty. Violence, crime, drug deals, evictions, sirens, police, ambulances—these are the sights and sounds of the neighborhood. The city is setting a murder record; these are "killing streets." Most of the families in my neighborhood are broken or shattered, the children passed from one relative to the next. And everywhere one goes, the ever-present homeless, holding out a hand, ask for some change, looking as though they have been through a war, as indeed they have: the war of the streets.

Today marked my first day of work at the Horace McKenna Center, a drop-in center and shelter for the homeless in the basement of an old Jesuit church, St. Aloysius Gonzaga Church, located on North Capitol Street. The church is nearly 150 years old; it was used as a hospital during the Civil War. Today, still within sight of the US Capitol, the people of the parish, who are poor themselves, minister to the homeless. Upon arrival, I was told the brutal fact: 15,000 people live on the streets of Washington. Perhaps as many as three million people are homeless nationwide. Congress estimates that there may be nearly 20 million people homeless by the year 2000. The situation is bad, but brace yourself: it's going to get worse.

The drop-in center is quite simple: a few rooms, some pictures of Christ among the poor, a wall of book-lined shelves, free coffee, some literature about available services, a clothing room, some file cabinets, and a storage area filled with canned goods for distribution. It is named after Horace McKenna, a man not widely known, but revered locally as a saint. Horace is one of Washington, D.C.'s most famous heroes. A Jesuit priest who died at age 83 in 1982, Horace dedicated his life to serving the poor. After working in southern Maryland throughout the 1930s and 1940s, trying to integrate the churches and serve the African-Americans of the region, he moved to

St. Aloysius' Church, where he remained, on and off, for the rest of his life.

In the 1960s, Horace began helping Washington's homeless poor. Soon, long lines of poor people streamed out the church, on a daily basis. He befriended everyone he met, served everyone who asked for his help, and never turned anyone away. He was convinced that Christ was truly present among the poor, and so he went out of his way to meet Christ there, to greet the human Christ.

I never met Horace McKenna, but I grew up in Washington, D.C., hearing about his good works and I attended his funeral, which I will never forget. He died in May 1982, a few months before I entered the Jesuit order. I was deeply impressed by the many people who flocked to bid him farewell—rich and poor, black and white, young and old, women and men. "We are bound together in our love and affection for Father Horace," the preacher observed that day. "We are one today because of him. In his own person, he had broken down all lines, barriers, and distinctions between us. He is our reconciler, mediator, and peacemaker. He is the door through whom we pass to friendship with one another." Dramatic words of praise. Everyone nodded in agreement. I remember thinking, Could such a person truly have walked these streets, in such an age, in such a city? By all accounts, the answer was yes.

Horace founded a variety of services for Washington's poor: S.O.M.E. (So Others Might Eat, a soup kitchen, clinic, housing and job program), Sursum Corda (a housing project located near the US Capitol; the Latin name means "Lift Up Your Hearts"), and Martha's Table (a soup kitchen and center for homeless women). He marched in anti-war and civil rights demonstrations; he was silenced for his opposition to *Humanae Vitae,* the papal encyclical denouncing birth control; and he always spoke out on behalf of the poor and homeless.

"You can't talk to a person about his or her soul if that person has no food," he would tell people. "The greatest undeveloped resource of our nation and of our world is the poor. If the church does not care for the poor, they will be neglected. This is the test of our faithfulness to Christ: how we relate to the poor."

He was quoted toward the end of his life as saying, "When God lets me into heaven, I think I'll ask to go off in a corner somewhere for half an hour and sit down and cry because the strain is off, the work is done, and I haven't been unfaithful or disloyal. All these needs that I have known are in the hands of Providence and I won't have to worry any longer who's at the door, whose breadbox is empty, whose baby is sick, whose house is shaken and discouraged, and whose children can't read."

From all accounts, he remained faithful—faithful to the Gospel, faithful to the poor, faithful to God. He loved others, reconciled blacks and whites, made peace wherever he went, and followed Jesus. He saw Christ present in the homeless and the poor. Indeed, he saw every human being as his very own sister or brother, a child of God. His life, from what I have learned, is a testament of service and commitment, of love and peacemaking, of speaking the truth and working for justice. He served the poor, said his prayers, laughed with his friends, and died with a deep belief in God.

The drop-in center and shelter in the basement of the church seeks to carry on his prophetic, holy work of service and justice for the poor, and does so in Horace's name, in Jesus' name. He may not be listed in the history books with Francis of Assisi, Dorothy Day, or Martin Luther King, Jr., but he surely lived as they did, walking in the spirit of Jesus. For the parishioners and the homeless who knew him, he was a friend who could be counted on in time of need. I can think of no better way to be remembered.

Certainly, the McKenna Center has its work cut out for it, but it is simple work: the work of charity and the work of justice, the work of loving the poor, which Horace did so well.

I spent today working with my friend Lisa Goode, a young woman who grew up in Sursum Corda, the nearby housing project, who was educated through the support of the parish, went on to college, and now has returned to work among the poor of her neighborhood. She knows the needs of the people, and brings to the work a deep compassion and spirit of fun. She is good news for the poor. I learn much from her. Brother Tom Williams, the director, has spent many years serving the poor in a refugee camp in Thailand. He brings a dedication to improving their lives, and a spirit of humility and down-to-earth, no-nonsense truth-telling that should push us all in the right direction.

Lisa and I drove out to the Food Bank, a community project which sells mass quantities of food at reduced prices. The food we bought will be sorted out and given in shopping bags to women with children who face eviction, who come to us each month by the score for assistance. Later, we drove around the corner to the nearby projects and distributed several boxes of bread that had been donated to us.

My first week at the Horace McKenna Center and I'm exhausted. Giving out food and clothing, answering the phone, attending meetings, hanging out with the homeless, picking up and delivering donated furniture, visiting with the elderly shut-ins—the list goes on. My job description, as presented to me, sounds like the workload of ten people. It includes: befriending the homeless, getting to know them personally, assisting them as possible; coordinating the night shelter for elderly homeless men and trying to find a home for each of them by the end of the year; giving out food, clothing, tokens; interviewing people for rental assistance; putting out a newsletter; attending advocacy meetings; assisting the pastor; leading a Bible-study group and the R.C.I.A. program (the "Rite of Christian Initiation," for adults interested in becoming Catholic Christians); tutoring various parishioners; and most important, working, somehow, to end homelessness and to get the government to provide decent, adequate, affordable housing for all.

As part of my Jesuit assignment here in D.C., I've also been doing some work at one of the Catholic Worker houses, helping out the coordinator of the house, Michael Kirwin, by answering mail, paying bills, and organizing the office, and so forth. Michael is something of a legend in this town. The story goes that as a graduate student at one of the universities, he began taking groups of homeless people into his dormitory. When the university officials found out about this, they were appalled. Michael could stay, but the others had to leave, he was told. So he left, and started a Catholic Worker house. He has been at the hard work of the Gospel for some fourteen years now. Besides offering hospitality, he goes out to the heating grates of the city streets every evening, and gives out soup and bread to the homeless. He lives a strict, voluntary poverty; any extra food is given away immediately. He never has enough money in the bank to pay all the bills. He has gone beyond poverty to what Dorothy Day advocated and lived—"precarity." Many come hoping to join him in his work, but find him too much. Recently, Michael took a very serious fall down a staircase and injured his back and legs severely. I'm here to help a bit while he is supposed to be resting. But Michael does not seem very concerned about himself; he's more interested in the house guests.

Lisa and I visited an 80-year-old woman who lives alone in an old apartment ten blocks from the US Capitol. She has no food, no gas, no electricity. Such terrible poverty! We paid her bills and bought her food. Meanwhile, one of the men I helped last week on clothing day was shot and killed yesterday in a drug deal. With the 100-degree heat, and the violence of the streets now a regular event, the city seems ready to blow up.

Today was the funeral of Matthias Tucker, an 82-year-old homeless man, who died last week in the hospital. He had been homeless since the mid-'70s and was a familiar face around the McKenna Center and a good friend of Father Horace McKenna. He used to wander away from Christ House, a hospice for sick, homeless people, and show up at the McKenna Center. At the funeral, I read from the Book of Wisdom:

> The souls of the just are in the hands of God, and no torment shall touch them. They seemed, in the view of the foolish, to be dead; and their passing away was thought an affliction and their going forth from us, utter destruction. But they are in peace. For if before people, indeed, they be punished, yet is their hope full of immortality; chastised a little, they shall be greatly blessed, because God tried them and found them worthy of God's self. As gold in the furnace, God proved them, and as sacrificial offerings, God took them to God's self. In the time of their visitation, they shall shine, and shall dart about as sparks through stubble. They shall judge na-

tions and rule over people and God shall be their God forever. Those who trust in God shall understand truth and the
faithful shall abide with God in love because grace and
mercy are with God's holy ones and God's care is with
God's elect. (Wisdom 3:1-9)

This passage speaks of Matthias Tucker. He had nothing: no
friends, no family, no money, no home. His funeral was attended by
five people, all shelter providers, and led by Fr. George Anderson,
S.J., the pastor of St. Aloysius' Church. At the end, Brother Tom
Williams, S.J., director of the McKenna Center, who was busy
attending to other homeless folks, asked me to ride in the hearse to
the graveyard to bury Matthias and to say some prayers for him. And
so I went with the undertaker, a man named Mr. Woodfork, to a
cemetery for the poor on the outskirts of D.C. I said some prayers at
the grave and gave Matthias to Christ. Then, I left, overwhelmed by
the reality of death among the poor, and the spiritual experience of
"commissioning" his body, this soul, this just, afflicted person—to
God. I truly believe this man who had suffered so much, like the
Lazarus of the Gospel parable, is now in paradise.

Work at the McKenna Center continues as usual. Today, I've
been sorting out the clothing room, and giving away pants, shoes,
shirts, and coats to the homeless, as well as "food baskets," grocery
bags filled with items like canned goods, cereals, spaghetti and iced-
tea mix. Today a poor, homeless woman came by with her two
children. Left to sleep in a school gymnasium converted into an
overnight shelter for families, she contracted pneumonia; then she
fled to a friend's house, even though he was a violent drug user. The
kids suffered throughout this whole episode. She came by today to

say she wants to leave, but there is no place for her to go. The shelters will not take her back because she had gone to her friend's house. "Could we help her?" Besides giving her some food, there was little we could do.

I picked up 2000 rolls and loaves of bread and Lisa and I then distributed them at Sursum Corda, the public housing complex nearby. We stood on one corner with our boxes of bread and gave away the food to women and children who lined up to receive it. Across the street, ten feet away from us, on the opposite corner, a group of young men and boys were buying and selling drugs. The whole scene summed up our world of inner-city poverty. A few days earlier, when I had driven through Sursum Corda, I was stunned to find policemen and narcotics officers standing at certain corners, holding machine guns or rifles in the air. A raid was in progress. In a flash, my mind returned to my visits to El Salvador. In a way, there is little difference between the war-torn realities of rural, Salvadoran villages and inner-city neighborhoods in the US. Both suffer from systemic violence, guns, poverty, hunger, and persecution.

I was deeply touched last week when I spoke with a young, homeless couple who had been sleeping on the grounds of the National Archives building. I gave the woman a carrying bag which someone had donated to us. As they sorted out their things, the man came across a dozen or more handkerchiefs in her shopping bag and asked why she carried them. "When you cry all the time, you need them," she replied quietly.

Being homeless would cause anyone to cry. The majority of these people have been suffering all their lives in poverty. Since 1981, the Reagan/Bush Administrations have cut the housing budget

77 percent—$25 billion a year. At the start of Reagan's first term, the US spent $7 on defense for every $1 spent on housing. Today, the ratio is $44 to $1. Millions of North Americans are threatened with eviction and becoming homeless, and almost everyone else opposes homelessness; but little is being done to stem the tide. Most of the money that should be going for housing for the poor, now goes to build more bombs and nuclear weapons. Horace McKenna would be appalled at this mad military spending and would surely be working hard to reverse the situation. He would want us to take up where he left off: to stand in solidarity with the poor and the homeless and the enemies of our nation; to demand money for adequate housing and food for the poor; and to work for the creation of a nonviolent, just society.

Every day, homeless people seek our help. "Do you know of any jobs, John? Do you know where I can get a place to stay? Do you have a blanket I could have? Do you have an extra coat? Do you have any work boots?" When I hear that request, I think of Horace McKenna, who used to say: "The poor can't pull themselves up by their boot straps because they have no boots!"

We are nearly overwhelmed with requests, and we are rarely able to help people find adequate housing or employment. Our days are spent talking with people who are homeless or who may soon become homeless. Often, we just listen to their stories and try to offer a word of compassion.

Many people can not afford housing—it's as simple as that. And the system does not care what happens to them. As the poor struggle to pay their bills, sooner or later they run out of money, and face eviction. We hear these stories every day. One woman named Mary, the mother of a little child, came to me after she had been given a summons threatening her with eviction. Her income averaged about $260 per month and her rent was $210 per month. Earlier in the year, she had been diagnosed with cancer and was undergoing severe chemotherapy treatments. Someone had given her an air conditioner to help her get through the 100-degree summer heat, but this led to a very high electric bill. She decided to pay part of it, and so did not pay all of her rent. Within a short time, she was far behind in her rent payments. The McKenna Center was able to pay the difference and she was not evicted; but she was one of the few we were able to help. We only have $2000 per month available for rental assistance, yet scores of single mothers who face eviction come to us from all over the city for help. The city averages over fifty evictions a day, and hires the homeless to do the evicting, paying them $10-$20 per eviction. Homeless people are recruited to make other people homeless. Meanwhile, business is booming across town at the Pentagon.

The reality of life on the streets comes down to one cold fact: homelessness kills people. Homelessness, like all poverty, is a matter of life and death, a form of low-intensity warfare. It is a spiritual matter. Housing the homeless is a matter of saving people from "an early and unjust death," as Jon Sobrino defines poverty in Latin America. Lately, George Anderson and I have been visiting David, a young homeless man who has no family and who is dying of both AIDS and cancer. One of the local hospitals was going to discharge him back to the streets, leaving him to die in the street. We were able to get him into Gift of Peace, a hospice for those dying of AIDS. He has been totally abandoned by friends, family, and society. His suffering is heart-breaking. Why was that hospital willing to put him back out on the streets? Why does our society allow the poor to die on its streets? Why do we look the other way?

In the short time that I've been working at this Jesuit center for the homeless, it has become easy to see God in our presence. Christ comes to us daily: homeless, broke, without any friends, evicted, wanted, an alcoholic or drug addict, unemployed, an illegal refugee, an AIDS victim, a mother with nine children and no food, a victim of violence. It is in these poor that Christ comes to us, within the shadow of the US Capitol. In these people, I see the effects of nuclear bombs already detonated. I see every day in the homeless what the future will be like for us all, unless we begin serious nuclear disarmament now. I recall Pope Paul VI's words: the arms race kills the poor. Since society spends most of its money on weapons of death, there is little, if any, for food and shelter.

Recently, I met with Mitch Snyder, the advocate for the homeless and member of the Community for Creative Nonviolence, to hear about his work with the homeless and to discuss my work at the McKenna Center. He gave me a full tour of the new shelter at Second and D Streets, Northwest, the fruit of his long fasts and demonstrations, the fruit of a dedicated community. Over 1200 people stay there, receive meals and medical care, and participate in many programs. He told me how important it was to simply sit and listen to the homeless, to offer them a place where they could go and talk with someone, which is precisely what the McKenna Center is supposed to do. In a few days, he and ten others will begin a 48-day fast to call for more money for housing and an end to homelessness. The fasters will sit on the steps of the US Capitol every day throughout the fast. God willing, they will break their fast on election day, November 8, 1988. Since I have Mondays off, I will try to spend a few hours every Monday this fall keeping vigil with the fasters.

One wall in the main office of the Community for Creative Non-violence living quarters is covered with shelves filled with glass boxes containing the ashes of those homeless people who have frozen to death over the years. No wonder Mitch is filled with such outrage and righteous indignation over the government's insensitivity toward the homeless. His vocation is to remind us all about the sufferings of the homeless. He remembers their sufferings and deaths because he looks at their ashes every day.*

Last week, an elderly woman walked into the church asking for food and assistance. It turns out that she has been homeless for nine years, that she gets some kind of government check in New York City, and that she has been riding buses around the country for all those years. She lives on buses. She has stayed in nearly every women's shelter in every major city in the country. I took her to Michael Kirwin's for dinner and then over to a church shelter for women. We sat in the car for over an hour, waiting to get into the shelter. We talked about her life, her travels and travails. The next morning when I went to see her, she had disappeared.

Last week Lisa and I helped organize a demonstration of elderly, public-housing tenants who live in a nearby high-rise apartment building that is falling apart from lack of maintenance. The apartment complex is located across the street from the brand new Department of Public Housing building, built last summer at a cost of several million dollars. On a Wednesday afternoon, we had planned to walk with our group of rag-tag demonstrators, some in wheelchairs, some with canes, across the street carrying our signs, and singing our

---

* Mitch Snyder died on July 3, 1990.

songs, to protest the conditions in the 20-year-old apartment building. Poor elevators, flooding, cracked floors, no garbage pickup, drug-dealing everywhere, no security personnel—such problems of neglect are typical of housing projects across the country; but it is, of course, particularly outrageous here in Washington, D.C., right across the street from the new, bright, shining public housing headquarters, five blocks from the US Capitol.

I was very excited about the whole venture: mobilizing the elderly poor to take on the D.C. Department of Housing. What a feat! Surely, our voice would be heard. We were David facing Goliath. But minutes before our protest began, the workers of the public housing headquarters poured out onto the street. Then, Alphonsus Jackson, the man in charge of public housing for the city, announced to us that a bomb threat had been called in, and implied that we were the ones who had made the threat! Everyone immediately suspected that he himself had called it in to discredit our demonstration and take away the sting of bad publicity that he would receive from the press coverage of poor, elderly D.C. residents suffering across the street from his swanky office.

We marched and sang anyway; we held our signs and spoke to reporters. I feel sure that somehow the problems will be addressed and improvements made. More important, our elderly friends felt empowered, even joyful! I will never forget their enthusiasm and collective determination. Together, they proved they could speak up; they could get the attention of the city. They discovered the power of public protest to get demands met. Surely, they will have to move mountains to get justice for themselves, but with their faith and determination, I'm beginning to think that the mountain of corruption which is public housing in our city and in our nation, may in fact, one day, be moved.

These days, I'm trying to focus on three intertwining tasks: 1) the works of mercy through my work at the McKenna Center and at St. Aloysius' Church among the poor: to feed the hungry, to give drink to the thirsty, to clothe the naked, to ransom the captive, to harbor the harborless, to visit the sick, and to bury the dead; 2) the works of justice: keeping vigil for peace and against injustice and war, passing out leaflets at the Pentagon and other places of government authority, and occasionally risking arrest in acts of nonviolent civil disobedience in order to resist the nuclear arms race and systemic injustice; and 3) what we might call the works of truth-telling, speaking on the issues of justice and peace, writing articles, newsletters and, once in a while, a book, recalling folks to the essence of the Gospel of Jesus Christ.

On Tuesday evening, I went over to one of the Catholic Worker houses for dinner with friends. Dinner was followed by a simple prayer service to renew my vow of nonviolence. It was a quiet evening; we took turns confessing our sins and failings, and admitted that we haven't even come close to the ideal of Gospel nonviolence. Finally, we renewed the vow in an effort to say to ourselves that, though we are sinners, we would be Christians, nonviolent followers of Jesus, peacemakers in the world. For me, it was a moment of surrendering my soul to Christ once again, giving my life to God and to God's nonviolent transformation of my heart and the world. I was so moved by my friends' humble testimony. It was an evening of grace in which everything came together, and once again I returned to my center—the nonviolent Christ—with a promise of love, a pledge of fidelity, a commitment to the truth of peace, even in the midst of my sinfulness and infidelity. Afterwards, we spent some time discussing how hard it is to be a Christian—particularly in this North American culture. An evening of peace, consolation, fellowship.

The work is non-stop: giving out food baskets, bus tokens, and clothing; moving furniture for people who have been evicted; talking with the homeless. Yesterday, I spent the afternoon with Mary, an elderly woman who lives across the street from my community. She is struggling to raise thirteen kids, all under the age of sixteen, and in the midst of this, she is being kicked out of her house. They are being forced out of their house due to encroaching gentrification. Fortunately, she will be eligible for some government benefits under T.A.P., the city's Tenant Assistance Program. And she's going to need them. Finding affordable housing for fourteen folks on a salary of nothing will be next to impossible.

One afternoon during the summer, I helped move some donated beds, chairs and couches into a small row house for the mother of some five kids. The other day she showed up at the Center crying, beside herself. While the younger ones were at school and she was out, her eldest son, a crack addict, stole all her furniture: the couches, chairs, pots and pans—everything was cleared out! She put her head on my shoulder and said this was the worst thing that could happen to any parent. "I want to kill myself," she said quietly. I tried to calm her down, to offer some words of hope, and with Lisa's direction, help get some new furniture. What a sad tale! What suffering for this poor woman! Her son, a victim of the drug culture, has torn apart his family's life. And yet, I hope she will be able to pick up the pieces and start again the struggle to survive. This is what life is all about for the poor of the world: a daily struggle to survive.

With the presidential election around the corner, the condition of
the fasters is worsening. Carol Fennelly is very ill but Mitch Snyder
appears to be holding up fine. On November 1, back at the McKenna
Center, we answered some 300 phone calls for the great Thanksgiving turkey-dinner giveaway. Some 200 poor families will receive full
turkey dinners, spices and all, thanks to Lisa Goode, Tom, Joyce,
Julie and all the volunteers. In between, I helped pay the rent for a
woman named Gertrude who faced imminent eviction. This is not
even a kind of "band-aid relief," and yet, these little acts of charity
will make a concrete difference in the lives of specific people that I
have come to know.

Yesterday, after a long day with homeless men and women, I
spent two hours sitting by the bedside of David Brizzi, the homeless
man dying of AIDS and cancer at the Missionary of Charity's hospice, Gift of Peace. David is virtually a skeleton, in agony, covered
with sores. I have never seen such suffering. He could barely talk. I
read several psalms to him, and some of John's letters from the New
Testament about the unconditional, total love of God. Truly, Jesus'
suffering on the cross is happening once again before my very eyes.
Here, before me, lay Christ-God, present in this brother's agony.
And so many good people, ministering to the dying. Gift of Peace is
a place of love and charity, and yet I know that not all Christians
have come to see those dying with AIDS as their brothers and sisters,
as Christ present among us.

Being with David left me feeling totally helpless and powerless.
All I could do was be there—sitting in a chair right next to his bed,
praying, showing my concern and love. I pray that the God of mercy
will shower him with mercies. David is truly the poor man Lazarus
of Luke's Gospel. May he be rich in the reign of God.

Two weeks ago, the famous election of George Bush. I did not vote. It was a small—even ridiculous—protest of the whole death-dealing, unjust system. I reject it all, in the name of love. I know that sounds awfully pretentious and arrogant and self-righteous, so I don't discuss it with others. But I can no longer buy the argument that one candidate is better than the other. I have slowly come to see reality from the perspective of the homeless poor who sleep and suffer in front of the White House, as well as the poor campesinos who suffer and die under US bombs in El Salvador; they have shown me that the whole system of the US military economy has got to go. I want to be part of this revolution, God's nonviolent transformation of the world; thus I am neither Democrat nor Republican, neither capitalist nor communist nor imperialist, neither conservative nor liberal. I am a citizen of the nonviolent reign of God. All my allegiance belongs to God. To make that citizenship real in my life, I try to practice it in little ways, such as withdrawing my participation from the charade of elections, as if voting once every four years is all I need to do to fulfill my responsibility to suffering humanity.

On the Monday before the election, some 2000 folks marched from an old motel converted into a shelter for homeless families to Capitol Hill. We walked through some of the poorest parts of the city—homeless people, advocates, activists. A good rally with an upbeat spirit, even though we all know the Reagan era of militarism is sure to worsen with the election of the former C.I.A. chief, George Bush.

The best part of election day, November 8, was the party held in honor of Dorothy Day's birthday at the Dorothy Day Catholic Worker House. There was no mention of the election at all, no TV sets blaring results, no politics in the whole house. A celebration in honor of a saint, a prophet, a Christian! Indeed, something very unusual on an election day in Washington. Probably the only household or gathering in the city that was not focused on the election.

In general, my spirits these past three weeks have been very good, I suppose because I am so happy and content working with the homeless, praying and living with such fine people in the Jesuit Community on K Street, actively resisting the injustice around me, and in general living a life much closer to the Gospel which I profess. I cling to my faith in Christ, and as I go about my work, I find I have been granted an unusually deep sense of peace, a feeling about the *rightness* of the direction of my life, though I continue to sin and mess things up here and there.

December has been such a hectic time; indeed, so have all these last few months. It's hard to know where to begin as I try to collect myself and reflect a bit. I've been running around, meeting so many people, doing so many things, trying so hard to be of service, truly losing myself in my work, trying to be a positive influence in the world of the poor, in the world of pain. Many experiences and people have touched me deeply. And of course, though I go to minister to others, I always find myself ministered to by the poor.

David Brizzi, the homeless man with AIDS whom we've been visiting at Gift of Peace, died this past Sunday at 1 a.m. He had been rapidly declining for some time. Since he had no family or friends, we had set up a visitation program in the parish. Every evening, someone went and sat with him for a few hours, up until the night he died.

This morning, we had a funeral Mass for him and I helped carry his coffin outside. The plain pine box was extremely light. His ravaged body was destroyed by the disease; all that was left were his bones. I pray that he is free from pain and sitting at the banquet table of justice with God. Indeed, I imagine that Christ himself must now be waiting on David. May he rest in eternal peace.

On December 1, the D.C. city government closed the Tenant Assistance Program (T.A.P.), the one program working to help the homeless get off the streets into affordable housing. The government would pay two-thirds of a formerly homeless person's rent so that the person would not end up back on the street. Ten thousand people who were waiting to be accepted into the program have now had their hopes dashed. The city claims there is no money left. Mismanagement, corruption, incompetence, lack of concern for the homeless— all these reasons conjoined to kill T.A.P. The evening before the announcement was made, I was in the main T.A.P. office at 5 o'clock with a poor, disabled, elderly woman who was applying for the program, when the director of T.A.P. called me in. "You're a Jesuit, I can tell you," he confided. "We're closing T.A.P. tomorrow." I nearly fell out of the chair. An impromptu demonstration was held the next day. Some 200 advocates and homeless people demonstrated inside the District Building, demanding to see Mayor Barry. We were pushed and shoved aside by cruel D.C. police and threatened with arrest. The spontaneous outburst lasted for hours. Many homeless people who had been promised housing were among the crowd, including several women who wept and wailed aloud. The whole experience was heart-wrenching. Oh, the injustice of this city!

It is now Advent and I'm settling down to a daily rhythm of working with the poor and reflecting and writing on that work in the Advent spirit of hope, patience, peace, and solitude. I had a good experience in the church shelter late on the night of December 2, praying over a passage from Baruch on hope and the call to be God's servant of justice. I was deeply consoled and pondered how God comes to me, how God reveals God's Self to me in the life of the poor. I must be careful in the days ahead not to lose my contemplative side through mindless activism, but always to look for the face of God in the eyes of the poor, to hear God's voice in theirs, indeed, to treat the poor as God.

Without contemplation in the midst of this whirlwind of justice work, I can become demanding, impatient, and even nasty. I know then that I have to take time to readjust and get realigned with the Light of the Gospel. I'm hoping to be used by God, to be *in* God. I pray the prayer of Willis Daniels, from the Gospel choir, "To the God who can make a way out of no way." That's the God I worship. The key point to remember is that this is God's work, that I'm not in charge, God is. Once I remember that I'm not the Savior, perhaps I can more easily walk in the Spirit of Peace—and let the Savior work.

God, help me to be your instrument, to do your will, to serve your people, to glorify you, to proclaim your Good News. Please bless my work, bless your poor, bless all enemies, bless all human beings that we may someday live in a world without war, a world with peace and harmony and love and justice. This is my prayer to You, God, in the name of Jesus. Amen.

The T.A.P. demonstrations have continued regularly. On Wednesday, 400 angry demonstrators disrupted the D.C. City Council hearing, and interrupted the incredible testimony of Alphonsus Jackson, the Director of Housing. It was clear, even to the City Council folks, that Jackson knew nothing about T.A.P., could not account for the millions of dollars that have disappeared, and could not explain why the program was suddenly cut. So much incompetence, and all of it leading to the further suffering of thousands of people. Some 200 advocates stormed the mayor's office. We sat in, and closed off the fifth floor of City Hall. No one was arrested. Great publicity followed the next day, calling attention to the situation. Further demonstrations then followed, including a symbolic eviction on Pennsylvania Avenue, in front of the District Building, in the middle of a snow storm. Seventeen friends were arrested. Meanwhile, Mayor Barry, who is bogged down in allegations of drug use and corruption, says there is no more money for T.A.P., and yet he has the audacity to announce plans to spend millions of dollars to build a new prison. His solution to the housing crisis is to build more prisons. Instead of homes for the homeless, he—and city officials—want new jails for the poor. We will never solve the root problems of our cities so long as we continue to build new jails and ignore the simple requirements of justice—food, housing, medical care. The officials in this city, like the leaders of our nation, are blind to the reality of justice.

Today, a week before Christmas, we gave away 250 turkeys and 100 hams and all the trimmings that go with them. I actually gave the frozen birds and hams away myself, to all the local poor who came to the church. They were so happy, so grateful (although I kidded many who were friends about eating meat, expressing my vegetarian shock; there was much chuckling about that). What an experience! Enacting Dickens' *Christmas Carol*. Pure joy.

Sunday, January 1, 1989

This morning I was off early to open up the drop-in center for the homeless, when all of a sudden it began to snow very large flakes. Beautiful! It covered the dirty streets and buildings and the whole messy area, transforming it into a resplendent winterland.

These continue to be very busy days for me: the work at the shelter never ends. Every bed is filled and I'm getting to know our guests quite well. We're continuing the never-ending work of paying rent for people about to be evicted, and giving out clothing and food. On Christmas Eve I spent several hours down on the Mall under a tent with 1000 homeless children. It was truly one of the most joyful experiences I've had with the homeless. Four hundred volunteers, Redskins football players, clowns, bands, Santas, celebrities, and tons of food and presents all for the kids. I spent the whole time at a table with a mother and her eight children—all homeless but enjoying the food and attention. A marvelous day. Martin Sheen, the actor and peace activist, joined us. Yet I know that today all those children are back in shelters. They should each be in their own homes.

Yesterday, I had a letter to the editor published in the *Washington Post* supporting Mitch Snyder and the Community for Creative Nonviolence activists who tore down the fences at four Metro (subway) stops on Christmas morning. Those fences had been erected to keep the homeless out. I wrote:

Their action was dramatic, but in light of the city's refusal to open new shelters in the midst of such an urgent crisis, it was necessary. It ranks on a scale with the nonviolent civil disobedience of Martin Luther King, Jr. and Gandhi....The city needs to open more shelters and provide affordable housing immediately. Otherwise, human beings will continue to suffer, and some will freeze to death. When the city provides adequate shelter for every person on the street, then perhaps there will be no need to tear down fences. When that day comes, there will not be a need for any fences.

I wrote the letter of support because of the strong negative reaction CCNV received for their protest. So far, no one has objected to my letter.

On the feast of the Holy Innocents, folks came from up and down the East Coast to pray and demonstrate at the Pentagon and the Department of Energy. At the D.O.E., peacemaker Elizabeth McAlister put up signs calling it "The Department of Extinction." We circled the Pentagon, and sang and distributed leaflets, as Pentagon employees entered the building. Some took our leaflets; others walked by in a huff.

Scores of friends have been over to the Sursum Corda housing project repairing an abandoned unit so that Mary and her thirteen kids from across the street could move in there. I spent an afternoon throwing out the trash while others painted, put up new windows, tore out old tile, and generally improved the whole scene. Mary will be evicted in a matter of days. Such is the government's understanding of Christmas.

Meanwhile, the news has come that Alphonsus Jackson, the troubled administrator of the D.C. Department of Public Housing, has resigned to take on the same job in Dallas. Perhaps there will be some relief for us now.

One morning during the holidays, as I walked to work, a friend who is homeless called out my name on the street. He proceeded to tell me that a church around the corner was giving out Christmas gifts. I asked if he was going there and he said, "I don't need any of those things. I've got soap, a razor, shaving cream, and a toothbrush. I need a home."

Yesterday, I was by myself in the McKenna Center. I must have answered fifty phone calls and spoken with fifty homeless people. For instance, a gentleman named Craig, who read about me in the *Post*, came in looking for me. He faces eviction today and has no job. A former drug user and dealer, he said he could easily start selling drugs again and obtain several thousand dollars by morning and not have to worry about eviction, but he really did not want to return to that scene. He felt like committing suicide, he said. He asked me to go ten percent with him; then he'd have the support to go one hundred percent. He had no money, no friends, and much furniture that he did not want to see put out on the streets to be stolen. I set appointments for him to get a job, and an apartment and a place where his belongings could be temporarily stored. He cried, and left.

Such is life for the poor.

For the poor, life is a no-win situation. There is no justice, little support, and often, few reasons to carry on the struggle to survive. I pray that he may survive, that he keeps hope alive.

This evening, I pray, God, that you will continue to be with me and help me to grow in awareness of your constant abiding presence. Send your Spirit of life down on me, take pity on me, and give me strength for the days ahead as I try to walk with your people. Dear God, I love you. I'm very weak and very frail and I'm trying to do so many things for your people, for your reign of justice and peace. I let go of my cares and anxieties; I offer you my future and my very life that you might use me to serve your suffering people and to help transform our world into a place of justice, peace and love. I ask your blessing on me and on every human being in the world. I let go of everything and pray for a spirit of emptiness, compassion and love that I may be Jesus present in the world. Jesus, you are the whole reason for living and being and acting. Everything I'm doing is for you, with you, through you, because of you. I am yours. I am trying to be your follower, your disciple, here and now. Come, be with me, show me how I can love as you loved, serve as you serve, speak as you speak, love others as you love everyone. O God, make me an instrument of your peace.

I write this on the weekend holiday in honor of Martin Luther King, Jr., in Atlanta, Georgia, where I've come for a two-day conference on homelessness. Housing activists, homeless people, and advocates have gathered here from across the country at the invitation of Mitch Snyder. A hectic, difficult, frustrating meeting. No structure, no agenda, no facilitators: Mitch stayed in the background, the homeless took the lead. After forty-eight hours of discussion, we decided to do three things: 1) to have a national conference of homeless people sponsored and funded by housing advocates; 2) to call for new legislation that would restore the millions of dollars that the Reagan/Bush Administrations took out of housing for the poor; and 3) to hold a national march on Washington, D.C., sometime in the fall of 1989, to demand affordable housing now as the way to end the crisis of homelessness. Our demand and our motto would be short and to the point: "Housing Now!"

Today, before catching the flight home from Atlanta, I watched the parade in honor of Dr. King and I prayed at his tomb. I heard Jesse Jackson preach at Ebenezer Church. He said that "Dr. King has more power in a crypt than Ronald Reagan has as president or ever will have." I thought of the power of nonviolence, the revelation of God, in the life of Martin Luther King, Jr., and I gave thanks and pledged to continue the journey of peacemaking.

As I watched young people, black and white, pass by his crypt, I could not help but rejoice in the life of Dr. King. In the midst of our mad rush to violence and war, our willingness to crucify the homeless poor, he showed us a way out. Dr. King dedicated his life to serving the poor by demanding justice and peace now. He did so through Christian nonviolence, the way of life that seeks justice for the poor through peaceful, yet provocative means. Dr. King taught us to be like Jesus—to defend the poor and to seek the truth, but to do so by accepting suffering rather than by inflicting it on others. He showed us how to make peace, by risking arrest and death through nonviolent civil disobedience, persistent reconciliation, and a refusal to study war any more. His life reveals the age-old truth that positive social change occurs only when good people break bad laws and insist through a peaceful spirit that justice is a human right. His dream of the beloved community of humanity gives me hope for the future.

My prayer is that we take up his commitment to justice and walk with the poor on that narrow road of nonviolence to a just and lasting peace. I pray in the name of Love that all people might be born again; that we might reform our lives; that we might make peace with the homeless, with each other, with God. As I look forward to Easter, I do so in the hope that Christ will rise in us, and enable us to live out the difficult but beautiful Gospel call of nonviolent love and peacemaking.

I pray that we might be who we are: all of us, brothers and sisters of one another; all of us equal in God's sight and already reconciled; all of us, God's own children, peacemakers.

2.
Stories from the Street:
The Hope of the Homeless

Summer 1988

The only things that the homeless have to call their own are their stories. Their stories are often tragic, but told with hope and love. They are, in other words, human stories.

At the Horace McKenna Center, the drop-in center and church-run shelter for the homeless in the basement of St. Aloysius' church in Washington, D.C., we try to listen to the stories of those who come to us—stories of suffering and displacement, pain and death, eviction and unemployment. In such stories from the street, we hear the voice of God, the voice which tells us what it means to be a human being. Such stories need to be heard.

The people who come to our drop-in center and our shelter usually come to us in the midst of some horrible crisis in their lives. They often speak of pain and tragedy. But they also come with a sense of hope that life will be kind to them, that good news is just around the corner.

"I have lived on the street for three years," says Kenneth, a friend who is homeless. "I've been in all the shelters, and slept along many streets around town. Once you're on the street and you have no place to call your own, you do not get the opportunity to get off your feet and out of the street."

"The street is filled with violence," he explains. "Six of my friends have died from one thing or another. One day, as I was leaving one of the city-run shelters, walking down an alley, a guy attacked me with a golf club. He broke my jaw to rob me. All I had was thirty-seven cents."

Oddly enough, I have discovered that the trial by fire which is life on the streets has given the poor new eyes to see the truth. When asked to tell their stories, the homeless will also share the lessons they have learned. They can, invariably, tell it like it is. Freed from most inhibitions and the cares of the world, our homeless guests— our friends—have within them the voice of truth.

"I think things are going to get better," one homeless friend says, "but only because they can't get much worse. The mayor and the president don't care about the homeless because the homeless are not the people who put them in office. Homelessness exists," he continues, "because the government is not committed to serving the average person, and meeting their employment, housing and health needs."

Recently, we showed a documentary film to our guests in the McKenna Center on the life of Martin Luther King, Jr. Later, we showed the movie, *Gandhi*. Needless to say, our homeless friends were impressed. "It's good to stand up for what you believe in," Kenneth said after the movie, "but I do not think the world is ready for the message of Martin Luther King, Jr., or Gandhi."

"The American dream is a lie," he continued. "The havenots can't get a job. The haves and the have-nots are totally separated, in this city and around the country. We do need a change. If it wasn't for racism, America wouldn't be as 'great' as it is today. We all have to change our lives."

William, another regular guest at the center, tells a similar story, with similar insight. He's been living in shelters for a year. "A lot of people—especially those who have a lot of possessions—do not understand that people in the street are hungry, that they have nothing. The only person we folks on the street can trust is the Lord.

"Being homeless is the most frustrating thing I've ever been through. I had a job, but for various reasons, the boss wouldn't pay me. I got mad, and I took him to the Labor Board. The next thing I know—I'm on the street. I spent three nights and days in the cold and I don't know how I survived. Then, Lisa Goode [of the McKenna Center staff] was able to help me get into the Gospel Mission [an overnight shelter]. When you're on the street, you're just looking out for number one. You're just trying to survive. And you get angry when people come up and criticize you because you have no money, no food, no home, no fancy clothes.... But I found out, that if you are in need, God will see you through.

"All the shelters are no good," William continues. "Drugs are everywhere, violence is everywhere. Sure, you can make money selling drugs, but what good is it when you're dead. I try to be careful on the streets. You can get mugged just standing on the side of a street. And if someone held me up, I wouldn't have any money to give them.

"I can't enjoy myself because I have no friends. I do not feel welcome in any church because everyone is dressed in nice clothes. But I've found that God answers my prayers; the Lord looks after me. If you don't have the Lord—I don't care how rich you are—then you don't have a thing."

The homeless have been given new eyes to see the world. One of the ironies of God's reign is that it belongs to the poor. The poor can see reality as it is, and thus they can see the truth of justice and injustice. The street itself is a school of injustice, which they resist as best they can, but which can sharpen their sense of justice in ways a university never could. Thus, the poor and oppressed inevitably have direct access to the truth, while the rich and powerful are blind.

"Politicians and Christians don't mix," William told me the other day. "If I had to choose between Christ or the president, I'd choose Christ. People can't rule the world even if they think they can or try to. We should work to solve our problems, to change the bad things we've done in the world, and get ourselves right with God. God didn't make the trouble with drugs and wars that our country is in. We did it all. And we had better start working to solve our problems and help those in need if we want to be right with God."

Hearing the stories from the street, letting them touch our hearts, allowing their pain and hope to become part of our own stories— these are the challenges which face us. It is the challenge before everyone: to hear the stories of the poor and to find a common thread between their stories and our own story. Listening to another's story of suffering is the first step on the road of compassion. Within a short time, as the road of compassion widens, one invariably will find a place for one's self in the stories of the poor.

The Bible maintains that God does not speak in great thunderous tones, but in a still, small voice. If one is looking for the voice of God today, one simply has to walk out onto the street to hear the Voice of the voiceless. For we Christians know that the stories from the street are nothing more and nothing less than the story of Christ. We know that Christ walks these streets in the hearts of these homeless, hungry ones, seeking shelter and food; inviting us all to a change of heart, and to change the system that makes people homeless and hungry in the first place. We know that this message of truth is conveyed today in those who have no place to rest their head. We know that the suffering Jesus, a victim of injustice, walked the streets of Jerusalem, carrying the cross, and as the risen Christ, he walked the road to Emmaus.

That same Christ is with us today. If we listen carefully, we can hear his familiar message in the homeless who walk our nation's streets: "Repent. Change your lives. Put away the sword. Love one another. Love your enemies. House the homeless, feed the hungry. Stop making war, start feeding the poor. The reign of God is at hand!"

I hope and pray that Christ may touch us so that we may touch the homeless, and be touched by them. I hope that we can all learn to hear the stories of the homeless and the poor and discover that those stories are our stories. On such a day, we will truly be granted eyes to see and ears to hear. On that day, all human beings will have their own homes and sufficient food to live in peace with justice.

One of most depressing sights in Washington, D.C., is the large shelter for homeless families which was formerly a motel called the Capitol City Inn. Some 200 people, mostly homeless, African-American children, live in this rat-infested, poverty-stricken hell-hole. They run around the parking lot, as men come and go selling drugs. The city government continues to make big promises about housing these suffering people, but then the officials look the other way and push the homeless children out of sight. It continues to board up house upon house, and build new prisons, and leave the homeless out in the streets to die from the cold or to wallow in un-safe, rat-infested motels. Yesterday, a fire broke out at the Capitol

City Inn. At least one baby is dead. Several children were injured. Another may die. The fifth baby to die there in a year.

Such is homelessness, an early and unjust death.

In this distressing guise of the poor, Christ comes to us daily, as Dorothy Day pointed out. But it is hard to find Christ coming with "good news," a word of hope. The homeless have barely begun to join together and demand their basic right to housing. Such a communal effort would mark the spread of resurrection among these beaten and shattered people. It is happening, but slowly. Groups such as the Union of the Homeless, and the Community for Creative Nonviolence, are spreading resurrection among these crucified people, and hope is there.

But it is so difficult to rise out of the rut of homelessness. Several years ago, after marching through the streets of New York City on Good Friday with several thousand Christians, and after having been arrested and booked for demonstrating against nuclear weapons, I joined a vigil of homeless people on the steps of St. Patrick's Cathedral. They had been sleeping on those steps for forty days, throughout Lent. After an Easter vigil Mass at the Catholic Worker, my friends and I walked around Manhattan looking for cardboard that had been thrown away to sleep on. Before going to sleep on the steps of the Cathedral, the homeless held a little prayer service which we joined. We prayed for ourselves, for all the homeless in the world, and for the Spirit of resurrection to come upon us and our nation, so that justice for the poor might become a reality.

Unfortunately, though it was the eve of the feast of the resurrection, hope did not emerge as a theme of the prayer service. It was a liturgy of despair, and understandably so. The cold concrete, disparaging looks on passersby, and the reality of homelessness left us feeling quite hopeless, even though Easter was upon us. After a restless night with little sleep on the street, our rag-tag group broke up, and a friend and I made our way down into the dark tunnels of the New York subway system.

It was early Easter morning, and there was not a soul in sight. The staircase down into the subway was dark, smelly, abandoned, even scary. We could see a light ahead, at the end of a passageway leading to the subway. As we got closer to the light, a homeless man appeared, covered in blankets. Suddenly, he threw up his arms, with the blankets hanging down around him like a wide open cape, and proclaimed to us, "Alleluia! Christ is risen! Happy Easter!"

My friend and I stopped in our tracks, amazed at the sight, over-whelmed at this news. We looked at each other, then looked at him, and replied, "Happy Easter."

It felt like good news. We had encountered an angel of light, and heard a ray of hope from a homeless person. Indeed, we were evan-gelized by the homeless poor. We found our hope.

I know there is hope among the homeless poor. In Washington, D.C., where there is much power and wealth and military might, few seem to exude a spirit of hope. Instead, we find cynicism and despair, and a general lack of enthusiasm for justice among people in government positions who work "for the common good." These days, it is primarily among the poor and homeless where one can find any hope. But when those who are able to share their resources with the poor do so, the hope of the poor catches on and spreads around like a pleasant, contagious disease. It can be like salvation. Homes are granted to the homeless; hope is granted to the hopeless.

It is difficult to comment on the spirit of hopelessness in our first world country. In many ways, it is so pervasive as to seem normal. "What is hope?" is a modern version of Pilate's question, "What is truth?" Do people really think there is something to hope for? Do people really believe there is Someone to place our hope in? Do people really believe in the resurrection of Jesus, in life after death (in life at all), in a world without war? What does such hope look like in the US, on the streets of Washington, or any other city street?

Hope comes alive in my heart when I see or hear the good news of resurrection played out in the lives of the poor. It happened when I heard that an old abandoned building was being rehabilitated into apartments for homeless women and children. Hope happens in my heart when I can find shelter or decent, affordable housing for a homeless person who comes begging in the cold. Hope is alive when poor people smile and laugh and resist and demand their rights and show mercy to one another and when I find that I can do the same.

Christ is risen from homelessness when the homeless are given homes. Christ is risen in Washington, D.C., when the homeless, the hungry, and the poor keep vigil at the Department of Housing or the US Capitol or the Mayor's Office and demand better service. Christ is risen when these suffering people are able to alleviate the suffering of one another and to do so in a spirit of nonviolent love. Such things are wonderful signs of hope in this city, a place where hope is a rare bird, rarely seen.

St. Aloysius' Church, our inner-city parish, has been sponsoring our shelter for elderly homeless men for the past seven years now. The parishioners worship the God of Justice and Peace—Christ in the Eucharistic Community—at one end of the sanctuary and serve Christ in the homeless poor at the other end of the sanctuary. Our little parish, comprising poor minority people, has become a beacon of light and hope in the city. People flock to the church to visit and to serve and to celebrate at one of the most joyful liturgical experiences I've ever been to. Every Sunday, a packed congregation sings the

Gospel songs of liberation and justice and listens intently to the preacher's message of justice, peace, and freedom found in the costly discipleship of Jesus, a discipleship which leads us to the cross, through nonviolent resistance to evil, and then on to eternal life with God. In this setting, people find hope for a new world because a new world is emerging in this setting. Christ rises among us and sends us forth to proclaim the good news of justice, peace and nonviolent love. The church becomes "the place we go from," as Dr. King used to say, and people go out to share the hope of God's reign coming among us.

Easter is breaking forth daily. People are getting involved in the lives of one another and the lives of the needy and acting on the Gospel message. In the city which shelters the president and the C.I.A. and accommodates the Pentagon and the Center for Naval Surface Warfare and the Department of Energy, Christ is rising among the poor who overcome the spirit of death in homelessness and violence. Such a spirit is contagious.

As William says, "I have a lot of hope because I believe in God." As Miss Ruth says, "If you stand on God's promises, you have nothing to worry. Put your hope in God and the Risen Jesus and watch how God transforms your life."

We can rejoice that our God is so good; that God is present among us in the least of our world, in the poor and marginalized, transforming our world. The Gospel of Matthew offers a vision of Christ's eternal presence among us, especially among the poor and the oppressed. This vision put into practice gives me hope:

The virtuous will ask, "Lord, when did we see you hungry and feed you; or thirsty and give you drink? [Homeless and give you shelter?] When did we see you a stranger and make you welcome; naked and clothe you; sick or in prison and go to see you?" And the King will answer, "I tell you solemnly, insofar as you did this to one of the least of these sisters and brothers of mine, you did it to me." (Matthew 25:38-40)

To heed the good news of nonviolent love, persistent reconciliation, service towards the poor and peace with justice! To stand with Christ and serve Christ among the poor! To follow Christ as he beckons us toward Life! To be found faithful to the calling! To be a person of hope in an age of despair! To be a servant of the poor, a servant of justice and peace, a servant of God!

May God hear our prayer of hope.

3

Making Peace with the Homeless:
A Shelter Is Opened

January 1989

We opened the shelter at St. Aloysius' Church last month on December 1, and welcomed five poor, elderly homeless men to dinner
and bed. My job is to coordinate the hospitality: bringing in ten or
twelve elderly homeless men, recruiting volunteers, making sure that
dinner will be ready, and working to get them their own apartments.

Tonight was the first night that Bill, a distinguished man in his
sixties, has spent indoors in four years. He is a graduate of George
Washington University, and because he possesses an alumni card,
has been able to spend his daytimes in the university library. It is
truly a blessing to offer him and the others shelter. Though it's not
the greatest place, it is much better than the street. The men sleep in a
little room at the back of the sanctuary. The parish has a real sense of
participation in this project, a sense of Christ's presence in our midst.
I've spent the last few nights in the shelter, getting to know the men,
and making sure I know all the details of running our little hospitality
center.

Compared with the city shelters, this is paradise. The men's shelters around town are violent, filthy, lice-ridden, and dehumanizing.
If I were homeless, I would, like Bill and some of these elderly men,

have opted to take the risk of living outdoors. We hope the personal care of our little shelter will offer a human touch and make for a peaceful transition back into a new life in an apartment.

The other night the Catholic Workers brought an elderly homeless man to the shelter. They had found him in the gutter of a back alley, covered in vomit and filth. Whenever they have a free evening, they ride around in a van seeking the most abandoned homeless people. I threw away his clothes, let him shower and clean up, gave him an entirely new wardrobe, and put him to bed for the night. He left the next morning and never returned.

One of the recent guests in the shelter was an imposing, elderly man who suffered from a serious mental illness. He imagined that every variety of government hound was after him: the C.I.A., the F.B.I., the I.R.S., even the Army. After staying with us for several weeks, and refusing to go for any medical treatment, he disappeared one morning. I saw him a few weeks ago on a street in the city, shouting into the sky. Then, last week, one of our co-workers saw him in the Hispanic neighborhood, Adams Morgan. His head had been brutally cut open, so she brought him to the hospital. After being treated, he disappeared out onto the streets again, refusing shelter and assistance. He suffers intensely and needs serious medication to ease his mental anguish. All we can do is pray for him and keep our eyes on the lookout for him.

Easter, 1989

Last evening, a long and moving Easter Vigil Mass, with the baptism of several babies and several adult friends. Then, I spent the night in the shelter with the homeless, but it wasn't a very pleasant night. One of the men, Charlie, was very agitated and upset. He has been homeless for at least ten years, possibly as long as forty years. We had rented him a room in the basement of a nearby house, but he would not take it. I really like him, but he is unable to manage indoors on his own. He became very disruptive, obnoxious, and violent. It did not feel much like Easter this morning.

Over twenty men have been guests at the night shelter in the church since December. These past months have had the usual crises, the usual good times and the usual difficult moments. The goal of the shelter is to provide a clean, safe environment for a small number of elderly homeless men. Through personal care and support, we try to place each person in a better living situation —preferably his own apartment. It looks like many will move on to better living situations, although not everyone.

Bill, who had been homeless for years, moved into his own apartment on Easter weekend. Tom was here for nearly four months, and just as he was about to start work, he disappeared. David eventually moved over to one of the local Catholic Worker communities. Gene had been homeless for four years, and has worked throughout that time as a volunteer for one of the church soup kitchens in town. He slept in the driveway of a bank until he came to St. Aloysius'. He, too, has gone to one of the Catholic Worker houses. Russell, a twenty-five-year-old who had been homeless two weeks when he came to us, was able to get a job as a receptionist at another church. He will soon have his own apartment.

So far, some sixty men and women have volunteered during these winter months to serve in the night shelter, as well as some forty high school students. The chores include setting up the shelter area, preparing the evening meal, turning out the lights at ten p.m., waking everyone up at six a.m. and preparing a light breakfast. We have survived power shortages, water shortages, break-ins, and burnt soup. Occasionally, a video movie has been shown and a birthday celebrated. On one night, as I was cooking dinner in the church, a big fat rat walked by. We bought traps and put them out, and luckily, he never returned.

Charlie, the elderly homeless man who stayed with us during the winter months, is back out on the streets, this time across from the church. He is unable to live alone. He is broken, his life shattered. I have been cussed at and cursed by him, and lavished with praise. I have tried to get him an apartment, have tried to befriend him, have tried to share my life with him as best as I am able, all to little end. He suffers from severe psychological problems that torture his mind.

Then, a few days ago, he came into the center and asked to speak with me. He said life on the street was tearing him apart. A group of kids had come up to him the other night and started spitting on him. One of them ran up and kicked him squarely in the shin, causing great pain in his poor leg. "It's hell out there," he said.

There is nothing left I can do for him except listen and continue to be there for him. He has turned away offers for help from many churches and social workers in town. When I tell people about him, I see them thinking, "Ronald Reagan was right; the homeless choose to be homeless." But that is not the case. Most of the homeless are there because of terrible, traumatic circumstances in their lives, events that have broken them. Most important, they are there because they are stuck at the bottom of a barrel, a militaristic culture which rewards wealthy, white males and leaves the poor to suffer and die in the streets. Charlie suffers from mental illness, and the combination of his poverty and illness will kill him. Our culture should come to a crashing halt to reach out and heal him through a massive community effort, but it will not. Charlie, like most homeless people, will be allowed to fall by the wayside and die.

I hope that a better fortune lies ahead for him, and us. May we have the courage to welcome him—and all the homeless—into our homes and hearts. Only then will we begin the task of making peace.

4.
Life and Death on K Street:
Community in the Heart of the City

Fall, 1988

My return to Washington, D.C., after years of schooling and teaching in accord with my Jesuit formation, is marked this time by a new geography.

I have moved into a Jesuit Community in a row house on K Street in the northeast part of the city. We are only a few blocks from the US Capitol, and yet it is altogether another world from Capitol Hill. This is a poor, African-American neighborhood where people are struggling to survive. Homeless people walk by to the nearby shelter, sometimes stopping in for something to eat or drink. Evictions take place all around us. Drugs are sold on every corner, including outside my window, as I write this.

But the community I live in, what a wonderful gallimaufry of Jesuits all dedicated to justice for the poor! The Maryland Province of the Society of Jesus has owned this house for ten years. At one time, it was a home called "Shalom House," sponsored by Horace McKenna, for homeless women. When the project moved on to better quarters, the Jesuit Community moved in. Some eight Jesuits live here, all devoted to the Gospel mission of justice, especially as it is written in the Jesuit documents. "The preferential option for the poor," "the faith that does justice," "the mission to proclaim the reign of God"—these are topics at every dinner.

I share a room with Peter Henriot, a lively, intelligent man who for seventeen years has been director of the Center for Concern, a social justice think tank. Joe Hacala heads the Jesuit Office for Social Ministries. For years, he worked among the poor of Appalachia. Dean Brackley is writing a book about salvation and liberation theology. He spent nearly ten years among the poorest of the poor in the South Bronx, organizing them to demand their rights. He is known for his comic book, "People Power," which outlines a process for social change and empowerment; it was widely distributed in the South Bronx. Frank Moan is the director of "Refugee Voices," which tries to raise the consciousness of the nation to the plight of the millions of refugees around the world.

Life with these Christians is unusually *compos mentis*. It is a human life, in other words.

We have no air conditioning; it's over 100 degrees outside and in. We take turns cooking, cleaning, handling the business. We gather regularly on Monday nights for community discussion and go away together for several days, four times a year.

Early every morning, before we go off to our various works, we gather for prayers and Eucharist. The readings this week centered on the call to hospitality and peacemaking in Romans 12 and the story of the rich young man and Jesus in Luke 18. They speak directly to me in a new invitation to serve the poor, to follow Jesus' Gospel call, to offer my life in service and costly discipleship, and to live in a community that practices hospitality. I claim the story of the rich young man for myself. Since before I entered the Jesuits, I have been keenly aware of my wealth and class, and have sought diligently to take the invitation seriously. While that rich young man turned sadly away from Jesus, I was determined, on the other hand, to renounce my wealth and privilege and follow Jesus even unto the cross. "Sell all you have and give it to the poor, and you shall have treasure in heaven, and come, follow me." Jesus also says these words to me. Therefore, here I am, becoming poorer, walking with the poor, living in a community of Jesus' disciples, following Jesus every day.

With this entry into urban Washington, D.C., I feel that I have finally done what I have been striving to do: to move across town from the rich, white, suburban life of Potomac, to the poor, African-American, inner-city struggle of northeast Washington, D.C., and to live there in a spiritual community of Christian friends. This new environment is challenging, but human to the core. The community life in this setting among God's suffering people fulfills the Jesuit vows of poverty, chastity, and obedience in community that I professed years ago. It fulfills the Gospel. Finally, I am where I belong.

During my second night on K Street, I awoke in the wee hours of the dark to the sound of gunfire in the street. The next day we heard the news: two men were shot with rifles and killed in the middle of the street, one block down at the bus station—a drug deal gone awry. The pools of blood have now been cleaned up, but I think of the event as I walk to work each day.

A few nights ago, a gentleman from South Africa showed up at our house. He is a law professor, one of the leading lawyers for the anti-apartheid movement in South Africa. The South African police had beaten him up and he lost most of his teeth; he knew that sooner or later they would come after him to kill him. His days were numbered, so he fled his country and was lucky to escape. Through various friends, he heard that we might be able to offer him hospitality. Of course, we would; we took him in at the K Street house. Arrangements are being made to have him interviewed for a teaching position at one of the Jesuit law schools; but meanwhile, he has been telling us horror stories about the repression in South Africa, and the determined faith of the black women and men who continue to hope in a future of peace freed from oppression.

Our community spent this past weekend away at the Jersey shore in a time of reflection, faith-sharing, story-telling, prayer and discussion about our common life: a time for spiritual communion and community-building. We sat together for long sessions, listened to one another, and commented on one another's sharing to affirm and support one another. Peter will be leaving Washington, D.C., after seventeen years of social activism and advocacy for justice to live and work among the poor of Zambia. Joe Hacala—sensitive, caring, committed—is considering a new position as the director of the Campaign for Human Development, the Catholic organization which funds charities that serve the poor. Bryan McNeil, a newly arrived and newly ordained priest from New Orleans, is beginning his ministry of lobbying Congress for disarmament and peace in Central America. Frank Moan, our wise and compassionate superior, so deeply committed to the refugees of the world, continues his advocacy work at "Refugee Voices." We have also been joined by Si Smith, the director of Jesuit Missions, a longtime advocate for justice for the poor, who is also compassionate and committed to refugees, and who brings a wide vision of the world as a whole from his years of service among the poor around the globe. Finally, Dean Brackley, with his youthful spirit and energy, his enthusiasm for social change, his commitment to the urban poor, plugs away with his writing project, wondering where life will lead him next. Life among such holy, humble people cannot be anything but holy, loving, caring, healing, and human. It is my first real experience of a biblical, Christian community. They are very supportive of my work with the homeless, my concerns for the people of Central America, my participation in anti-nuclear vigils and actions, in all the activities that make up my vision and life. I feel as though I have found a place to call home, a group of people whom I can call my brothers, friends and fellow disciples of Jesus. I am happy and consoled to know that yes, indeed, I can be happy as a person committed in community to the Gospel vision of justice. These good people are happy and committed; they witness to me though they do not even know it.

Thank you God for these days, these friends, this life.

Community life continues to be a blessing, a struggle, and a joy. Joe, who does the house shopping, is a genius at his chore. He likes to shop at midnight, after a hard day's work. He searches out the best bargains, gets what's on sale, and keeps the cost of living in the house very low. This, in addition to his work at the Jesuit Social Ministries Office, his duties at the parish, and his public speaking and organizing work around the country.

I'm not so good at my chore: I'm in charge of cleaning the first floor bathroom and mowing the (small) front lawn. I'm the "groundskeeper." Ultimately, that means I pick up the trash that lands on the front of the house each day. One day, I prided myself on a job well done: the hedge was clipped, the lawn mowed, the sidewalk and garden weeded, a beautiful job. Then, Joe politely informed me, I had pulled out all his new flowers. (So much for my green thumb.)

Meanwhile, the bathroom presents a much more serious task. Every time I face the dirty toilet for a thorough scrubbing, I remember the scene from the movie, *Gandhi*, in which Gandhi discusses cleaning the "latrine" and doing it with joy. I have a hard time doing it with joy, but I'm learning. I know Gandhi would find some humor in scrubbing down our tiny bathroom that is used by so many housemates, guests, neighborhood kids who visit, and others. But Gandhi may be right: cleaning the toilet has a way of distracting one from all the other essential issues of the day. When confronted with that task, I find myself in prayer with St. Paul: "I look on everything as so much waste, if only I can have Christ, and be given a place in him." (Phil. 3:9) Everything else falls into place and for once, I am focused on life in the present moment.

Not only has this house brought me down to earth with the human touch of these friendly folks, but I find myself learning to live like most of the human race with the most basic assignments. Like everyone else, I take turns cooking. Since I have never cooked before, I am finding this a daunting responsibility. Usually, ten or twelve people are at the table each evening. As I try new recipes and find the table fellowship affirming, I am gaining confidence in my cooking. So far, no one seems to have gotten ill.

The chores continue: cleaning the toilets regularly; picking up the trash on the sidewalk in front of the house; doing laundry; vacuuming; and more. Chores done in community with a cheerful heart make this dwelling place truly a place of peace. This past weekend, we spent a day together doing our fall cleaning and then shared the latest events in our faith lives. It was a peaceful, healing, human experience. How I wish others could learn to live in such peaceful, human, communal ways.

This weekend, we held another community weekend together: faith-sharing, Eucharist, long meals together, spiritual conversation. One day last week, before we went away together, Frank, Dean, and

I had a lively and intense discussion during the morning Mass about the reading from the first letter of John:

> This is the message as you heard it from the beginning: that we are to love one another.... This has taught us love—that Jesus gave up his life for us; and we, too, ought to give up our lives for our brothers and sisters. If anyone who was rich enough in this world's goods, saw someone in need, but closed his or her heart to that person, how could the love of God be living in him or her? Our love is not to be just words or mere talk, but something real and active. (3:11, 16-19)

We all agreed with the truth of this passage, and we admitted to our shame that we do not fulfill this way of life as well as we could. How can our life together—"our love"—be "something real and active"? How can we love one another better, as Jesus did, even to the point of giving up our lives for others, for the poor and oppressed, for our sisters and brothers? When will we fully share all that we have, including our very belongings, with those in need? Such questions are at the core of the Scriptures, and once again, we found ourselves challenged by God's Word. We found ourselves pledging to take God's word seriously and try to live that Word in our own lives. Throughout our weekend away, we continued to ponder the challenge of this vocation, and asked God for the strength to be faithful to it.

Recently, we wrote a letter to a group of housing realtors who have been pressuring our neighbors to sell their homes and move away. We chided these realtors for their practice of gentrification, which only succeeds in making the poor poorer. They leaflet inner-city neighborhoods, encouraging poor people like our neighbors to sell their homes for several thousand dollars. Then, the realtors resell the row houses for three or four times the money. We called this business "unjust, immoral, and sinful." "Your emphasis on buying and selling, turning a profit, and making a fantastic investment," the letter stated, "all speak of your complicity in one of the most serious social evils in our country today—the housing crisis, with its related homelessness that is so much a part of the fabric of life in our city and neighborhood. Rooted in a profit-making orientation at the expense of the poor, gentrification has helped create and continues to perpetuate this evil in our midst."

Much to our surprise, the realtors responded and asked if they could meet with our community to discuss the letter and this matter of gentrification. We agreed. When they gathered in our house, we told them stories about landlords who sold neighboring row houses to make money, thus forcing our neighbors to move from their homes, some into city shelters because of the lack of affordable housing.

Two of the realtors who visited us were incapable of hearing our point, that the poor are suffering because of their business. But one seemed to be touched and said he would consider our concerns. Every one of us took turns speaking about the plight of the poor, and the immorality of their business. Before they left, I spoke of my experience with the homeless, and said, "You have a special responsibility to make low-income housing available to the poor. If you can't do that, you ought to seek another line of business that does not oppress people. Perhaps, you ought to work with the homeless and try to find them homes." They listened passively and politely left.

It is summer and today was the annual K Street Front Lawn Picnic and Party for the fifty or sixty neighborhood kids who come to our house every day throughout the year. These children invariably live on the street, playing ball, riding their bikes, hanging out. We have become quite close to some of them. Many of them have lost one or both parents. One youngster saw his father murdered by his mother at the dinner table; a few months later, he saw his mother murdered by another relative. We have tried to befriend that child, and others, to help heal the pain of poverty and violence which has destroyed their young lives. The party is a way to cheer them up in the midst of this sweltering Washington summer. For us, we find, it is a way to be faithful to our Gospel. We remember the words of Jesus, who said, "If you're going to throw a party, don't invite people who can pay you back. Invite the poor, who cannot pay you back in this life, but who will in the next." Our party not only brought out the kids, but neighbors of every variety. Indeed, people driving by who saw the party, parked their cars, got out and joined us for a meal, a glass of lemonade, and some singing.

As Dean said later, such is the reign of God. Indeed.

5.
Proclaiming God's Reign:
A Church of the Poor

Summer, 1988

Besides the work with the homeless at the Horace McKenna Center,
my vocation includes serving the people of St. Aloysius' Church,
especially by assisting Fr. George Anderson, S.J., the pastor. He is
a wise man, dedicated to the people of this inner-city neighborhood,
committed to justice for the poor, and rooted in a deep faith in the
living God. He entered the Jesuits late in life, after getting his doctorate in English literature. For ten years, he served as a prison
chaplain on Riker's Island in New York City, and ever since, he has
been here at St. Al's, helping us all to be faithful to the Gospel. He is
a simple man, a contemplative, a true pastor, loved by the people.
His sense of humor lightens the crises that unfold each day around
the parish. As pastor, he reaches out to the poorest of the poor and
makes them feel welcomed and dignified, but he is the first to say
that they are the teachers, the real ministers, the very presence of God
among us. Like Horace McKenna and Dorothy Day, George Anderson sees Christ among us, in the eyes of the poor.

People flock from miles around to come to this church because
they know they will hear the Word of God preached in a setting
where it is lived. How different a church this is from the wealthy

parishes in suburbs across the country. Here, at St. Al's, the collection is so minuscule as to be laughable. It is clearly not the point of the gathering. St. Al's is that rare bird: a parish become faith community, a sign of God's reign amid the chaos and violence of the world, a gathering of people transformed by God's love. St. Al's — a church of the poor—is a sign of hope. I do not write this in a spirit of self-righteousness or pride. Rather, I'm trying to describe our common experience of God. When the Gospel choir starts the Sunday liturgy, the sanctuary ignites as if the people are on fire with the Spirit of God. It is electrifying, pentecostal, and all the while, rooted in justice and peace and the Gospel's message for today. It is real and makes the Gospel real for us. These people are poor and struggling and faithful. When they gather in Jesus' name, God is present; rather, God makes God's constant presence tangible, even visible in the eyes of each other. When the bread is broken and the cup poured, scales fall from our eyes and we see the risen Christ among us and we are filled with joy. St. Al's is a model parish. I think God feels at home here.

The other day, at George's invitation, I visited Mr. Washington, an elderly man who lives in one of the neighboring projects. Some twenty-five years ago, he was sitting in the back of a car when a robbery occurred down the street. The robbers began to shoot people and one of the stray bullets struck Mr. Washington in the back. He nearly died, but somehow, he survived. Over the years, he developed gangrene in his legs and both eventually had to be amputated. The gangrene still threatens him. He is very ill, yet he has a strong spirit which was very evident on my first visit with him. "I never complain," he said to me the other day when I asked how he was holding up. "Life is too short to complain. I'm just living, one day at a time, and trusting in God." These are the people one encounters at St. Al's. I am privileged to be able to visit such steadfast people.

I've also been asked to help facilitate the children's summer school program, "Vacation Bible School." The choir director has been teaching the parish youngsters about the Bible; I'm in charge of the "vacation" part! After a week of story-telling, drawing, reading, singing, and playing, we went swimming at a friend's pool, quite an event for these inner-city kids, most of whom have never gone swimming. The peals of laughter and delight! It was exhilarating; I think I gave ten of them their first swimming lesson. They were beside themselves with joy.

Such frivolity is a significant act of service by the parish, I think. It provided a great relief for these inner-city children who know hardly any relief from the poverty and pain around them. Their lives are an uphill struggle to survive, and given their fifty-fifty chance, many of them will not survive. One day of swimming became a day of celebration, a breath of fresh air in their lives, a brief respite from the war daily waged against them. Praise God for such a day! May every child in the world know such days of joy and laughter! May a day come when children around the world live every day in joy, peace, and laughter.

Recently, a much beloved parishioner, an elderly woman we call Miss Ruth, had to travel to South Carolina for a funeral. She has been raising her five-year-old great-nephew, and she asked if I would take him for a few days while she was away. In his short life, this little boy has already had his share of uphill battles—fighting poverty, violence, racism, and despair. I found myself saying, "Of course, I'd be happy to take care of him," and yet I had no idea what

I was getting myself into. But this is part of the life of the inner city. Many elderly women share the responsibility, the hard work, of raising their own children's children and each other's grandchildren. I was their neighbor and friend; of course, the boy could stay with me and my community.

And so, for five days and nights, he was with us at the K Street house. He traveled with me, went to work with me, ate with us, and slept in our prayer room on a mattress. I took him to school, and picked him up, put him to bed and made sure he was ready for kindergarten. One afternoon, Lisa Goode and I took him and some other kids to a Disney film. They loved it. The boy is hyperactive and extroverted—and great fun to be with—but by the end of the visit, I was exhausted. Yet he was raring to go for more adventures. I do not know where Miss Ruth gets the energy to handle this dynamo. It was a blessing to have him with us, and he gave me a tiny insight into parenthood, a good (although limited) experience for a celibate.

The real discovery, however, was the heroic work which these neighborhood women perform as they raise generations of children. One neighborhood woman is raising as many as ten kids, most of them not her own. In this respect, such women resemble the heroic women of South Africa, Nicaragua, El Salvador, and the Philippines. Such women are the true heroes, the real saints, the gentle revolutionaries who have staked their lives on their children. They do the best they can in a rough situation to guarantee a future for the children of our broken city. They are strong models for everyone, courageous women who respond to difficulties with towering courage and strength. Their efforts shall not go unrewarded.

With the help of the local Catholic Worker community, St. Al's has started an evening soup kitchen for the homeless. There are few places, if any, in D.C. where a homeless person can go to get a free, hot meal in the evening. For several weeks now, on Wednesday evenings, nearly one hundred homeless men have lined up along the side of the church building for dinner. The homemade food is served cafeteria style, and the guests sit at large tables together. Lemonade is served, and fruit and a candy bar are offered on the way out. The loving spirit of the Catholic Workers, as well as the delicious menu, invariably bring rave reviews.

But it is difficult work. Last week, several young men became quite disruptive during the meal. One threw a plate of lasagna at a volunteer. Then, at the entrance to the church, three men began beating up a fourth man, probably over a drug deal. Before we were able to pull them apart, the beaten man was covered with blood. As I called for an ambulance, the three hoodlums ran away. The beaten man was lucky to be alive. He could easily have been killed. Such is the reality of death in this city, the "murder capital" of the nation, where there was an average of over one murder per day last year.

We were extremely shaken by the violence, and once again, threw ourselves into deep thought over how to serve these broken people in a nonviolent way that shows respect and honors their dignity, yet prevents and diffuses violence. I trust God's blessing on the project, and am grateful for the leadership and loving, peaceful example of the Catholic Workers. The answer lies in the steadfast presence of nonviolent love which these Christians have manifested. They are loving and respectful, yet they resist violence, even and especially among the battered poor. Such loving service can stop violence in its tracks and begin the process of healing the broken bodies and spirits of the poor. What better place to practice this Gospel life than at St. Al's in Washington, D.C. Perhaps right here, in the shadow of the US Capitol and its imperial might, the light of God's reign might break forth and transform our lives, and perhaps the nation and the world.

St. Aloysius' Church is alive and kicking. The lively music, the warm embrace of the community, the powerful preaching of the Word, the generous hospitality, the outpouring of service into the city, the gathering in song and praise around the altar: these are signs of life in a dying city, not to mention a dying nation. This church is a spiritual home for many people. It is a home where the poor find the good news preached to them, and more important, a home where they see it practiced around them. It is a place where people can be good news for each other. At St. Al's, the light is shining. There is good news. This is a cause for rejoicing.

6.
The Street as Apartheid:
South Africa in Washington, D.C.

December, 1988

One way of understanding the horror of homelessness is to see it as a form of apartheid. South Africa's system of institutionalized racism was named "apartheid" because the word means "to separate apart." Racist government officials who founded the system in 1948 wanted blacks to be separated from whites. They pushed aside black people and created society so that those who were white benefited; those who were black struggled just to stay alive.

North American society demonstrates its disdain for the poor by closing down low-income housing, using tax money on weapons of destruction instead of housing, pushing people out onto the streets and then ignoring them in their suffering. By allowing homelessness to continue, society separates the poor apart from the rich, and in many cases, minority races from the white majority.

Homelessness, like apartheid, is institutionalized injustice. Our system is set up to help those who have money and homes. Those who are on the streets get a cold shoulder from passersby and learn the painful lesson that they are not wanted.

These insights came home to me in an encounter at the McKenna Center on the day after Thanksgiving, when a small, African-American man walked into the McKenna Center office. I had been working by myself in the "receptionist" office and had been inundated with requests for food, shelter, money to help pay the rent, and transportation assistance to new jobs. William sat down and said he had needed help to pay his rent. He had an unusual accent, almost British, and I inquired where he was from. He had come from a refugee camp in Botswana, but was from Soweto, South Africa, where he and his wife, Anna, had suffered arrest, imprisonment, and torture for their work to have English, not Afrikaans, taught in the elementary school which their children attended. They had fled for their lives, leaving everything, including their two little children. The white authorities jailed him for six months. Most of his right ear was cut off, as he showed me. His back had been whipped and he had been beaten. He cried, he told me, for his torturers, who could be so blind as to treat another human being that way. Anna had been beaten as well. She was kicked in the head repeatedly, losing her front teeth in the process.

They had been in Washington, D.C., for nearly a year, getting by with the help of various relief groups. For the last few months they had been on their own, trying to survive on welfare (which they receive because of their special refugee status) in a crack house! In a few weeks, he said, they would be evicted from that denizen of drugs and put back on to the streets. From apartheid in South Africa to a crack house and homelessness in Washington, D.C.! They were about to discover a new apartheid: life on the streets of Washington, D.C.

Later, after we talked and he left, I decided to drive over to visit the place where he and Anna have been living. I could not get them out of my mind. The house was a boarded up row house, with ten or fifteen rooms, each holding a family. They had no heat, no stove, no hot water, and no safety from the violence of the drug culture. William and Anna shared one tiny room and a few possessions, and put up with the drugs, the fighting, and the police. I immediately began making phone calls and within a few days, they moved into a Catholic Worker house across the street from our Jesuit community. One of the doctors from Health Care for the Homeless agreed to examine them and a top immigration lawyer offered to look over their papers. And now, we are discussing how to bring their two little children to the United States.

It's been a real blessing befriending these South Africans who have walked into our lives. South Africa has certainly come into my life in a very concrete way these last few months. First, with the visit of an exiled South African lawyer who stayed with our community; then Tim Smith, a Jesuit from a segregated area of South Africa who spent a week with us; and now Anna and William. I'm grateful to God for these friends and I hope I can learn from them and respond to their needs, especially as a way to resist the evil of apartheid. They offer me the chance to practice the moral of the Good Samaritan parable with all its political ramifications. Perhaps our hospitality to them may help resist and abolish apartheid.

March 1989

On February 19, William and Anna received word from South Africa that their two little children, Mandla, age five, and Thokozile, age seven, and their aunt were shot and killed by South African police on February 1 while they were attempting to cross the South African border into Botswana. Their eighteen-year-old cousin had managed to climb the fence into freedom in Botswana. The aunt was lifting the seven-year-old girl, Thokozile, over the border fence when they were all shot. The cousin was wounded, but managed to crawl to safety on the other side.

We have been devastated by this news. The entire parish had raised funds in hopeful anticipation of flying the two children to Washington, D.C., to be reunited with their parents. Anna and William are grieving. How can a government shoot children? How can people be so cruel?

When William and Anna entered our lives, a new realm of suffering and hope touched us. We saw the suffering which is apartheid and how it scarred their lives, their bodies, their souls; but we were touched by their faith, hope and love. As they were recovering their strength, and Anna had her teeth replaced as we prepared for the children's advent among us, we thought: Here is a chance to overcome the deadly evils of the South African state. We will get these children out of South Africa's apartheid and reunite them with their parents.

But how little we here in the United States know about South Africa—the terrorism of apartheid! When the news came, we were cut to the heart, broken-hearted. "Life is so harsh, the times so evil. People are so cruel," we said. The brutality of apartheid in a far-off land had touched our lives in D.C.

As I go through Lent, and ponder the brutal torture, imprisonment, and capital punishment of Jesus—an innocent person who spoke for peace and justice—I remember his steadfast spirit which stood up to injustice and resisted evil. I remember that Jesus overcame the horror of his crucifixion. But the deaths of these two little ones, of the South African people—how terrible is evil in the world!

I do believe in God, and I do believe that one day apartheid will fall, that injustice will be overcome, that death shall be forever transformed into life. I recall the words of Dr. King, as he spoke a eulogy for the four little girls killed in the bombing of a Birmingham Church in 1963: "God has a way of bringing good out of evil. History has proven over and over again that unmerited suffering is redemptive. The innocent blood of these little children may well serve as the redemptive force that will bring new light to us all."

In that same hope, I rededicate myself, with my friends and church—in the name of the children, in the name of Jesus—to resisting and abolishing apartheid and to creating a new South Africa and a new world, where justice, peace and equality prevail.

June 1989

At the invitation of the Sojourners Community, people from all over the country gathered in Washington, D.C., to march for a free South Africa on the anniversary of the massacre of the children of Soweto. The night before, in a Baptist church a few blocks from the White House, a black preacher from South Africa warned the white South African government: "The victory is ours! God has already won!" Other church leaders joined in the chorus to demand an end to US support of apartheid, an end to our association with the racist regime of South Africa, and the full use of sanctions against that government.

The next day, some five thousand of us, black and white, South African and North American, gathered at the Washington Monument and marched to the White House. In single file, each one of us passed by the front of the White House, offering the name of a child jailed or killed in South Africa. Then, some forty-four of us, including Joyce Hollyday and Jim Wallis of Sojourners, sat down in front of the White House. We each held a sign with the name of a murdered child from South Africa. My sign read simply, "Mandla."

We were arrested, and brought to the Anacostia Park Police Station, where we were briefly held in a cell. Afterwards, while I waited along the Potomac River for a ride home, I watched the sun set in the distance. Thinking of William and Anna and their children and all the people of South Africa, I was very glad to be in such company, glad to have sat down at the White House, glad to have spent the afternoon in a holding cell. It was a small gesture, a small risk (we will probably not have to go to jail for this action), but it was another beginning, a good first step in the nonviolent struggle against the US support of systemic racism.

Certainly, this small stand against South African apartheid is connected to my work with the homeless here. All these issues are related; indeed, they are all one. "Injustice anywhere is a threat to justice everywhere," Dr. King said. Apartheid must be dismantled and homelessness must never be permitted by any society. All people in the world should be free to live anywhere they desire in a decent, affordable home with food, medical care and education available to everyone. I believe this vision of a new world of justice can be realized. Together, we can make it happen. The systems of institutionalized injustice will one day be transformed.

May there be many more such prayerful, nonviolent, direct actions until apartheid—at home and abroad—is abolished.

7

Notes from the D.C. Central Cell Block:
In Jail with the Homeless

April 12, 1989, 1:00 p.m.

A friend of mine, a Trappist monk of Gethsemani in Kentucky, recently sent me a copy of Henri Nouwen's new book, *In the Name of
Jesus: Reflections on Christian Leadership.* It is a moving and striking account of what it means to be a Christian leader in a world of
extremes—rampant poverty, outrageous riches and nuclear weapons.
Lately, I've been carrying the book around (with the Scriptures) in
my pocket, reading as I go. Sometimes, I steal a few moments from
the drop-in center to ponder its insights.

During the last few days, we have been preparing to combat the
city government's latest outrage: redoing the famous "Initiative 17," a
law which requires the city to provide shelter to anyone in need.

A City Council hearing began at city hall this morning. Hundreds
of homeless people, church-shelter providers, and advocates came to
testify and speak out against the callousness that would close the few
(and miserably inadequate) shelters we already have now. Seven
people froze to death this past winter; without available shelters,
more people will die. It is as simple as that. Yet the D.C. government
looks the other way, cutting its funds for the poorest of the poor.

As the hearing began in the fifth-floor council chambers, ten people sat outside in the hallway singing "We want housing now." Police officers were milling about, as well as reporters. One officer in charge announced that if the protesters did not move, he would put them outside.

I was not planning to be arrested with the civilly disobedient, but I decided to sit with them for a few minutes of song. I had come to support my friends who were testifying. A reporter began asking me questions, so I stood aside and tried to explain what was happening and why we were so upset at the city proposals.

All of a sudden, fifteen police officers pushed me away from the reporter into a group of other supporters who were standing on the edge of the hallway. Before I knew it, I was shoved into an elevator with nine other onlookers. We were brought to the first floor, hand-cuffed, loaded into police vans, taken away and thrown into jail. No questions asked, no warning given, no rights upheld.

Such is life these days in Washington, D.C.

Although I should be outraged, angry or at least shocked, actually, I am not at all surprised to find myself here. I did not intend to risk arrest in an act of nonviolent, civil disobedience, but somehow, I have begun to expect that my association with the homeless poor is going to have consequences. So, in some unconscious realm, I fully expected something like this. If one is going to walk with the homeless, one had best be prepared to suffer. And here I am, today, all of a sudden, in jail.

The police officers took my pens (as well as my watch, my belt and shoelaces), but someone in our group managed to keep hold of a pen, which he has lent to me. Meanwhile, I have my copy of Henri Nouwen's book and some paper to write on.

As I write this, some twenty of us (men and women, black and white, homeless and non-homeless) are locked in the D.C. Central Cell Block, two small, ugly jail cells. Despite the injustice we've experienced, we can still laugh, tell jokes, talk with the officers, and ponder the charade of the city hearing. Presently, my cohorts are asking for a "cell with a view," and some flowers for the table.

From this vantage point—a jail cell in a city where 15,000 homeless men, women, and children walk the streets, and where funds for the homeless are being cut—jail seems like a good place to be. As Gandhi would say on such an occasion, "It may be the best protest I can make at this time."

Jail is also a good place to ponder what it means to be a Christian leader, a servant of the poor, a disciple of Jesus. Perhaps, all priests, religious women and men (especially Jesuits!), bishops and cardinals should spend time in jail for speaking out against the injustices of the day, or being in illegal solidarity with the oppressed. After all, we follow a tradition—a Way of life—which led Christian leaders of this century—Gandhi, King, Day, Jaegerstaetter, Parks—to spend time behind bars. Our leader, Jesus, suffered the scandal of arrest, jail, trial, and capital punishment. This is the Person we claim to follow. Somewhere along the way, at some point in our Christian lives, we need to catch the troublemaking, illegal Spirit of his life.

In his book, Henri Nouwen gets to the heart of this point:

I am deeply convinced that the Christian leader of the future is called to be completely irrelevant and to stand in this world with nothing to offer but his or her own vulnerable self. That is the way Jesus revealed God's love.

Protesting the crimes of the day—and the horrific crime of a military economy that has brought the world to the brink of destruction and caused the suffering of millions of human beings—is one way to experience what it means "to be completely irrelevant," for it naturally leads to the irrelevance of jail-time.

The first ones to tell us today that our protests were irrelevant were the government officials, followed quickly by several police officers. The officials are setting aside the people's votes and concerns and the officers long ago gave up any hope of changing city corruption. "What good is your meaningless protest against the city government?" they say through the bars. "The hearings will continue; your points will be ignored; the funds for the homeless will still be cut!" When I hear such talk, I am glad that I was arrested, but I know too that such despair will not have the last word. That's what the irrelevance of the resisting Christ teaches me: resurrection is guaranteed for those who cast relevance to the wind and take up the cross of loving, truthful nonviolence.

How much Jesus must have heard this same kind of talk! "What good is all this resistance, all this troublemaking?" they must have shouted to him. "If you really are the Savior, if you really had any sense, you'd become a powerful leader who takes control and reforms the system." He must have faced constant opposition from despairing people clinging to the last vestiges of power. It is a temptation that plagues church leaders to this day.

But Nouwen is insistent. His book, the fruit of his move from the world of academia into the world of L'Arche, a community of disabled people, declares that Christianity calls for an unusual fidelity:

> The leader of the future will be the one who dares to claim
> his or her irrelevance in the contemporary world as a divine
> vocation that allows him or her to enter into a deep solidarity

with the anguish underlying all the glitter of success and to bring the light of Jesus there.

Nouwen calls for a movement "from the moral to the mystical," if Christian leadership is to be faithful in the future.

The only way to survive jail for nonviolent protest is to move into the arena of the mystical and the contemplative. And considering the times we live in, jail is a real possibility for all those who try to put the Gospel into action. Without accepting one's powerlessness and trusting in the love and truth of God, one will go crazy in jail. One's true desire to be powerful, in control, effective and popular will come crashing through the four walls of powerlessness, inefficiency, scandal and the inability to change the world.

Nouwen maintains that true discipleship to Jesus involves the movement from leading others to being led, as Jesus said, "where we'd rather not go." "The long painful history of the church is the history of people ever and again tempted to choose power over love, control over the cross, being a leader over being led. Those who resisted this temptation to the end and thereby give us hope are the true saints."

Nouwen speaks with a peaceful integrity that penetrates to the truth of life as a disciple of Jesus, a life I want to experience, beginning in this jail cell.

I hope many heed his message. Perhaps then, Christians will eagerly join the world of "the hungry, the homeless, and the locked-up," as my cohorts refer to themselves, and be less reticent about the cost and results of true discipleship.

June 20

Last week, the ten of us who were rounded up by the city police for "trespassing" at city hall, during an open public hearing of the City Council, showed up in court. After a day of discussion with the judge and the prosecutor, as we were on the verge of starting a trial, the judge dismissed the case against us. We were arrested "illegally," she said. Case closed.

As we left, we shared our hope that we might always risk nonviolent, illegal solidarity with the homeless and the poor, whatever the consequences.

The next day, most of my companions from court were arrested again for blocking traffic in the middle of Pennsylvania Avenue, outside of city hall, the District Building. Once again, they are trying to prevent the closing of the city shelters for fear that such an irresponsible act will lead to the deaths of many more homeless people.

We may not live to see our goals fulfilled, but we will be as faithful to fulfilling the vision as we can.

8.

The Case of the Moving Furniture:
On Trial for Affordable Housing

December 1988

On Wednesday, October 19, 1988, with six other friends, I was arrested on the grounds of the US Capitol for calling attention to the plight of the homeless poor and the need for affordable housing. At precisely twelve noon, Sue Frankel-Streit, Joe Byrne, Anne Tucker, Richard Powell, Connie Lamka, Gabriele O'Brien, and I unloaded a pile of furniture, including two couches, chairs, tables and lamps, in the middle of the intersection between the Supreme Court, the Library of Congress, and the US Capitol. We sat in the couches in the middle of the street and sang songs of peace and justice. After singing and praying for a minute, we were surrounded by some thirty officers and arrested. We spent the afternoon being "processed" and then most of the night in jail. The next morning, we were arraigned in the D.C. Courthouse. We were threatened with one year in jail and $1000 in fines. We pleaded "not guilty" and set a date for trial.

What an experience! We took to the streets in dramatic fashion, using the creative nonviolence of Dr. King, Gandhi and Dorothy Day, to demand affordable housing. Our action was part of a series of daily actions for housing taking place at the US Capitol in the weeks prior to the election. Previously, a group of housing advocates from North Carolina let loose seven chickens on the Capitol lawn and unfurled a banner which read "Money for Housing is Chicken Feed!" Another group symbolically evicted Senator Jesse Helms from his office. They dressed as furniture movers and entered his office like lobbyists about their business, posted an eviction notice on his door, and started moving furniture into the hallway, as stunned secretaries looked on. They continued for fifteen minutes before they were stopped. Earlier, others dropped a banner from the public balcony in the Senate, demanding that Congress create decent, affordable housing for the poor.

Our action has been the most involved so far because we are all local D.C. folks, and had easy access to significant "props." We met the night before and discussed a variety of possible actions, until slowly the symbolic eviction emerged from the discussion. None of our supporters thought we could carry through with our plan, and I was skeptical myself. The police knew something was going to happen because daily actions had been promised throughout the fall; but on this day, an unusually large number of reporters and supporters were congregating at 11:30. Carrying a couch, Joe and I ran into the intersection when there were few cars around. It all happened very quickly. The traffic stopped immediately, and then proceeded around us (as if nothing unusual were taking place). Suddenly, the police were everywhere, closing the intersections and confiscating the illegal furniture. We kept on singing.

Of course, our shenanigans were intended to point out the lack of affordable housing, Congress' refusal to do anything about the housing crisis and the dramatic number of evictions taking place daily around the country. In Washington, D.C., we estimate there are fifty to seventy-five evictions a day.

When we stand trial, we will say firmly, "We are indeed not guilty. Congress and the US government are guilty of ignoring the housing crisis. In fact, they are the deliberate cause of it."

Needless to say, it was one of the most exciting and fulfilling days of my life. The action offered a daring, creative symbol for the country; it dramatized the plight of the poor. I had a deep sense that the act itself was born of the Spirit. As we brainstormed the night before in the shelter run by the Community for Creative Nonviolence, the idea literally emerged on its own. No one person thought of it. It dawned on us as we discussed the things we wanted to say and do. Slowly, together, we saw the light and agreed to go forth with the vision given to us, hoping the country would see.

Typically, I sat there, as the discussion progressed, mumbling to myself my pessimistic thoughts. "It'll never work; don't waste your time." But everyone was so enthusiastic, I couldn't not join them. In the Spirit of community, I discovered the strength to go forward. Then, I saw the action happen. I became a believer: affordable housing is possible for every human being if we choose to create it.

January 24, 1989

An amazing week of grace. Last Wednesday, the seven of us began a four-day trial for "obstructing traffic" on the grounds of the US Capitol. It was the week of Dr. King's birthday and also the week of a presidential inauguration. Hardly any press covered our trial, and yet, in all humility, I think it was a significant event. Every day the courtroom was packed with friends who came to hear our testimony and show their support for us and the homeless. And every day, I saw my parents sitting in the back of the courtroom, encouraging me with their loving support.

The first step in the procedure was to pick a jury. We were asked to introduce ourselves to a roomful of forty-eight potential jurors. We each told of our religious motivation and years of service among the poor and destitute of Washington, D.C.

At one point, a potential juror stood up and said, "Your honor, I could never convict such holy people." We were touched, we reflected later, but we did not consider ourselves holy. It is the life work of the Gospel which is holy. We were merely doing our duty as human beings trying to help other human beings.

The prosecutor began: we were indeed guilty. We had "unlawfully, knowingly, and intentionally occupied the roads to substantially obstruct or hinder their use." We were guilty, he said. The implication? We deserved months (possibly years) in jail.

He called forth a police officer who was present that October afternoon. He called forth another officer to testify that the police indeed did pick up furniture in the middle of the street. And he brought out a video machine and showed the police videotape of us singing in the middle of street and as we were led away into the waiting police vans.

"They are guilty," he told the jury. "The prosecution rests."

It was our turn. We stood in our own defense, and in defense of the homeless. "This is not merely a case of traffic violation," said Joe Byrne of the Olive Branch Catholic Worker. "The reasons we did what we did were because we felt it was demanded of us; because all of us work with the homeless and this was a way of dramatizing their plight, a way toward solving it; because those people inside the Capitol building, our congressional representatives, need to see in a very dramatic fashion the plight of the homeless so as to effect legislation towards solving the crisis; because homelessness in this country has become a national emergency and all other recourse has been tried and found wanting. Our simple effort was the best way of addressing this emergency that we knew of."

Sue Frankel-Streit of the Dorothy Day Catholic Worker took the stand and testified about her work sheltering homeless families, going out at nights to feed the men on the heating grates, and advocating on behalf of the poor.

Then I took the stand. The question was put to me: "Why did you do what you did?"

"I went to the US Capitol after much prayerful consideration," I answered, "because of what I have seen and heard, because of the hundreds of homeless people I have worked with over the years, because of the scores of people that I have tried to help as they faced eviction.

"I went because these statistics about a national crisis are not just statistics for me; they are real. These figures come down to real people that I know.

"I have come to see homelessness and the housing crisis as a spiritual matter; it's a matter of life and death. People die on the streets. I've known homeless people who have died. I had to act now to call attention to this matter of the spirit.

"We were saying, 'Congress, look at an eviction; look at homelessness. By spending our resources on weapons of war, you neglect the poor and cause people to suffer. Stop it; stop the evictions; stop the housing shortage. Stop turning away from the sufferings of our sisters and brothers.'

"We are a people who follow in the tradition of Jesus and Dr. King. We take seriously the tradition of active, nonviolent social change. We look to Dr. King's example to find out how to improve society. He worked for civil rights; we say housing is a civil right and so we've taken to the streets through the power of nonviolence, like Dr. King, to demand that basic right for the poor.

"Finally, I went to the Capitol in response to the burning question, 'What does it mean to be a moral person, a religious person, a Christian?' to the question of our age, 'What does it mean to be a human being?' I've concluded that being human means caring for others; standing up for the rights of all, especially the poor and marginalized; and working to make the world more just and more peaceful."

I took my seat; the trial continued. Vicky Luna, of the National Union of the Homeless, spoke from her experience of being evicted, and her work to organize other evicted peoples to acquire their own homes.

Dr. Janelle Goetcheus of Healthcare for the Homeless and Christ House, a medical facility for the homeless, testified to the medical effects of the crisis of homeless. She spoke from her experience of working as a doctor in five city shelters and going out in a medical van to the streets, parks, and grates in the evenings to offer help.

When asked to relate her memorable moments, she replied, "They are all memorable. I would have to talk about every moment of every day. I just came from the biggest shelter in the city, and as I was leaving an elderly woman was coming in who had just been discharged from a hospital having just had a heart attack. She was discharged back to the streets.

"Nearly any illness that you can think of is exacerbated by being on the street. From all our studies, we have concluded that it is a fatal condition to be homeless; I am just speaking medically. Homelessness is a life-threatening condition. We see people dying in the shelters and dying out on the street, but it is going to get much worse."

We rested our case. Then, the prosecutor stood up before the jury and argued why we should be found guilty, why we were criminals.

Finally, it was my turn to stand before the jury, on behalf of my friends, and offer a closing statement:

"I come before you this afternoon on behalf of all seven of us to ask you to find us not guilty of any crimes, indeed to proclaim to the city and the nation as a whole that we are not guilty. And I would like to discuss this fact that we are not guilty in light of two points, first the letter of the law, and second, the spirit of the law.

"Regarding the letter of the law, the evidence proves that we are indeed not guilty. We seven did not do what we are charged with doing. We did not make any serious, substantial hindrance or obstruction in the road. The videotape and photographs showed a bus, limousine, car and other vehicles moving around us; traffic continued and everything kept going. And besides, if we had wanted to obstruct traffic knowingly and intentionally we would have brought more furniture or blocked traffic with our truck or gotten fifty other people to sit in the street or lie down in the road. But that is not what we did and not what happened.

"Our objective was not a matter of traffic violation. We presented a minor, temporary and symbolic presence in the street, a fleeting, momentary, nearly ridiculous, symbolic demonstration pointing to a more noble goal. We are not guilty and your job is to say so, to say, according to the letter of the law, we find the seven defendants not guilty.

"But I would also like to speak about the spirit of the original law which was written hopefully to help serve human life. And in light of that spirit of the law we believe that you must also find us not guilty, in view of the fact that the root of all law is justice.

"We did not do anything criminal. We went into the street on October 19, 1988, to testify to the urgent crisis of homelessness, to a life-threatening emergency, and we said to Congress dramatically: 'Look at evictions; look at homelessness. For the love of God, do something about it. Make housing available now.'

"We therefore did not commit a crime. The crime that has been committed and that continues to be committed is that our government allows some of our brothers and sisters, other human beings, to walk the streets homeless without getting homes for them.

"Congress lets it happen; it turns the other way. The government walks over the homeless. Our government rushes ahead with its mad military spending for more horrible bombs while offering pennies for housing for the homeless poor. Actually the figure is two cents per tax dollar for housing, while fifty-two cents per tax dollar goes for military spending.

"This, I beg you to see, is criminal activity. It is also inhuman, immoral, unjust, evil and in the biblical sense, sinful.

"Ladies and gentlemen of the jury, it is a crime that fifty evictions take place each day in this city, not to mention the hundreds and thousands of daily evictions around the country. It is a crime that three million people walk the streets of this nation without a home. It is a crime that Congress can report nonchalantly that there may be nearly twenty million homeless people by the year 2000.

"The lack of affordable, appropriate housing is the crime and we went into the streets as good, upstanding human beings, doing our patriotic and religious duty, to say this to the country and to the Congress in particular. We can no longer allow this crisis, this high-level crime, to continue any longer."

The judge sent the jury off to find a verdict. We waited all afternoon. No verdict. Then, today at about noon, we gathered in the court to hear the verdict. "How do you find the co-defendants as to the charge of obstruction of the roadway?" the clerk asked the foreman of the jury.

"Not guilty!"

We were overcome with joy and gratitude.

The judge spoke up. "To the former defendants, I would like to extend my thanks to all of you for your conscientious, dignified, and decorous behavior. I am often enriched by the people who come into my courtroom; I would go so far as to say that I am enriched daily but by none more than the seven of you. I would like to ask for your prayers for me and the work of this court and to tell you that you can be assured of my prayers for you and for your work. Thank you, you can be on your way now, once and for all."

This evening, two jurors called wanting to know how they could get involved in work with the homeless.

This was a historic verdict, it seemed to us, a sign of victory for the homeless and the poor. It did not solve the crisis, nor did it convert us to believe in the judicial system which is very corrupt, but it sent a signal to Congress that there is a crisis and the government better start working seriously to solve it. It marked not the end of our struggle, but rather a new beginning, a sign to keep working for the day when all God's children would have affordable, decent housing.

March 4

The judge who presided over our case has written to me that she has purchased a copy of my book on nonviolence, *Disarming the Heart,* as well as *By Little and By Little: The Selected Writings of Dorothy Day.* "*Disarming the Heart* is a fine work—forcing readers like me to confront the dichotomy between how we live and how we ought to live, if we take the Gospel seriously."

I had written to her suggesting that judges should refuse to try cases of conscience and social justice, civil disobedience cases that involve nonviolent activists who pursue housing for the homeless and disarmament for peace. My hope, I wrote, is that not only will the judges then draw attention to the need for justice and peace, but they will even be inspired to come down from the bench and join us in the streets as we seek justice for all. "Let me say," she concluded in her long letter, "it is my hope that all prosecutors will someday be out of business because of the commitment of people like you to bring about a peaceful change of heart in those who engage in violence. For the example of your daily commitment to the poor and homeless, I remain gratefully yours in peace and love."

Part Two:
The Witness of Nonviolence

My optimism rests on my belief in the infinite possibilities of the individual to develop nonviolence. The more you develop it in your own being, the more infectious it becomes till it overwhelms your surroundings and by and by might oversweep the world.

Mohandas Gandhi

If our cause is a mighty one, and surely peace on earth in these days is the great issue of the day, and if we are opposing the powers of darkness, of nothingness, of destruction, and working on the side of light and life, then surely we must use our greatest weapons—the life forces that are in each one of us. To stand on the side of life we must give up our own lives.

Dorothy Day

The first thing to be disrupted by our commitment to nonviolence will not be the system but our own lives.

Jim Douglass

9.
Disarming the Arms Bazaar:
A Word of Peace in a Place of War

They arrested the apostles and had them put in the common jail. But at night, the angel of God opened the prison gates and said, "Go back and stand in the Temple, and tell the people all about this new Life." They did as they were told; they went into the Temple at dawn and began to preach.

Acts of the Apostles 5:18

Mornings at the McKenna Center are usually crowded with conversation and chores. One morning this fall was typical. Several women were sitting in a waiting room as I put together and gave to them bags of grocery items that we had stored for such emergencies. Each woman was in the process of rearing children, keeping an apartment, and trying to make ends meet in order to thwart eviction. The money runs out fast; a load of groceries makes it easier to get through the month.

But that morning was different. After several hours of this, I changed from my work clothes into a jacket and tie, courtesy of the McKenna Center clothing room, and took a local subway across town to one of the classiest hotels around. I met a friend at a nearby subway stop and we entered the hotel. The chandeliers and gold fixtures were a stark contrast from my work place and abode, but I was more struck by the crowds. Over 5000 people had traveled from all over the nation to attend the Air Force Association's annual arms bazaar at this monstrous first-world hotel. All the major nuclear and conventional weapons' designers and manufacturers were there to display their wares to prospective buyers. Martin Marietta, General Electric, TRW, McDonnell Douglas, Eaton and many others were there, trying to capture new contracts. It was to be a week of buying and selling, with a lot of fun and frolic as well. Feasts, dances, speeches, and entertainment were planned. It was a "National Assembly" of the military-industrial complex.

My friend and I sauntered our way into the lobby, where we discovered a lounge area. We sat for a few moments and watched the hordes of people milling about.

Finally, we stood up, walked into the center of the fray, unfurled a large, colorful banner that read, "Swords into Plowshares," and began to speak. "We call upon everyone here to stop producing, buying and selling nuclear weapons and weapons of any kind," I proclaimed. "These weapons threaten to kill all people and are an offense to God. Please, on behalf of the poor of the world, dismantle your display booths and go home. Let's close down this arms bazaar. Jesus taught us that the way to peace is through nonviolence, through loving our enemies. The use of these weapons will only bring terrible violence and destruction. For the love of God, let's put an end to this whole lethal business."

As I looked out at the crowd, I could see that people were listening. Many seemed stunned by our sudden theatrics; many others were amused; a few were disgusted, some definitely curious.

As we continued our pleas for peace, we were surrounded by security guards, police, and undercover officers. We were warned to cease or face the consequences. As calmly as I could, I said,

"Officer, these people are buying and selling weapons of mass destruction that threaten humanity. Please stop them. If you won't, we intend to do what we can."

Needless to say, we were arrested and handcuffed and led out the front door to a nearby police van. But all the way, I continued to call upon people to follow Jesus' way of nonviolent love. I said that I was a Jesuit who serves the homeless here in Washington, D.C., and that all the money for these weapons belongs to the poor.

Our witness was, in many ways, simple and ridiculous. We spoke to the crowds for a mere two minutes before we were hustled out of sight. If I had worn clerical garb, I would not have even had the opportunity of those few seconds. We were "disguised" as businessmen just so we could get in.

So many people—particularly my community members—have said to me since then, "What did it accomplish? What good did it do?" It was a difficult experience indeed. I cannot recall ever being more nervous and terrified. I have traveled in dangerous war zones and walked through my violent neighborhood, but as I sat in that hotel lobby preparing to unfurl a simple banner, I trembled. I shook with fear.

All that fear and anxiety passed, however, the moment I began to speak. It was then that I felt the Spirit of God empower me with peace and calm. I was given the words to say and the spirit in which to say them. We were booked and jailed and had some lively exchanges with our guards later in the day. The jail cells were disgusting and puny, but we fell asleep easily, exhausted from a long day. At 12:30 a.m., we were awakened and released. A few hours later, we were back vigiling and holding signs at the hotel. The charges had been dropped.

But what did we accomplish? What good did we do? Part of me says, "Such deeds accomplish very little, but they still need to be done," and a larger part of me says, "Such an action does a world of good for the world." My friends and I have tried a variety of legal avenues over the years to rid the planet of nuclear weapons and the thinking that leads to their existence. We have written letters to government officials and newspaper editors, met with government officials, and given talks. Still the arms race continues, worse than ever. And the arms bazaar is thriving. It could even be said that the whole nation/state system of the world is one big arms bazaar, with nations buying and selling and using weapons of death. Someone needs to stand up and say, "Enough is enough. Let's get rid of these deadly monstrosities and learn to live together without killing each other." When enough people say that and act on it, peace will be at hand.

We were peaceful, respectful and nonviolent, and we disrupted the entire comings and goings of the arms bazaar, albeit momentarily. We were trying to be obedient to God in an age of nuclear idolatry. We were trying to be faithful to the nonviolent Jesus who entered Jerusalem's holy Temple, spoke out against its oppressive business and committed a symbolic act of civil disobedience by overturning the tables of the money-changers.

Civil disobedience is risky. I find that it simply cannot be measured by our pragmatic, American standards that always look to results. While participating in it, I had no desire to look for results. What was important was that we were sharing the truth of disarmament as best we could, in as disarming a way as we could, with a crowd of human beings who, for a variety of reasons, are dedicated to arming the planet. They risk the consequences of genocide and global destruction for what they see as the truth; we risk the consequences of personal inconvenience and our own suffering for what we see as the truth. The act itself of witnessing was what counted to us; it was the right thing to do. We did what we could—calmly, peacefully, openly.

Through our night in jail, friends began to hear of our action, to ask "Why?" and to learn about the weapons business. People became aware of the arms bazaar in the process. Also, in a concrete way, we supported and perhaps inspired further resistance. As we held our banner and spoke with police officials, another friend, Marcia Timmel, in a far corner of the hotel, pulled out a hammer and pounded on an eight-foot-tall model of a Minuteman missile (which had been assembled for the arms bazaar at a cost of $10,000). Marcia poured her blood on the model (a kind of "golden calf") and left leaflets explaining the Gospel call to disarm and live. (She faces a trial and several months in jail for this "Plowshares" act.)

The following day, six others penetrated hotel security and stood up in the middle of a packed luncheon—it was Yom Kippur—and threw ashes on themselves, put on sackcloth, and called people to repentance. They were led outside and released. During an evening candlelight vigil, one woman spontaneously decided to sit in the hotel driveway as limousines pulled up for the final, gala dinner dance. One elderly woman with a cane and a bad back stood in the driveway to offer her resistance. As a car pulled up, she moseyed over to block its passing and gently stretched out her hand, motioning the car to halt. The driver and riders were astonished (we could see their jaws drop).The demonstrators cheered at the beautiful display of nonviolence. The sit-in contingent was eventually removed and jailed, and those keeping vigil sang and stood in silence with their banners. Further actions occurred on the last day of the bazaar, and people are committing themselves to plan for next year.

At the heart of our witness and the acceptance of its consequences was a spirit of love among us all that was very significant. We had come together in prayerful preparation beforehand and committed ourselves to nonviolence. While under arrest and in jail, we continued our witness through prayer and fasting. It is hard to convey how powerful such an experience can be—the powerful sense of truth and the presence of God with us. There were no reporters, no TV cameras; we were ignored by the media. Yet we believed that the action would bear fruit, that it was perfectly right to do what we did.

Our experience did not stop the arms race, but it was a noble try. It was the fruit of the small daily efforts to stop the arms race in our own hearts. Our hope is that the struggle in our personal lives to be nonviolent will touch the hearts of others and help transform the arms bazaar that the world has become into a beloved community of friends. Our witness of nonviolence ultimately comes down to one day in the life of a continuing struggle of faith, hope, and nonviolent love.

The witness of those who spoke out against the arms bazaar will bear fruit, I am convinced. Every year more and more people will step forward to question, in the name of Jesus, in the name of a world without war, the whole bizarre affair. Someday, thousands of Christians will stand up with banners and dismantle model weapons and sit in at places that promote war. Someday, the hotel will no longer be willing to host such an event. Someday, hotels and military installations will all be transformed into low-income housing for the poor. It is bound to happen because it is already happening. The arms bazaar is being disarmed and the spirit of nonviolent love is spreading. This good news gives us the strength and hope to continue on in our journey in the reign of nonviolent love.

Our experience only confirms our resolve: the risks are worth taking. The vision is worth seeing. The reality of nonviolence is worth living.

10.
Mondays at the Pentagon:
A Prayerful Vigil for Peace

Every Monday morning, rain or shine, snow or sleet, for several years now, a small group of churchworkers from the metropolitan Washington, D.C., area keeps a prayerful vigil outside the south entrance of the Pentagon.

The group stands along the side of the walkway, greeting Pentagon employees as they go to work. Their protest is subtle, silent, and peaceful. Their signs are simple; so is their message. "The Way to Peace is Peace." "We Want Peace, Not Nuclear War." "Disarm Now and Live." "Create a Peaceful World for the Children."

The reaction by ingoing employees is mixed. Some are outwardly hostile, most ignore the vigilers, and a few quietly walk over to them to express gratitude and agreement.

After years of walking past the Monday morning vigils, most Pentagon employees do not even bother to look up from the concrete as they walk by.

Yet those keeping vigil keep coming back, offering a friendly smile and a "good morning" to those going in. They also offer a leaflet explaining why the work of the Pentagon is evil and must cease.

"It's hard to develop a suitable dialogue," said Paul Magno of the Olive Branch Catholic Worker as he handed out leaflets one Monday morning. "It would be great to sit down with these folks for twelve hours, but that's just not possible."

"There are a lot of good people going to work at this place," said Anne Tucker, a 61-year-old mother and long-time advocate for the homeless, "and we've come to ask them to consider other types of work, work that is life-giving and peaceful, not deadly."

"I think it's important to initiate a dialogue with people working in the military," said Marcia Timmel, who works at the Zaccheus soup kitchen in downtown D.C. and keeps vigil every week at both the Pentagon and a nearby abortion clinic.

"My experience is that most of these people are as sincerely committed to peace as I am, but somehow through fear of communism or inferiority or whatever, they've come to the conclusion that the way to achieve peace is by making war. I want to challenge them to explore that concept," Marcia said.

The Monday vigils, which last from 7:30 a.m. to 8:30 a.m., conclude with a few minutes of silent prayer.

Thousands of employees pass by the banners and hundreds take the leaflets each week, but most do not stop to converse with the peacemakers.

"Everyone here wants peace," said Richard Powell, a 58-year-old member of the Dorothy Day Catholic Worker, "but these folks seem to be locked into a job. This is their security, and it's hard for them to envision changing jobs to work that does not threaten human life. But if the nuclear arms race isn't reversed soon, we're in for a terrible catastrophe, and who wants that? We've got to change our priorities and we've got to do it now."

"We started coming here almost two years ago now," said Paul, "because we think it is an important place to be and to communicate with one another. We want to share with others our vision of a disarmed, peaceful world. I try to invite people to get peaceful jobs, instead of working at the Pentagon."

"We want to reach the ones with doubts," said Anne. "Twenty thousand people work here; not all of them have the same level of commitment. Maybe we can find some of the cracks. These are good people with energy and talent. They have the best intentions. We believe they are just misdirected."

Each of these demonstrators works through the churches to serve the poor. Most have studied intensely the issues of war and the nuclear arms race. They are quick to note the amount of money that goes to plan and organize war instead of housing the homeless poor.

The demonstrators are trying to change the spending policy of the country. They note that fifty-two cents per tax dollar goes to the military and to weapons, while only two cents per tax dollar goes to affordable housing, and two cents for food for the hungry.

They point to statistics which prove the injustice, the very immorality, of money spent for bombs versus money spent for homes. For $22 billion, they cite as an example, we could build 524 more Trident-II nuclear missiles which are designed to allow the US to strike first in a nuclear war. Each missile has 250 times the destructive power of the bomb dropped on Hiroshima in 1945. A total of 845 Trident-II missiles are planned by the Pentagon. Yet for the same $22 billion, we could renovate and completely modernize 1.3 million units of public housing, creating thousands of new jobs in housing construction and other industries that provide materials and services for homes.

They invoke the message of Martin Luther King, Jr., in dreaming for a different kind of country where the Pentagon would be a day-care center for children and all weapons would be dismantled.

"It is a vision worth striving for," said one demonstrator; indeed, a vision worth dying for, but not killing for, they contend.

The vigil-keepers are friendly and cheerful, and eager to share their vision. Their minds are set on the future, as they labor with a message of peace.

Until then, they will keep gathering every Monday morning in silent prayer at the Pentagon. Perhaps some day, their prayer will be answered.

11

Good Friday in New York City:
Nonviolence Means Carrying the Cross

Holy Week, 1989

Jesus died on the cross a common criminal, a victim of capital punishment, a disgraced enigma to his friends and followers, an outcast. He suffered the fate of other revolutionaries. He had tried to speak for justice, for truth, for the love of God, but the ruling authorities (the Roman and Jewish leaders) realized that he was a threat to their power, and so he was disposed of. Broken and crushed by this "disgrace," his (male) friends fled, perhaps fearing the same outcome for themselves if they were seen standing by Jesus, the political prisoner, in his final agony. Through it all, Jesus never denied his mission or betrayed his God. He was faithful, spoke the truth, and accepted the consequences. In the midst of his tragic end and apparent failure, Jesus did not know what would happen. He remained in the dark. And yet, he fulfilled and exemplified all his teachings on nonviolence and unconditional love in the midst of that pain and darkness.

Jesus did not strike back! He prayed for his persecutors, forgave and loved his enemies, remained nonviolent to the end, and showed us all how to die well. He showed us what true love is all about—the love that suffers even death for the sake of justice and peace, for the sake of all humanity, a suffering love which does not return violence for violence. It is this final, complete love in the midst of such rejection and abuse which reveals his Godliness—God in trouble for being God, for being human, for loving above and beyond the expected boundaries of love.

"My Bible tells me that Good Friday comes before Easter Sunday," Martin Luther King, Jr., used to say. "To be a Christian," he said, "one must take up the cross, with all of its difficulties and agonizing and tension-packed content and carry it until that very cross leaves its marks upon us and redeems us to that more excellent way which comes only through suffering." On another occasion, King told a crowd a followers, "When I took up the cross, I recognized its meaning.... The cross is something you bear, and ultimately something that you die on.... Before the crown we wear there is the cross that we must bear. Let us bear it!" he declared. "Bear it for truth. Bear it for justice, and bear it for peace."

To bear the cross for truth, justice, and peace will be a very painful, messy, political, lonely affair, as King learned. To bear the cross will mean going against the grain of society, upsetting the status quo of injustice and violence. Bearing the cross will upset every aspect of one's life. It will affect all our relationships with others, one way or another, upsetting their lives too. It will cause disagreement, division and rejection. One will feel as if the bottom has fallen out of one's life, or, to use imagery from the Hebrew Scriptures, as if one is deluged by flooding waters or surrounded by burning flames. It is the public, political, social reality of telling the truth and insisting on the reconciliation of all sides, even at the price of crucifixion. It will mean living as the object and scorn of the powers and principalities, the system of death which controls the planet.

Bearing the cross means entering the nonviolent struggle for justice and peace and risking crucifixion by the state. Bearing the cross means being a bearer of peace every day of our lives in our violent, warmaking, nuclear world. Bearing the cross means taking a chance that we will suffer physically, and even be killed, for our insistent vision of peace and justice. It means risking the possibility of becoming the latest victim of the world's violence, but doing so in a spirit of love. Martin Luther King, Jr., knew this. The saints and martyrs down through the ages understood this logic of nonviolence as well. Jesus took this risk and went to Jerusalem. He was faithful to God, took his chances, called for the conversion of humanity, willingly accepted the consequences, and paid the penalty by being publicly executed. We are his followers.

Our task today, in a world armed to the teeth with nuclear weapons of self-destruction and every type of bomb and war machine, is nothing more and nothing less than that same kind of death-defying, life-giving, risky business of proclaiming the truth about peace and justice in a nonviolent spirit.

This week is Holy Week, and large groups of college students have been keeping vigil around Washington, D.C., with the Jonah House peace community from Baltimore and other anti-nuclear activists. We prayed at the Pentagon and in front of the White House. On Good Friday, in the wee hours of the morning, I drove to New York City, to join good friends—and several thousand Christians—in the annual Good Friday peace walk, a modern-day "Stations of the Cross" through the streets of the city, from one end to another. We started at the United Nations Plaza and stopped at every conceivable point of crime: a multinational corporation doing business with racist South Africa; a pornography store; an armed forces recruiting station that supports US intervention in Central America; a nuclear weapons manufacturer; a newspaper which publishes heavily biased "news" that favors that military establishment. A cold rain and black sky set a somber tone for the entire day.

The fifteenth station marked the resurrection of Jesus, and so we sat in at the Riverside Research Institute, a Star-Wars, nuclear-weapons think tank on 42nd Street and were subsequently arrested by the police. About one hundred of us were brought to a nearby precinct and booked. It was a fitting end to such a day. We politely but publicly said NO to the madness of global violence, on the anniversary of the execution of Jesus the peacemaker and truth-teller. In our own way, we tried to take up the cross of nonviolent love and follow in his footsteps.

In the midst of each Gospel account of Jesus' arrest, trials, torture, crucifixion, and death, in the midst of the chaos and cruelty of those days, we read how the Roman soldiers made fun of Jesus. They mocked him, insulted him, pretended he was a king, laughed in his face—in short, they totally humiliated him.

> The men guarding Jesus amused themselves at his expense. They blindfolded him first, slapped him, and then taunted him: "Play the prophet; which one struck you?" And they directed many other insulting words at him. (Luke 22:63-65)

When we walk down 42nd Street each Good Friday on a walk for peace, we try to recall this humiliation and pain undergone in the spirit of nonviolent love for justice and peace. We try to see how this violence continues all over the world today and to call for an end to such evil activity. Our Good Fridays are times of remembrance and recommitment to the Way of the nonviolent cross. For others, even in our midst, the re-enactment is closer to the original story.

One Good Friday, years ago, we were arrested in the lobby of the Riverside Research Institute for opposing Star-Wars research. We were led in groups of five by various New York City police officers into waiting police vans. I sat inside with several friends until slowly the van was packed with our protesting companions. We were not handcuffed and the police were extremely courteous and polite to us. Just as they were set to drive us off to the precinct, two police officers brought in one young, African-American man—handcuffed. He was put in the back of the van. After five or six white police officers entered the front of the van, we drove off.

A friend of mine next to me whispered, "Just watch the racism at work here."

An officer called back, asking for the handcuffed passenger's name.

"My name is Theodore," came the response. "I want to be with these people. I'm against war. These people are doing the right thing."

The officers broke up laughing before our eyes and proceeded to make fun of him by mocking him, pretending he was a lawyer or a businessman or a jobholder who was also a peaceful resister. It was a short ride, but it seemed to last an eternity as the officers continued to abuse him verbally. Someone of our company asked, "Why is this man handcuffed? Why do you treat him like that?" "He resisted arrest," one of the officers replied curtly.

When we arrived at the police station, we were led into the lobby and individually given a summons to appear in court. The handcuffed one, however, was immediately processed and taken off to jail. The lawyers in our group were unable to help him. It appears this poor man (who may have been homeless) walked nonchalantly into the lobby, saw our demonstration, and sat down with the rest of us. Before he knew it, he was under arrest, lifted up, and struggling to stay seated.

One of the consequences of our actions for peace is the opportunity of seeing what happens every day to the poor. The poor suffer the brunt of society's racism and violence and are wisked off to prison before they know it. Such injustice happens all the time. Perhaps in seeing what they suffer and how they are persecuted, middle-class, white resisters like myself are empowered by the Spirit to go with them, to stand with them, to defend them, to speak for them, to enter into their struggle for justice, and most important, to resist the violence. Seeing them, we also see Christ. That Good Friday experience highlighted for me the truth that every day is Good Friday for the poor. Our protest is an attempt to speak up for justice, and a way to enter this Good Friday world of the poor.

As we stood in the precinct lobby that day, one friend explained to a passerby, "What we're really looking for is justice." Some police officers overheard this comment. Turning to another, one laughed and whispered, "And all they're going to get is *just us*!"

To a certain degree, the police officer was right, but only to a degree. Could it be that on the path into the reign of God and God's nonviolent justice one must inevitably, in our day, encounter police officers and their vans? Apparently, this was the path of Jesus before he entered into God's glory. Perhaps it will be for us, too.

Every day is Good Friday for the poor. How fully we respond to the needs of suffering humanity can only be decided in the silence of our hearts. In that silence, the voice of Jesus still speaks today, "If

12.
Peace in a Time of Resurrection: Beating Swords into Plowshares

It happened like this. In the evening of that same day, the first day of the week, the doors were closed in the room where the disciples were, for fear of the Jews. Jesus came and stood among them. He said to them, "Peace be with you," and showed them his hands and his side. The disciples were filled with joy when they saw the Lord, and he said to them again, "Peace be with you. As God sent me, so I am sending you." And he breathed on them the Spirit of peace.

Jesus' gift of peace to his disciples is the gift he has never stopped giving. At a time when they were full of despair and sorrow, when all hope had scattered and vanished, Jesus appears, and, with a word, gives peace to their souls, a peace that fills them with joy. His gift of peace is his very presence, an act so astounding that, moments before, it seemed impossible. His presence, his return to them, his victory over death, broke all the rules, as well as the veneer of hopelessness and despair. His resurrection brought a peace his disciples had never known, a peace that would never be taken from them again. It was the gift of the Risen Christ, the gift of love which conquers all hopelessness and despair, the gift of love which proves victorious over sin and death, the gift of love which reaches out and reconciles people to each other and to God, once and for all time.

Jesus gave a gift of peace to them which the world could not give. It was the gift of fully realizing that they lived in the reality of the reign of God, a reality where everyone is sister and brother to one another, all children of a loving God.

From that moment on, his disciples were never the same. They received his gift of peace and the commission to witness before the whole world what God had done in the resurrection of Jesus of Nazareth. The rag-tag band of followers were transformed into a dynamic, spirit-filled company of witnesses, eager to live as Jesus lived, to seek justice for the poor as Jesus sought it, to love through self-sacrifice as Jesus loved, to die nonviolently for others as Jesus died, and to rise to fuller life as Jesus rose. They took to the streets, filled with the peace of the reality which is God's present realm. They spread the Good News that the time of sin, despair, violence, and death was over. They lived in a time of resurrection.

Our time is such a time. Jesus Christ continues to appear to his followers today and give them a peace they have never known. Today, we Christians are so filled with the joy and peace of the reign of the Risen Lord that we cannot help but want to share that peace with all the world. Christ's message of peace continues to be Good News of great joy to those who have ears to hear it.

The peace of the world, on the other hand, is a non-peace, the non-peace of stalled diplomacy, war and violence, the non-peace that comes from a nuclear arms race which spreads a shadow of fear over the hearts of the human race. It is a non-peace which causes us to get defensive, to "deter," to arm ourselves to the teeth out of fear, to plan first-strike nuclear war, to invade smaller countries to protect our economic interests. This non-peace has cast such a pall over the gift of Jesus that it is hard to get a handle on what Jesus was talking about, indeed, to see Jesus standing before us, hands out, side open, offering his greeting.

In light of his word of peace, I am reminded of the greeting I heard a few years ago on Easter, a greeting of peace and resurrection that has touched me deeply.

It happened like this.

A friend of mine, Patrick O'Neill, along with seven other people, stood up on the Feast of the Resurrection and said to the whole world, "Peace be with you," as simply and as boldly as that. The act of these apostles may have been lost on many, but it struck me and leaves me astounded.

On Easter morning, Patrick and his friends, the so-called "Pershing Plowshares," entered the Martin Marietta plant, where Pershing II nuclear missile components are packaged, near Orlando, Florida. They opened one missile kit, removed some of the parts and hammered on them "so as to beat the Pershing sword of death into a plowshare of peace." Martin Marietta security found them one hour later, kneeling together in prayer and song. They were arrested, tried, and sentenced to several years in prison. As I write this, Patrick is in jail.

Hearing the news from a friend, I was struck dumb. Their action spoke of peace to me and hit me like the reality of an impossibility—Resurrection. I had seen Patrick a week before. He looked as he always looked: tall, skinny, with black curly hair and Buddy Holly glasses. We had lunch together with some friends. He was always laughing, making others happy. Now, Patrick was in prison, condemned by the courts and, before I knew it, locked up for years.

A few weeks after the event, Patrick's letters started arriving in my mail. They read like Paul's letters from prison, about a conversion that had taken place, of a new Spirit unleashed, a Spirit that offered a new alternative towards Peace in an age of non-peace, the age of the nuclear quagmire. One year later it is Easter again and, looking back over these letters, I can see the peace that was given by that act of resurrection. "By our actions," Patrick wrote, "we have taken a personal responsibility for disarmament and we can only hope that you'll be empowered to do likewise. Yes, our actions were radical, but in reality far less radical than those of our 'leaders' who each day allow the suicidal arms race to continue and escalate, while the poor starve and suffer. These are the nuclear hostages—those who die even when the bombs aren't exploded."

He sent their "Declaration of Conscience," a statement the Pershing Plowshares made on that Easter Sunday. "In a time of the militarization of thought, of oppressive silences and twisted words that call the Pershing—offensive in speed, range, accuracy—a 'defensive' weapon, we decry these realities; we express our desire to repent of the deeper violence that 'secures' power and property while it bankrupts the spirit of a nation pledged to a welcome for the world's oppressed and to life, liberty and happiness for all. We act as a prayer that our hearing and vision be healed, that those we call 'foreigner' and the invisible poor of our world may be seen, recognized and named our sisters and brothers, that we be led out of the darkness of despair and apathy into the light of hope.

"We act in hope that this Passover may be a new liberation from the consumer lifestyle that enslaves us; from the fear and false securities that paralyze us; in the conviction that, in the midst of multiplied and impotent words, we must risk our bodies to conquer despair. We hope that, in a vulnerability open to the power of God, we can be healed of our violence and, empowered by love, break through the walls that divided 'friend' from 'enemy.'

"We act in love, in this Easter, this 'dawn' of new life: responsible love—recognizing our relationship to these weapons which we must transform, to their creators, all of us in our shared violence and apathy, to their victims who cannot act; communal love—conspiring, breathing together, that we may be one, East and West, North and South in a more human and faithful world; obedient love—enfleshing the prophets' command, 'They shall beat their swords into plowshares and their spears into pruning hooks; one nation shall not raise the sword against another, nor shall they train for war again.'

"In choosing to disarm our own fear and to say NO to one weapon at its source, we celebrate the renewal of life; we choose the way of love that we and our children may live."

These words, held high by their act of disarmament, began to ring in my ears like the chorus of alleluias so familiar during the Eastertide. "Where did these folks learn to speak with such authority?" I secretly uttered under my breath. "Isn't this just Patrick, my friend, and his companions? Where did they learn to speak like this?"

More letters arrived. They continued to read like notes from Franz Jaegerstaetter or Alfred Delp, with the conviction of Bonhoeffer, Gandhi, Day, or King. "Too many people appear to be hung up on this question of 'law'—and obedience to it. Eight women and men decide to hammer on a few components of one of the most deadly weapons in the world and they are arrested and thrown into jail. Yet the same set of laws which label the Pershing Plowshares as criminals supports the legality of the nuclear-arms race. In essence, nuclear war and the preparation to conduct one are, in fact, 'legal' acts! Certainly none of the eight of us would be inclined to beat tuna fish cans into plowshares at the local A & P! We're not anti-law. But when the law states that nuclear war is legal, we have a moral obligation—and a legal responsibility—to break that immoral law. We must not worship idols, false gods, gods of metal."

From his jail cell, he asks a question: "If Jews in Germany during World War II took hammers to the gas chambers and ovens in Nazi concentration camps—for purposes of destroying them—would that have been wrong? These weapons have no right to exist."

"I'm willing to acknowledge that we did indeed go 'one step too far,' " Patrick wrote one day, "if you're willing to apply the same value system to the Pentagon, the Kremlin, and Martin Marietta. Pentagon strategists claim that peace is the 'goal' of their work. Martin Marietta leadership appears to believe that Pershing II is the best 'method' to achieve world peace. (Pentagon strategists envision nuclear victory with losses of no more than twenty million lives!) Considering that the world is at this moment ten minutes or less from nuclear incineration, isn't it appropriate to say that the Pentagon, the Kremlin, and Martin Marietta are the ones who have really gone too far?

"The actions of the Pershing Plowshares were designed to expose the insanity of nuclear-war planning in a most basic way—WE DISARMED A SINGLE WEAPON. The government claims that we did $15,000 worth of 'damage' to a few components of a Pershing II Missile—one Pershing costs $4.6 million! Not much of a dent in their production, huh? We were not vandals or terrorists bent on destroying everything in sight. Our hammering lasted about five minutes. We know that beating swords into plowshares can only be done on a mass scale when we change our hearts, increase our faith, and begin to love one another. Until then, the Pentagon and the Kremlin will keep building many more swords to replace the few we convert into Plowshares.

"It's such a strange feeling to see the truth," he writes from jail, "because you become so overwhelmed with the seemingly total lack of decency in this world—which Dorothy Day called 'a filthy, rotten system.' I just can't understand why so few people appear aware of all this insanity—40,000 daily deaths from starvation and over one trillion dollars spent each year on weapons of death. I ask myself, Can this be true? Is it really happening? The insanity of it all drives us to seek and act in faith and in truth.

"These last six weeks have been the most difficult of my life. My body and mind are spent but my faith is hardy. I miss my friends and loved ones very much; I miss the birth and life blood of spring; my garden; hitchhiking; a bike ride or a run; a quiet moment; many things which I normally take for granted. There is much human suffering in this place.

"During the last six months, I have served time in ten different jails, prisons and 'correctional centers' in four states and the District of Columbia. The federal prison system says I was 'in transit.' Boy, was I! I was physically and emotionally exhausted when I got here. I was and continue to be spiritually strong!

"I have struggled for many years and sought God every step of the way, asking God to take this cup from me.... This time in prison and the weeks 'in transit' have been a lonely and painful experience. I pray daily for the faith to rejoice in my suffering as Peter and the Apostles did when they were brought before the High Priest of the local party of the Sadducees. (Acts 5:39-42) What faith they had! I really do reap comfort from that chapter. Christianity is not a call to comfort and security, but rather a faith which is based on one's willingness to bear his or her cross and also on one's willingness to take an often painful journey with Christ.

"My heart aches when I think of the sufferings of the poor in a world so plentiful with God's gifts. Instead of using God's gifts to nurture life, we are taking much of what God gave us and using it for war preparation. Think of all the great minds which are wasted designing and constructing weapons—thinking up more devious ways to murder God's creation instead of trying to solve the many problems that plague our world. We have clearly reached a point of moral bankruptcy. As one of my co-defendants said, we are on the 'last page of human history.' I think of all the resources we extract from the earth and use to build war machinery, the wasted lives of those who die in war and because of war. What my seven friends and I did was just a very basic and reasonable action in light of all this insanity. We dented a few pieces of metal—metal which is screwed and welded together to make a weapon which could kill millions of people. Think deeply about that, my friend; think too of the poor, and then you will see more clearly the necessity of actions such as ours. We took a very small step and now we must be separated from those we love for awhile. It's painful, yes, but a far smaller sacrifice than so many are willing to make for war.

"The fate of God's earth is up to us. As Thomas Merton said, 'The duty of the Christian is to do the one task which God has imposed on us in the world today. That task is to work for the total abolition of war.' "

After he was denied parole and realized he would be serving a much longer sentence than he had originally expected, Patrick wrote, "The persecution Jesus promised is REAL, yet as I've said before, it's such a small, insignificant sacrifice compared to the enormity of suffering we're trying to stop. Our crosses will surely become much heavier as the burden for the poor increases."

His words remind me of other words of Thomas Merton: "The Christian must have the courage to follow Christ. The Christian who is risen in Christ must dare to be like Christ: he or she must dare to follow conscience. The risen life is not easy; it is also a dying life. The presence of the Resurrection in our lives means the presence of the Cross, for we do not rise with Christ unless we also first die with him.... We have been called to share in the Resurrection of Christ not because we have fulfilled all the laws of God and humanity, not because we are religious heroes, but because we are suffering and struggling human beings, sinners, fighting for our lives, prisoners, fighting for freedom, rebels taking up spiritual weapons against the powers that degrade and insult our human dignity."

One year later, and the full import of this resurrection act and peaceful felicitation hits me. Patrick and his friends reveal what the first Easter was all about. The risen Jesus disarmed his disciples. He gave them, now disarmed, peace. His way became theirs. They were disarmed and went about shouting it to the world, a message of peace, that was Good News. Somewhere along the line, Patrick and his friends were touched, disarmed by the Peace that comes from Resurrection and though they have suffered and struggled, they are growing strong and hardy in the presence of the Risen Christ. Patrick and his friends speak, through their act, Christ's greeting of peace to the world, a greeting that disarms and empowers with the Spirit of love. They went forth to announce their message, willing to accept the consequences of suffering in love for all people, because they had risen to new life in Christ.

The early Christians, according to the Scriptures, called themselves "Witnesses of the Resurrection." Today, Christians might simply be called "People of the Resurrection," those who heed the Gospel call to nonviolence, the people who go to those places of death and transform them into places of life. In such places, they pound on nuclear weapons with hammers, to beat swords into plowshares; they shelter the homeless and feed the hungry; they keep vigil at execution sites or weapons factories; they sit down and block the doorways at Star-Wars think tanks or the Pentagon. In other words, they re-present the peace of Christ which is present here and now.

We are called to be such a people.

Patrick reveals to me what the Christian, the one in whom Christ is risen, looks like in our day and age. The Easter Sunday of Patrick O'Neill and his plowshare friends plays out a modern-day version of Jesus' resurrection greeting of peace. It is a greeting and a prayer, an act of hope that points a new way to peace in our time of resurrection.

The peace that Patrick and his potent Shalom! leaves with me is the peace that comes with the Spirit of disarmament. Through their act, Christ appears to me and disarms me. Christ's disarming love among his people is indeed what makes the great Christian witness of peace in our time. The Risen Christ is appearing before us, disarming us, and sending us out to do likewise. The task at hand is to allow Christ, as the poet Hopkins says, "to easter in us." Let us be sure to believe and accept Christ's disarming greeting and we will indeed, in fact, be filled with a joy that will last forever. Let us follow the disarming Christ who goes before us and act with the Christ in the reality of resurrection, announcing peace to all peoples.

Such acts, such disarming scenes, will surely fill our hearts with love, joy, and peace; and when played out in our faith lives, cause us to sing, with the psalmist of the Easter season, "Alleluia."

13.
Living in a Kairos Moment:
The Call for Nuclear Disarmament

The times we live in are both devastating and hopeful. Things are worse than ever, and are getting worse. At the same time, new, hopeful possibilities for peace and justice appear on the horizon. This is a special, historical moment, a time of opportunity.

Martin Luther King, Jr., spoke frequently of such a historical sense of time. He used the German word *zeitgeist*, meaning "time spirit" or "the spirit of the age." King felt the force of history moving in the late 1950s, leading people to greater liberation. He thought that historical moment had touched him personally, and he was right.

The New Testament uses the Greek word, *kairos*, to speak of a special moment, a decisive, critical moment, "a crisis hour dense with the possibilities of grace," "that time which is now." Compared to the word, *chronos*, or "chronological time," *kairos* refers to the movement of the Holy Spirit in a special, urgent way. Jesus began his public life by proclaiming, "The *kairos* is fulfilled, and the kingdom of God is at hand; repent, and believe in the gospel." (Mark 1:15) For Jesus, "the time is now."

Around the world, oppressed peoples have been speaking about such a *kairos* moment. Hundreds of South African black Christians collaborated, in the mid-1980s, on their *Kairos* document, which declared apartheid a sin and a heresy, indeed, the anti-Christ. Theologians and concerned people in Central America followed with their own *Kairos* document, calling for an end to US military intervention in their lives. After several years of preparation by activists and theologians from seven third-world countries—South Africa, the Philippines, South Korea, Nicaragua, El Salvador, Guatemala, and Namibia—another document appeared, entitled, *The Road to Emmaus: Kairos and Conversion.* This prophetic word calls Christians of the first world to conversion, to stop persecuting God, as Saul had been doing, and to begin standing with and defending the poor and oppressed.

Theologian Bill Kellermann has similar questions regarding the effect of the *kairos* on North American Christians. "In church history," he writes, "it is recognized that there are extraordinary times when the church's very identity is imperiled. If its confession is not made unequivocally clear, nothing less than the meaning of the gospel within the church and before the world is at risk. This special time, a *status confessionis*, is brought on by a historical crisis within the church or without. To discern and name the crisis is incumbent on the community of faith, and to distinguish, as clearly as it possibly can, between truth and error, even between life and death."

Christian activists and organizers from around the country have been quietly meeting each year for several days of retreat in the hills of northeast Pennsylvania to discuss and pray over these questions. Kellermann puts the question this way, "Is this a confessing moment in the church in America? Is a historical crisis upon us? Has the faith of the church been confused and compromised by a cumulation of silence, seduction, and outright subversion?"

Karl Barth and other theologians, living under the Nazi reign, thought such a time had come in May 1934. They issued the Barmen

Declaration, declaring that the *status confessionis*, a time for confessing allegiance to Christ, had come. Most of its authors were subsequently imprisoned or killed by the Nazis.

Kellermann writes of four elements in our own historical crisis that give reason for a special response to a *kairos* moment. First-strike weaponry, the threat of ecological collapse, the structured injustice of the global economy (in which 40 million people die from hunger each year, due to the consumeristic, materialistic lifestyle of the first world), and the war on the poor (the "low-intensity" conflict that leaves thousands dead in the streets). With such an array of death before us, there is surely cause for renewed action, renewed confession, indeed, renewal. That is the essence of *kairos*: to hear the Word anew, and to act afresh in a new way to create a new time, a new world.

Jack Nelson-Palmeyer, author of *War Against the Poor*, offers three important reminders as we grapple with the question of our own response to the *kairos*, our own *status confessionis*: 1) We do not choose this as a *kairos* time. Our task is to respond to the Spirit moving in the times. 2) Our confession and response to the *kairos* is an attempt to live our faith and speak the Word in our historical moment, in our place, and our time—in the United States. 3) Responding to the *kairos* is a response by people of faith to the churches, not to the state.

Given the signs of the times, the terrible capacity to destroy the planet, the movement of the Spirit among us, the developments in the world for justice and peace—a *kairos* is upon us.

Perhaps the umbrella issue which encompasses this *kairos* moment is our continued willingness to destroy the planet: the nuclear arms race and its subsequent fallout. In recent years, I have traveled across the United States and prayed at various nuclear and military installations. The effect of such a pilgrimage on one's soul can only be called sobering. It impresses the urgency of the moment—the willingness to destroy the planet—upon one's heart and mind, and calls forth a response.

At King's Bay, Georgia, I was arrested with seventy others for blocking the entrance of a new Trident Submarine Base. Pax Christi USA and the local Metanoia Community had organized the protest. "One Trident submarine," organizer John Linehan reported to us, "with 24 Trident II (D-5) missiles, each with 8 warheads, will be able to destroy 192 targets, each with a blast 38 times more powerful than the Hiroshima bomb." One Trident submarine, in other words, would be the "equivalent" of 7,296 Hiroshimas. The fleet of 20 Trident submarines that are being completed, at the cost of $85.3 billion, will be the "equivalent" of 145,920 Hiroshimas. When the Tridents are used, God's creation will be destroyed, we were told.

Shortly afterwards, I kept vigil and passed out leaflets at the Trident Submarine Base in Bangor, Washington, where the Ground Zero Community has had a nonviolent presence for almost two decades.

Along the way, I prayed at the Trident Submarine plant in Groton, Connecticut; the nuclear Navy ports in Norfolk, Virginia; New York City, and San Diego, California; the Riverside Research Institute in New York City; the nuclear-weapons test site near Las Vegas, Nevada; the Livermore Laboratories in Berkeley, California, and the nearby Concord Naval Weapons Station; and in Washington, D.C., the Department of Energy, the Naval Surface Weapons Station, the US Congress, the White House, and the Pentagon.

The actual experience of seeing in our own country these nuclear arsenals and the offices where nuclear holocaust is planned was overwhelming. Disbelieving my own eyes, I asked myself, "Is our nation really that dead set on nuclear war? What about those disarmament treaties that US administrations have signed with the Soviet government? What about the wave of peace that is sweeping the world? Just what is going on in the nuclear-arms race? Don't we really want peace?"

The answer, unfortunately, is no. Robert Aldridge's book, *Nuclear Empire* (New Star Books, Vancouver, Canada), makes clear that not only is the apparent progress for disarmament limited to dismantling old and obsolete weapons systems, but the United States is perilously close to "first strike" capability—the ability to launch a nuclear attack against the Soviet Union or some other nation before they can defend itself.

The real arms race continues unabated, as new technological and geopolitical developments shift the action to new weapons systems and new parts of the globe. More and more, the action is shifting away from Western Europe and into the Pacific and Indian Oceans; away from land-based missile systems and to submarine-based first-strike systems and the Strategic Defense Initiative, Star-Wars; away from the NATO alliance and Western European listening posts, to sophisticated new, computerized, navigational and decision-making systems.

In other words, we are closer than ever to nuclear destruction; we race toward it full speed ahead.

Aldridge ought to know about such things. The author of two other books on nuclear weapons, *First Strike!* (1983) and *The Counterforce Syndrome* (1979)—both bestsellers in Japan—he is an engineer and former designer of ballistic missiles for the Lockheed Corporation. His book, *Nuclear Empire,* presents a detailed, brilliant, and devastating analysis of the nuclear imperialism of our country. He goes through the sobering facts, point by point; and the evidence against the genocidal policies of our government is staggering.

This sane book begins with a brief historical overview of US nuclear weapons policy from Hiroshima to the present day, and then examines how a limited, conventional war could escalate quickly into a nuclear exchange. "Deterrence is the *declared* or *announced* nuclear policy," Aldridge points out, "while first strike is the actual, or *action*, policy. In order to fully understand the nuclear picture one must grasp this basic precept that what is announced is not always true."

Henry Kissinger and other former "National Security Advisors" writing in the 1980s put it another way. The US practices "discriminate deterrence"; that is, it aims to deter "social revolution" in the third world, through the "low-intensity conflict" of military aid and regular bombings in countries like El Salvador and the Philippines. Regarding US nuclear policy, "discriminate deterrence" means that US nuclear weapons can be used first wherever desired in a first strike.

Aldridge quotes a 1982 speech by Secretary Caspar Weinberger: "The only war we want is the war-which-never-was. But the war-which-never-was is a war which was never fought because we were prepared to fight and win it." Such Pentagon statements, Aldridge warns, should not be interpreted as confusion or restraint regarding nuclear weapons. "Those statements are designed to confuse the public," he asserts.

Aldridge then explores the US nuclear presence in the Pacific and its wake of devastation; its significance particularly in New Zealand;

and the seizure of the small atoll, Diego Garcia, 1,200 miles south of India, for use as a forward base for Trident submarines.*

Next, Aldridge analyzes the Trident II as a first-strike weapon and the cruise missile as a major factor in the Pentagon's first-strike strategy, which will be in full operation by early 1991. Not only is the Trident II very costly (its funds, if redirected, could easily eliminate world hunger and many diseases), not only does it increase the risk of nuclear war by motivating the Soviets to attack, but it could easily be triggered by one of its submarine commanders, acting under pressure.

Aldridge then investigates the latest advances in missile navigation and targeting technologies, NAVSTAR (Navigation System Time and Ranging, which would direct the course of nuclear weapons), and ELF (Extreme Low Frequency, located in Wisconsin and Michigan, a system which would orchestrate submarines for a first strike); new developments in anti-submarine warfare; and the components of the Star-Wars system. "SDI is a major escalation of the nuclear arms race that will negate any concept of deterrence while allowing America to attack the USSR with impunity," Aldridge maintains. Even with the fall of communism and the ground-breaking developments in the Soviet Union in recent years, including the START treaty, the US will continue the nuclear arms race because it is profitable and because such massive military force can be used to threaten any third-world nation, from Panama and El Salvador to Libya and Iraq. When five percent of the world's population controls

---

* Bob Aldridge and Ched Myers have further documented US nuclear mischief in the Pacific in their latest book: *Resisting the Serpent,* available from Fortkamp Publishing Company.

well over fifty percent of the world's resources, big guns are necessary to keep the balance tilted to one side.

Reviewing the Pentagon's reliance on artificial intelligence and computers to start nuclear war, Aldridge writes, "We are literally placing the existence of all life on this planet at the mercy of an electronic robot's ability to imitate the human brain." And he breaks the myth that the president is the sole person responsible for "pushing the button." In the technological never-never land of today's weapons systems, there are more human and mechanical button pushers than there are buttons.

Finally, Aldridge describes a supposedly flawless, underground, nuclear test that he witnessed; he makes the case that policing a nuclear-test ban would be very easy, and that people should urgently demand such a treaty.

Nuclear Empire concludes with a simple reflection on why an unarmed peace is safer for us all than an armed peace. Aldridge offers a word of hope and a simple way out. "The only way to prevent nuclear war is to halt deployment of those destabilizing first-strike/first-use devices, while at the same time intensifying negotiations toward dismantling the existing nuclear systems of both superpowers. In the meantime, Congress should demand answers on nuclear delegation, and legislate against any use of nuclear weapons without approval from a special legislative panel.

"I view fear and self-interest as the two overriding obstacles to justice and peace. These prevailing attitudes must be turned around before we can expect serious negotiations. That turning around hinges on a factual understanding along with developing compassion for others. A few people on this planet already have this insight. A heavy burden rests on them to motivate the remainder, if humanity is to have a future."

Aldridge's work has become a primer on the US war machine and its nuclear imperialism. Well-documented analysis supports his thesis that the United States administers a nuclear empire which is global in scope, and which is policed and protected by the US military. The reality of the evidence is shocking; the endless quotes by US administrators and Pentagon officials, devastating.

In ancient times, a prophetic word like Aldridge's books might have caused the people to weep and repent. A sane people, after realizing their insanity, would put on sackcloth and sit in ashes. *Nuclear Empire* places a truth before us: if we do not repent of our nuclear madness, if we do not allow ourselves to be healed from our nuclear addiction, some of us may be reduced to sackcloth and ashes. But most of us will be killed.

Aldridge has done his part. If we are wise, we will buckle down, learn what's really going on in the nuclear world, dedicate ourselves to forfending nuclear war and transform that world. We have our work cut out for us.

A good place to discern our response to this *kairos* moment of nuclear catastrophe is the desert. Throughout history, the desert has been a place of spiritual growth and testing, a place where the Spirit of God dwells. In that empty land, with its cactus and wild flowers, snakes and hills, we can hear the Word of God. Jesus went there, "driven by the Spirit," as the Scripture says. John the Baptist lived there. Early Christians fled there to get away from the historical crisis of doubt and betrayal. We, too, can go there to hear a word of peace.

The desert (of the Southwestern United States) has become, however, a very significant place within this country itself, and perhaps the world. Every three or four weeks, the United States tests a nuclear weapon at a test site in the Nevada desert. Our country continues to rush ahead with its addiction to violence and death, and gets closer to genocide with each test, with each new weapon, with each bow before the altar of nuclearism.

As a people, we need to come to grips with the spiritual consequences of our nuclear testing. What happens to our soul as a people when we so willingly bomb the land with hydrogen bombs more powerful than all the explosives used during World War II combined? What does such activity say about the value we place on life itself? Such a symbol of our willingness to destroy the planet calls us to go deeper into the way of nonviolence as a whole new way of life embraced together by all people. These days, it is as if the very stones are crying out, "Now is the time (your *kairos* moment). Don't miss your last way out."

Jesus spoke such words when he arrived in Jerusalem, just before going to the Temple and turning over the tables on the systemic evils of his day. Luke reports: "As he drew near and came in sight of the city, he sheds tears over it and said, 'If you in your turn had only understood on this day the message of peace! But, alas, it is hidden from your eyes.' " He went on to describe the inevitable consequences of their violence—the destruction of Jerusalem, the murder of thousands—"...and all because you did not recognize your opportunity when God offered it!" (Luke 19:41-44) The people did not recognize their *kairos*, their chance to embrace the way of nonviolence that Jesus offered them.

The times we live in are our *kairos* moment—our last chance to embrace the way of nonviolence that is offered to us. Jesus offered it to us; Gandhi, Dorothy Day, Martin Luther King, Jr., and many others have continued to show us our opportunity. The Spirit of God, moving in the gentle breeze of the desert, calls us to heed the opportune moment of peace, and not to blow it all away with the winds of nuclear destruction.

Will we seize the moment, take our chance, risk nonviolence? Can we respond in faith in a new creative way to this powerful movement for good or for evil among us at this time in history? Will we disarm, stop testing nuclear weapons, repent of our first strike and low-intensity conflict policies, give away our possessions to the poor, rededicate ourselves to the service of humanity, and adopt nonviolence?

The silence of the desert is a good place to hear the still, silent voice of God, offering us a way out of our addiction to violence. With the loud noise of nuclear bombs going off every few weeks, the voice of God can be easily drowned out. We become deafer than we already are. Yet, that voice still pleads for disarmament, and offers us the way of nonviolent love as a solution to all our problems. If we are ever going to have ears to hear the voice of God greeting us in the Nevada desert with a word of peace, we will need to take a chance on peace and disarmament. Perhaps we should all go into the Nevada desert to search out the call to peace and peacemaking.

The main entrance to the Nevada Test Site, an area the size of Rhode Island, is near the town of Mercury, sixty-five miles north of Las Vegas. The barren, desert valley stretches out for twenty miles on either side of the highway north of Las Vegas, and on the outskirts, enormous, beautiful desert mountains stand out. Joshua trees, cacti, and yucca plants mark the stark desert surroundings. Some of the mountains are snow covered, while others change color depending on the time of day and the amount of sunlight.

I have prayerfully kept vigil with friends at the entrance of the test site, in the middle of that desert valley, just as a nuclear bomb was detonated in the mountain floor some fifteen miles away. We could not feel the ground shaking, although the shockwave registered nearly 5.5 on the Richter scale, and the violence done to the earth traveled along the mountain range and could be felt in the tall casino buildings of Las Vegas. The feeling one gets in such a place at such a moment is overwhelming. The beauty of the earth and the evil of US warmaking collide. One feels intense sorrow that we are so dedicated to destroying God's gift of creation. The desert valley is turned into the valley of the shadow of death. The realities of our world are revealed for what they are: an addiction to violence and death that has reached catastrophic proportions.

Although the power of the evil is unimaginable and overwhelming, one discovers in such a vigil the revelation of God's grace in the community of nonviolence and resistance that emerges. If this community is faithful to its calling of nonviolent love, it will eventually embrace the local police, military officers, test-site employees, and all those within the desert area working on nuclear weapons so that nuclear-weapons testing will stop. Love is the key to opening this door to a new day without nuclear testing.

One cold, Lenten morning, I joined a community of peacemakers gathered for a Eucharistic liturgy in the desert. It was dark and cloudy, very cold and windy. As we broke bread together, the sun came out. We spoke of "the very stones crying out for peace and an end to nuclear testing." The day before, we had each gathered a stone from the desert and painted a message of peace on it. After the Eucharist, we processed to a cross erected in the desert, and left our stones in a circle around it. (One week before, another retreat group had left a set of painted stones, but after the group left, the police authorities confiscated the stones and took them onto the test-site grounds). We walked in procession to the entrance of the test site, and in small groups, proceeded to cross the line on to the base, risking arrest. As my group crossed the line, we knelt down and offered the Lord's Prayer. Just then, snow appeared everywhere. We stood up as a heavy snow fell upon us and were arrested for trespassing. We took that as a sign that the environment was supporting our nonviolent protest.

We were arrested, handcuffed, held for a short while, booked, and released. The charges against us were subsequently dropped because the state authorities do not want these "cases" to go to trial. They know that trials will draw more publicity to the evil that is being prepared in the desert. The best way to continue the deadly business of testing nuclear weapons is in secret, and the nuclear industries and the US government want to continue their testing without the general population's fully understanding the implications of that work.

In our own time, as more and more people begin the process of questioning our nuclear imperialism, the prophecy of Hosea has begun to ring true: "I will allure her into the desert and there I will speak to her heart. And I will make a covenant with the birds of heaven and the creeping things of the earth. I will remove all weapons of war from the land, all swords and bows, and will let my people live in peace and security." (Hosea 2:14,18) The echo of Isaiah's promise also speaks to our situation, and offers hope that peace is ours if we choose it: "Once more God will send the Spirit. The desert will become fertile, and fields will produce rich crops. Everywhere in the land righteousness and justice will be done. Because everyone will do what is right, there will be peace and security forever." (Isaiah 32:15-17)

Part Three:
The Prayer of Nonviolence

While you are proclaiming peace with your lips, be careful to have it even more fully in your heart.

St. Francis of Assisi

Acquire inward peace, and a multitude around you will find their salvation.

St. Seraphim

My greatest weapon is mute prayer.

Gandhi

14.
In Step with the Spirit of Peace: Retreat Notes (August 1988)

Sunday, July 31, 1988
The Feast of St. Ignatius Loyola, founder of the Society of Jesus

My soul is deprived of peace; I have forgotten what happiness is; I tell myself my future is lost, all that I hoped for from the Lord. The thought of my homeless poverty is wormwood and gall; remembering it over and over leaves my soul downcast within me. But I will call this to mind as my reason to have hope: the favors of the Lord are not exhausted. God's mercies are not spent; they are renewed each morning, so great is God's faithfulness. My portion is the Lord, says my soul; therefore I will hope in God. Good is the Lord to the one who waits for God, to the soul that seeks God. It is good to hope in silence for the saving help of God. Sit alone and in silence. (Lamentations 3:1-31)

I have come away from Washington, D.C., to make my annual eight-day retreat, here in Wernersville, Pennsylvania, at the Jesuit novitiate and retreat center. I am exhausted, and feel the need to rest in the Spirit of God. Like everyone, I struggle to become more and more aware of the abiding presence of God. Yet I am blessed to meet Jesus every day as I come face to face with the poor. I experience the presence of God in the K Street Community, in the Eucharist; in the peace movement, and in my prayer of silence. And so, I have come here to dwell in silence, in the peace of God.

I walked down to the community cemetery to visit the gravesite of Joe Grady, a Jesuit scholastic who died at a young age a few weeks ago. Joe had just begun his theology studies, but was diagnosed with leukemia. After years of suffering, he was healed of cancer, but he caught a severe case of pneumonia, which finally killed him. He died in great peace, trusting completely in God to receive him with love. Now his body awaits the resurrection in a simple pine grove with other Jesuit saints.

Monday

"The Lord is my portion," says my soul.

A restful night, morning prayer, meditation, Eucharist. A morning spent gently recalling the consoling moments and days that have filled this year—even in the midst of the pain and ebbing, the confusion and inner turmoil that I have known over the years before returning to Washington, D.C. The consolation I now know in my life work!

A dynamic homily this morning set me thinking about the question: What does it mean to be a prophet of peace? Who are the prophets in my life? Am I listening to them as they speak the truth? How can I say yes to God's call to be a prophet—since all Christians are in varying degrees called to the prophetic work of denouncing evil and announcing good news? How can I undertake prophetic work, when in fact I'm a sinner, a frail spirit, caught up in competition and selfishness?

My director has given me a fine piece on prophecy by the theologian Sandra Schneiders:

> We [have] to question seriously our own credentials for this lonely and agonizing vocation to be a prophet. Indeed, anyone who aspires to be a prophet is completely uninformed or clinically insane. Probably, one of the surest signs of the call to prophecy in the Church today is the same terror in the face of such a task that made Moses stutter, Jeremiah rebel, and Jesus sweat blood. The more afraid we are of the consequences, the more unworthy we feel in the face of our own sins to call anyone to repentance, the more deeply we love the Church and reverence its ministry of leadership, the more resolutely must we face the implications of the vocation to prophecy in the contemporary Church. This will only be possible if our wholehearted commitment to Jesus gives rise in us to a passionate and ultimately fearless identification with the reign of God, that regime of reversals whose great sign is the resurrection of the executed prophet.*

Such a statement rekindles in me a desire to a greater fidelity to speak the truth in love to power. Franz Jaegerstaetter and Oscar Romero come to mind, executed prophets who are rising in the general consciousness of Christian people. But there are so many others who have fulfilled that vocation: Gandhi, King, Steve Biko, Rutilio Grande, Ita Ford, Maura Clarke, Dorothy Kazel, Jean Donovan.

I set my soul, therefore, to a greater determination to defend the poor and the earth, to call for a non-nuclear, non-warring world, to make the light of Christ shine in the world. By writing, public

---

* From *New Wineskins* (Mahwah, N.J.: Paulist Press, 1986), pp. 310-320.

speaking, teaching, and, most important, acting at places of criminal-
ity, I hope to be found faithful. And always, if possible, to speak
from the world of the poor. To walk with them, to stand with them,
to speak with them, and thus with God.

Tuesday

> Lord Jesus, I have the joy and the responsibility of believing
> that ever since my baptism, we are one. Don't extinguish the
> light of your presence within me. O Lord, look through my
> eyes, listen through my ears, speak through my lips, walk
> with my feet. Lord, may my poor human presence be a re-
> minder, however weak, of your divine presence. For, to the
> degree that others notice me, it is a sign that I am, unfortu-
> nately, still opaque and not transparent.
>
> The Prayer of Cardinal Newman

The Gospel today speaks of Jesus walking on the water. A
strange tale that only recently has come to the light of understanding:
the evangelist is trying to explain that Jesus' life was a ministry of
reconciliation between enemies. Jesus ministered to the Jews on one
side of the Sea of Galilee and walked the water to minister to the
Gentiles on the other side. His life was a life of peacemaking and resistance, doing the unbelievable without fear, "walking on water," in
other words.

It's 1 p.m. on a beautiful, sunny day. I'm sitting in Holy Spirit
Chapel praying for new strength and courage to walk the waters of
peacemaking. I put the question to the Walker of Waters: "Jesus, is

there anything you want to say to me today, or that you want me to do?"

I am called to walk the waters of peacemaking—fearlessly, effortlessly, bold in the Spirit, filled with faith. For me, those waters are the real experiences that lie ahead in the immediate future: life in my neighborhood, among the urban poor; life in my community; life in the parish; life in the world of the homeless; life in my pilgrimages to Central America and the Philippines or wherever I'm led; life protesting the nuclear arms race, war, and injustice; and whatever else may unfold on my journey. To walk from one side of hostility to the other; to heal both sides; to bridge the gap of prejudice, class distinction, and nuclear deterrence by walking the waters of peacemaking. To go to the other side and work a miracle.

At the heart of the revolution of the heart is the revolutionary Christ. The Gospel is pure revolution: the call for a pure revolution, for nonviolence, resistance, truth. The revolutionary Christ asks me through the Scriptures, "What have I done for the revolution of nonviolent love, what am I doing, and what am I going to do?"

First, I want to avoid making a statue of Jesus to mumble sweet, mawkish pieties to—as we do to King and Gandhi and all those who are holy. Jesus is alive and wants us to take up the work of revolutionary nonviolence, the Gospel. I want to be a *real* follower of Jesus, one who makes people feel the presence of the risen Christ in our midst.

Later. A silent, focused meditation in the chapel on Jesus walking those waters. Jesus sent the disciples ahead to the other side. He sent them *together*, and then he walks on the water. They are caught in a storm, then they see him and are filled with fear. They are in a boat *together*, crossing the sea, filled with fear, and unable to stay focused on their mission. Jesus is trying to get the disciples to take up the work of reconciliation, to go from one side to the other. Reconciliation like peacemaking is always dangerous stuff; it's like being out at sea in a storm. The only way to live nonviolent resistance, to practice the reconciliation which Jesus teaches is in *community*.

Jesus says further, "Do not be afraid; have faith." As we practice the reconciliation and nonviolence of the Gospel, we must 1) not be afraid, and 2) have faith. We must concentrate on these two commandments as invitations to a life of peace, as a loving response to our loving God. Finally, Peter starts out on the water and finds himself walking because he keeps his eyes on Christ. He believes in Christ and the impossible becomes possible. The moment he loses faith, he starts to drown. We must truly believe in Christ, then we will find ourselves walking the rough seas of reconciliation and justice. And when we do, we must keep our eyes on Christ, and complete our mission of reconciliation with total faith in God to see us through.

Wednesday

Christ's call to nonviolence is truly revolutionary. Gospel nonviolence is God's revolution. Last evening, I came across an interview with Brian Willson, the peace activist who lost his legs on September 1, 1987, when he was run over at the Concord Naval Weapons Station in California by a train carrying weapons to the Contras in Honduras. "I believe in a revolutionary consciousness for North America," he told *Sojourners* magazine. "In the revolution of consciousness, people take their own power and listen to themselves, to the intuitive self, the inner voice, the higher self." He continued:

> I think I grieved over the loss of so many legs in Nicaragua that I had already grieved over the loss of mine.... I believe these kinds of things [such as his injury] are going to happen if we're going to stop violence. In other words, we're going to have to start taking risks to stand up for the truth. Those of us who are speaking truth are going to be intimidated, jailed, injured, and killed. But when you start living the truth, and what you really believe in, the risks don't matter anymore.... We resist not because we like to resist, but because we love life and we must resist policies that destroy life.

There is a photo of Brian dancing—with the use of crutches to balance his artificial legs—on the steps of the US Capitol. He quotes Emma Goldman: "If I can't dance in it, it's not my revolution."

How nonviolent in heart and soul he is! How prepared he was to face death! Not a trace of bitterness and anger, and meanwhile, he's calling for a new revolutionary consciousness, the nonviolent transformation of America.

A deep, challenging invitation. He sounds to me as though he's asking me to come out and walk on water with him. Can I be like that? As nonviolent, truthful and loving? As ready for the consequences of anti-war activity? Do I realize what the consequences of my actions could be? Can I risk the consequences of solidarity with the poor? Am I ready for rejection, injury, or even death? Will I say, "Receive me Lord" as Ita Ford did when she almost drowned in El Salvador? Could I be ready like Franz Jaegerstaetter and Oscar Romero were? Or do I think that such things will never happen to me? What Brian Willson speaks of is at the heart of my prayer and my life: the willingness to lay down my life in the nonviolent struggle for peace, for justice for the poor, for life for suffering humanity. I pray to embrace the way of nonviolent resistance and peacemaking, the cross. This—or else my life makes no sense.

And too, I want to dance and celebrate in the nonviolent revolution. My prayer, then, is the prayer of these last few years: to undergo a new conversion, to become like Christ, to become the person I am called to be, the person I am, a child of the nonviolent God, a person loved and lovable and loving towards all.

My prayer: to be ready and willing to die for truth, for peace and justice, for love. To be willing to walk out on the water when the Lord says, "Come."

Christ, if you want me to be a saint and a martyr, a gentle revolutionary, an apostle or prophet of nonviolence, if you want me to be your disciple, if it's really you out there on those waters—just say the word. Ask me to come out there with you and I'll come.

I pray to have a strong faith that could sit on train tracks or do a plowshares action or serve the homeless poor or sit in at the Pentagon or walk through El Salvador, all for Christ's reign of peace and justice on earth. I was very scared when I lived in a refugee camp in El Salvador and I get very scared every time I am arrested for witnessing at a place of nuclear crime; every time I stand up and speak out for peace; every time I go to confession; every time I ask for my Jesuit superior's permission for something Gospel-oriented; every time I speak to my family and friends about my latest adventure; every time I walk outside my neighborhood in Washington, D.C., I wake up in the morning and I'm scared to go out and live, because I know that real living in this day and age means dying to one's self. I have to become who I am called to be, who I am—a revolutionary peacemaker, an apostle of nonviolence, a servant of the poor, a friend of God, a human being.

Thursday

Ched Myers' new book, *Binding the Strong Man,* is a powerful exposition of the Gospel of Mark. He writes:

> The cross was in Mark's day neither religious icon nor metaphor for personal anguish or humility. It had one meaning: that terrible form of capital punishment reserved by imperial Rome for political dissenters. This discipleship is revealed as a vocation of nonviolent resistance to the powers.... It also entails solidarity with the "least" in society, equality and compassion within the family and community, economic justice and sharing, and service rather than domination.... Jesus' way of the cross stipulates that the primal structures of domination can only be overthrown by the practice of personal and political nonviolence, from the "crib" to the "courtroom." This way contradicts all our orthodox notions of social and economic security, and it has been profoundly difficult to accept by his followers in the story and throughout Christian history.*

"To pray," he continues, "is to resist the despair by which the powers rule, in our hearts and world—the despair that tells us that genuine political transformation is impossible.... As residents of an

---

* See Ched Myers, *Binding the Strong Man* (Maryknoll, NY: Orbis Books, 1988).

imperial culture that routinely imposes crosses upon the poor," he concludes, "it is time we 'take up our cross,' learn to pray, solicit Jesus for vision, and practice the way of nonviolence."

At 4 a.m., I prayed over this way of the cross and the refusal of most Christians today to take up that way. I prayed that we Christians accept it, follow it, and risk the way of the cross. This is why the Holy Spirit got me out of bed so early: to invite me into the risk of the cross. My prayer has become a reflection on what that means exactly in my life, how I should continue along the road that I've taken as well as turn down a new road.

After dinner and spiritual direction, I went for a long walk outside to watch the sunset. My director has asked me to read and meditate on the Passion of Jesus. And so I've spent the evening walking through those scenes: the agony in the garden (the very human terror, the fear of torture and death); the arrest; having his hands tied; jail; the dungeon; the two trials (a farce; injustice beyond measure); being mocked, abused, tortured, whipped, made to wear a crown of thorns, stripped, crucified. A sea of blood everywhere.

The grace I seek: to be in solidarity with Jesus' Spirit as he undergoes the cross, in order to risk a similar fate for the sake of the reign of God.

I remember my first night in jail, in Harlem, where I ended up after sitting-in with friends at the Riverside Research Institute in New York City. Tonight, Jesus says to me, dying on the cross, *"This is your liberation! This is the liberation of everyone!"*

I am stunned and confounded by these words. I have studied and practiced the Gospel call to nonviolence and resistance for years— and I find myself thinking that I know all about it. But tonight, as in most nights, I am back to square one: Is this it? *This* is liberation?

This is the way out? *How* can this be? As Ched Myers asks, "Who of us is prepared to accept that this is the way to liberation?" And I come back to the realization that I know nothing about the Gospel, that I have only just begun to put it into real practice.

I thought of that night in jail and asked God, "How can my being in jail even for one night advance your reign and help overthrow the rule of violence and nuclear madness and death? If this is the way, why aren't more Christians doing it?"

Thinking of the cloud of witnesses who have gone that bloody road of suffering without retaliating—King, Gandhi, Jaegerstaetter, Romero, the Central American martyrs, and so many others—I hear them say to me: "This is your liberation. This way is the liberation of all." The implication: his death, undergone in the spirit of unconditional, nonviolent love, is my liberation (thus, my salvation); and his death is the invitation to undergo or risk the same arrest, jail, trial, torture and death. Jesus, covered in blood, writhing in pain, dying on the cross: the fullness of the reign of God; the revelation of the Human One come in all power and glory. The reign of God is revealed in Christ crucified. If I want to experience that reign, I must be with Christ, on a cross, in civil disobedience, paying the price for Divine Obedience, in defense of the poor and oppressed, in service to life, in loving resistance to the powers of war, violence, oppression and death. This transforming spirit of nonviolent love is the most powerful force there is.

My response: "I believe, Lord; help my unbelief."

Later. After a walk under the stars and an hour sitting before the crucifix, I find myself transfixed with the call to be—like Mother Theresa, the Missionary of Charity—a Missionary of Justice, a Missionary of Nonviolence, a Missionary of Resistance to Evil. I asked

Christ, "What do you want me to do to help you in your transformation of the world?" and heard an answer, *"Practice nonviolence. Put my Word into action."*

Friday

A 4 a.m. meditation on Christ crucified across the world: in South Africa, in Central America, in the Middle East, in the Philippines, in Northern Ireland, in Afghanistan, on death row, in the womb, on the streets of our country and in refugee camps around the world. I remembered a picture of Christ crucified with a nuclear bomb exploding in the background. Sitting with Christ in his suffering, in his spirit of love, praying for the grace to risk the same fate for the nonviolent pursuit of justice and truth, I felt consoled and at peace.

11:30 a.m. A Good Friday Contemplation, holding the dead body of Jesus, seeing the failure and glory in his blood. I read Paul's letter to the Ephesians and Peter's first letter about the blood of Christ being our peace, and reflecting within myself: I do not want to deal with or look upon blood, the suffering and death of anyone, and I do not want to go through this ugly death, this pain, for political or spiritual reasons or for any purposes. I am slow to feel compassion. I want to turn away like the other men in the story (as opposed to the women who stay there). Then, like Ignatius, I prayed, "God, place me with your son." I want to follow you, Jesus; I am willing to drink the cup of suffering love which you drank. Give me the courage and the strength to be your disciple in the world, and I will do your work.

8 p.m. A Holy Saturday prayer, anticipating tomorrow, the anniversary of Hiroshima and the feast of the Transfiguration. My contemplation: standing outside the tomb of Jesus, imagining all the wars of the world, the injustice that covers the globe and the mad rush to nuclear holocaust. Trying to imagine Hiroshima, knowing that it would take a lifetime to imagine that hell, not to mention the bombings of Dresden, El Salvador, Vietnam, or the holocaust of Auschwitz or Dachau. Praying for peace, for the world's conversion to nonviolence, accepting Christ's powerlessness. Imagining God looking at our world: its forty-five wars happening right now; the homeless and displaced and hungry and sick and imprisoned, so many neglected and abused; the work of the Pentagon; the fleet of Trident Submarines; the first-strike weaponry of the D-5; the willingness of first-world nations to obliterate third-world nations at a moment's notice. Christ in the tomb: a world of no hope, where war is victorious; where death, imperial oppression and nuclear bombs have won out. The overwhelming sense of it all!

"To see reality in our time is to see the world as crucifixion," writes Jim Douglass.

In the midst of this world, the church—blessing the wars, practicing injustice within its own walls, forcing out the poor, the marginalized, women; a war church; a community of disciples living as if Christ is still in the tomb, as if the resurrection never happened. I can so easily understand the thousands of people who leave the church, scandalized by its love of power, its infidelity to the Gospel, its dead liturgy and blindness to the truth of Jesus' Way of peacemaking. I prayed that it might become what it is called to be: a peace church. I find myself deeply consoled at the prospect of staying within the church, and from there, living out the Gospel in all its glory, in all its radical spirit, in all its shining truth. I shall stay and live out the Gospel witness as a peacemaking Catholic, a Jesuit priest, and a servant of the poor because I too, like the church, am broken and sinful yet called to be faithful. Perhaps a lifetime of suffering within the church may lead to a deep change, such as the ordination of women, the servanthood of its members, and the transformation of structure into a community of service and sharing.

I found myself pondering the Plowshares movement as a revelation and experience of such a peace church, in particular, the four activists who boarded the U.S.S. Iowa on Easter Sunday, 1987, and hammered on the missile containers. Then it occurred to me: THIS IS THE RESURRECTION. Jesus is risen in Phil, Margaret, Andrew and Greg and in all those who beat nuclear swords into plowshares. They reveal the reign of God present and active on earth. The resurrection is happening in the Plowshares communities and actions, and also in the little acts of nonviolent resistance at all such places of nuclear crime and injustice. And so, I prayed that Jesus would rise in me, to put the resurrection into practice in my life, that I might experience resurrection.

Sunday, August 6, Hiroshima Day

5:30 a.m. I got up an hour ago, tired and anxious. I have fear and anxiety over a talk I am to give next week at the peace gathering, and more important, at an upcoming journey to El Salvador, and whatever else lies ahead in my life. I prayed in the silence of Holy Spirit chapel, and considered the women of Mark's Gospel who encountered the angel at the tomb. They were filled with fear and anxiety. It might be that such emotions go hand in hand with resurrection. I prayed that I might continue to walk with my fears and meet the risen Jesus along the way.

11:30 a.m. As I continued to ponder the resurrection of Jesus in prayer, the phrase "I know my Redeemer lives" became the mantra I repeated over and over. In the face of Hiroshima and Nagasaki, and the world at war today, I know still that my Redeemer lives and wants me to move on with the lifework of peacemaking and justice-seeking.

How God must grieve over our violence! How God must long for us all to turn from the ways of violence to the Way of nonviolence. How we mistreat God's gift of nonviolent love! Given the direction of our nuclear intentions, unless the world adopts nonviolence now, it is doomed to perish. Today I will undertake a simple fast as part of my repentance, to forfend the violence within me and around me in the world.

Ched Myers writes in *Binding the Strong Man*:

Mark's resurrection tradition offers no visions of glory or triumph, only the promise that Jesus is still on the road, and that we can see him again in Galilee. And where is Galilee? It is the place where Peter and the disciples were first called to follow Jesus. Which is to say, the discipleship narrative is beginning again. The story is circular! No wonder the women bolt, mute from fear at this realization.... (16:8) This last passage is the most fearful of all, for a martyr figure beckons them (and us) to take up the journey afresh—now fully conscious of its cost! What an ambiguous ending! It leaves us not with a neat resolution but with a terrible ultimatum: we can see the risen Jesus only on the way of discipleship.... The genius of Mark's "incomplete" ending lies precisely in the fact that it demands a response from the reader. The story of discipleship continues, and we cannot remain mere spectators.

I pray that I may see the risen Jesus on the road of discipleship.

Monday

The hidden ground of love. Praying to be, like Merton, constantly aware and walking in that hidden ground of love. An appropriate way to draw the retreat to a close and to begin anew my journey into the Gospel of peace.

The first reading from 1 Kings 19: 4-8 in today's liturgy offers a metaphor for this retreat and my life:

Elijah went a day's journey into the desert, until he came to a broom tree and sat beneath it. He prayed for death, saying, "This is enough, O Lord! Take my life, for I am no better than my ancestors." He lay down and fell asleep under the broom tree, but then an angel touched him and ordered him to get up and eat. He looked and there at his head was a hearth cake and a jug of water. After he ate and drank, he lay down again, but the angel of the Lord came back a second time, touched him, and ordered, "Get up and eat, else the journey will be too long for you." He got up, ate and drank; then, strengthened by that food, he walked forty days and forty nights to the mountain of God.

This is the way my life has been in recent years, from my college experiences at Duke University in Durham, North Carolina, through the Jesuit Novitiate in Wernersville and philosophy studies in New York City, to teaching high-school students in Scranton, Pennsylvania, to my life among the homeless and the poor in Washington, D.C. On occasion, I have prayed for death, claiming exhaustion, weakness, and no end to my sinfulness and the violence of the world. But God continues to send angels to me. They awaken me, give me food and drink, and strengthen me for the journey ahead. I can list the angels in my life, from Daniel Berrigan, Phil Berrigan and Elizabeth McAlister, Shelley and Jim Douglass, to other Jesuits like Bill Sneck, George Anderson, Richard McSorley, to my family and community and co-workers at the McKenna Center. I am filled with gratitude for God's persistent care, for the loving concern of those angels of grace. With this retreat, I am ready to start anew, to walk the forty days and forty nights of Gospel peacemaking to the mountain of God.

Disarm me, God!

Come, put away the sword I still carry somewhere in my heart. Take away the violence that lingers in my soul. Make me an instrument of Your peace. You have a plan for me: fulfill it! In this world of armaments, disarm me and I shall be able to disarm others.

Come, God. There is still a trace of war and madness in my veins. Purify me, O God, and I shall let loose disarmament in the world that will cause people to praise you freely. Purify me of all violence and I shall stand before the powers and principalities without fear and free those trapped in the structures of fear and violence.

Come, God. Disarm me without my knowing it, and then, show me that you are the Disarming One, nonviolent from the beginning of time until the end of time. Disarming Presence, Unconditional Love, Great Reconciler, Suffering Servant, Patience Personified, Peaceful Mother, come, bearing peace.

Come, God. Disarm this restless heart which wanders off into apathy and selfishness, but which longs to rest in You. Lead this heart into the fire of your Love, where it can be consumed in the Flame of Nonviolence, setting fire to other hearts nearby. Let your unilateral disarmament engage me, win me over, force the scales to fall from my eyes and the weapons to be released from my hands. Push me into the violent hearts of others that I may take on their anger and release them from the chains of hatred and the bonds of violence.

Disarm me, God, and I shall disarm others. Disarm me, God, that I may be one with all humanity, all your sons and daughters. Disarm me, God, and bring me into Your reign, to live forever in peace and love.

God, you see all that I am. You know my thoughts, my heart, what I say and what I do. I know you love me and I place my trust in you. Therefore, I do not fear any human being. I do not fear anything. I do not fear the power of death. Help me then to resist death and all the fears that bind human beings. Help me to break through human fear into true human relationships, into true solidarity with the poor and oppressed of the world, into voluntary poverty, into a deep, prayerful peace in my heart, into acts of nonviolence that can spark a transformation of the policies of death and oppression into food and housing for the poor. In the moment of confrontation, when I am publicly challenged, mocked or attacked, in those days ahead when I may be arrested and jailed for my nonviolent resistance, in those encounters when I embark on a new relationship with my oppressed sisters and brothers, in the hour of my death, let me pass from all fear to complete calm, peace, and trust rooted and grounded in you and your love. My daily prayer is: I shall fear no one. I shall place all my trust in You. I shall walk into the public world proclaiming my love for all people, especially the poor, resisting death and oppression and choosing life. I shall not be afraid. Jesus, I am coming. I will follow you. Receive me into your reign of love and peace.

God, I beg You: give us your peace. Grant us your spirit that we may all repent from the ways of violence and convert to your Way of Nonviolence.

God, the world is filled with so much violence, so many wars, so much hatred, anger and bitterness. Wipe it all away. Create clean hearts. Help us to realize the unity and reconciliation you have already given us. I ask you to do this, not only in my own heart, more and more, but in every human heart on the face of the earth.

Please, God, help us to love one another and to put away our pride and desires for power, domination, control, order, imperialism, and money. Help us to let go of our power and to disarm ourselves, unilaterally, as you did and continue to do every day. Help us to stop our plottings. Put an end to the torture, bombings, assassinations, kidnappings, electrocutions, abortions and wars which we devise and plan and perpetrate. Raise up new prophets, apostles and martyrs of nonviolence who will show us the Way in these dark days in which the world is overshadowed by nuclear annihilation. Raise up strong, loving, simple, humble Christian communities in every neighborhood of the world where people can come together and say "No" to violence, and "Yes" to life, nonviolence, and community.

Grant us peace in our hearts as we enter into voluntary suffering, as we follow the way of the cross in the world. Though it looks as though our efforts fail or achieve only small gains, bless our desires for peace, purify our hearts and make us true peacemakers.

"The Reign of God is the poor's. If you have something better to give to them, give it. But remember, the reign of God is the poor's." Ned Murphy, S.J., said this the other day and how true it is. "We're asking the wrong question when we ask, 'What is God's will for me?' The question to be asked," he said, "is, 'What is God's will for the poor?' And the answer is very clear: God's will for the homeless is homes. God's will for the hungry is food. God's will for the oppressed is liberation. God's will for the poor is the good news of justice and peace."

Jesus, you were quite clear when you spoke to your followers: "Sell your possessions and give alms," you told them. "Get yourselves purses that do not wear out, treasure that will not fail you in heaven where no thief can reach it and no moth destroy it. For where your treasure is, there will your heart be also.... In so far as you neglected one of the least of these, you neglected me.... Sell all that you own and distribute the money to the poor, and you will have treasure in heaven; then, come, follow me."

O God, there is so much poverty in the world, so much senseless suffering due to our greed and our arrogance. I think of the millions of homeless children, women and men here in this city, in every city in our country, and throughout the world, not knowing where to turn, hungry, cold, scared, living and dying in the streets, in the shelters, in the refugee camps and the war zones.

And I see our attention, our time, our energy and money being spent on frivolous, selfish concerns: expensive clothes, liquor and gourmet food, fancy cars, entertainment, large estates, yachts, and of course, weapons to protect those possessions. Billions of dollars thrown away while so many poor people suffer unjustly.

Empower me to give homes to the homeless, food to the foodless, love to the loveless, clothes to the clothesless, hope to the hopeless, peace to the peaceless. Inspire everyone to renounce their bourgeois lifestyles and turn to the suffering poor with the hand of peace.

God, I saw you in the eyes of the poor on the streets of Washington, D.C., today. I see you in the victims of our nuclear madness, our arms races, our culture of death and destruction. Help me to reach out to you in the poor. I too am in need of your reign. I know they will share what is theirs with me. Help me to accept your reign, God, from them, by becoming poor with them, one with you. Let me receive the blows and persecutions, not them. Let me stand up for them, speak up for them, and nonviolently resist the powers and principalities that would kill them. Make me a defender of the poor, servant of the poor, friend of the poor, lover of the poor. O God, make me a human being.

16.
Good News to Dry Bones:
Taking Ezekiel at his Word

Peacemaking in America necessarily means a ministry of prophecy, not in the sense of predicting the future, but in the sense of speaking truth to power. But how do people who want to reflect the peace of Christ speak prophetically in America?

Recently, I decided to reread the book of Ezekiel. Surely, Ezekiel's testimony, a legacy of prophecy, could shed some light on this vexing question. I found the book startling, to say the least. A cold reading of Ezekiel is enough to jar anyone. If Ezekiel spoke that strongly in those days to that culture—a culture of violence, idolatry, and sin—what are we required to say in these days in this culture? Surely nothing less radical, nothing less powerful, nothing less profound.

Ezekiel's testimony is filled with reproaches for Israel's sins and foretells the inevitable devastation that will naturally occur as the sin of violence continues. His message includes a call to hear the promise of salvation, a promise that requires fidelity to God's covenant. Ezekiel dreamed of a future in which God's people would be faithful, loving, nonviolent—indeed, a true beloved community, the reign of God on earth.

From the beginning, Ezekiel is clear because God had been very clear to Ezekiel. God wanted him to go and speak to the people—to proclaim boldly and publicly the truth of their times—that their deeds of violence and idolatry were doomed to failure (because violence can only breed violence) and that unless they embarked on the path of repentance and fidelity, their end was near.

God spoke to Ezekiel, "I am sending you to those who have turned against me.... to say, 'The Lord Yahweh says this.' Whether they listen or not, they shall know there is a prophet among them.... Do not be afraid of them.... You must deliver my words to them whether they listen or not." (2:1-6)

Later, God told Ezekiel that some people do indeed listen to God's words, "but they do not act on them. They cannot tell the truth and their hearts are set on dishonest gain." God said, "As far as they are concerned, you are like a love song beautifully sung to music. They listen to your words but no one puts them into practice." (33:32) God was greatly upset at their lack of response. "I shall make a covenant of peace with them," God decided. (43:24) "People will learn that I, their God, am with them, and that they, the House of Israel, are my people—it is the Lord Yahweh who speaks." (34:30)

Ezekiel was sent to preach to a "dry bones" people, to those who had given up any hope of a peaceful, wholesome future. God told Ezekiel that those bones represent the whole House of Israel, the ones who kept saying, "Our bones are dried up, our hope has gone; we are as good as dead." God wanted to breathe new life into those people—those dry bones—and so God sent Ezekiel to them. "Say to them, 'the Lord Yahweh says this. I am now going to open your graves; I mean to raise you from your graves, my people, and lead you back to the soil of Israel. And you will know that I am Yahweh, when I open your graves and raise you from your graves, my people. And I shall put my spirit in you, and you will live....' " (37:1-14)

Ezekiel proclaims to the people of his day—and to us—that God is alive and sees the evil deeds that nations do in darkness. According to Ezekiel, God is politically aware. God sees the violence done by God's people and God will not stand for it. God intends to transform the world of death into a realm of life. Jesus' risen life of nonviolent love is God's response to the dry bones of Israel.

As Christians, we believe that we are living in that new covenant of peace, an agreement sealed in the blood of Jesus and in his resurrection. God will be faithful to God's end of the bargain, we are told, and merely asks that we remain faithful to our side of the covenant, by renouncing war, violence, and injustice. But a reading of Ezekiel is sobering: look how much worse we Americans behave today, to the point of threatening to destroy the planet and all humanity! Our nuclear age makes Ezekiel's nightmarish prophecy pale in comparison. Does the God of Ezekiel have an opinion about this? Is the living God concerned with our addiction to death and despair? Might God want us to speak to America, as Ezekiel was asked to speak to Israel, about God's covenant of nonviolent love?

Through modern-day prophets such as Dorothy Day and Martin Luther King, Jr., God asks us to put God's word into practice with our own lives, to be peacemakers, to speak that word of peace to others. That challenging word is the Word of the Gospels, the voice of Jesus calling us to a life of active nonviolence. Like Day and King, we imperfect people are to deliver God's message to the people of the United States, our sisters and brothers. Our message is a simple word: "Put away the sword. Love your enemies. Repent, and believe the good news of peace and justice."

We are asked to proclaim a vision of the reign of God on earth, a reign brought close at hand through the life of Jesus who exemplified human fulfillment of God's covenant. We have been asked to create a new community of life and peace, foretold by God to Ezekiel in the last line of the book. This "city of the future" is to be called, "Yahweh-is-there." Are not we Christians to be that city? Is not that future now?

To hear the Word of God in America is to be a prophet of God who puts those words into practice with one's very life. It is an impossible task, but Ezekiel was asked to do it, and he did it. In these powerful days, God insists on no less from us. Perhaps we can look to Ezekiel to muster the courage and daring to offer our lives in a prophetic word of peace. Through serving the poor and peacefully demonstrating at places of violence and nuclear crime, we are called to be good news to dry bones. By proclaiming the truth of justice and peace, we are called to be good news to dry bones. By living in a spirit of steadfast hope, we are called to be good news to dry bones.

May we hear the Word of God and with all the love in our hearts, tell it like it is.

17

The Prayer of St. Ignatius Loyola, Updated

Soul of Christ, Sanctify me.

> In solitude, in prayer, in contemplation, make me holy, at peace, free in your Spirit. In the quiet of this moment, breathe through me, live in me, dwell in me. Be pleased to make your home with me. Let me live in the awareness of your peace and nonviolent love forever that I may serve all my sisters and brothers throughout the earth.

Body of Christ, Save me.

> Give me a place in the beloved community of human beings, your children, O God. Let the church of peace and nonviolent love—your very body—be my home where I live and breathe, freed from all fear and every sign of death. Help me to find refuge in a human community where everyone is nonviolent and just towards one another.

Blood of Christ, Inebriate me.

> Let me be filled with life, your life-giving Spirit of peace-making, in the Gospel life of healing, reconciling others, loving the enemies of this nation, resisting death, and prac-

ticing nonviolence. Let me be healed and filled with your love for others so that now, not I live but Christ, you live in me. May your Spirit of peace ever guide me.

Water from the Side of Christ, Wash me.

Word of God, cleanse my spirit with your light, your clarity, your love, and truth. Renew me with a new understanding. Give me a new mind and new eyes to see the world from your perspective. Give me a conscience that serves, respects, and defends all life. Wash away every speck of violence in my being so that I may shine with your Spirit of nonviolent love.

Passion of Christ, Strengthen me.

May your suffering love and forgiving Spirit strengthen me to risk pain and death for the sake of justice and peace on earth. Let me live as you live and as you died—loving, faithful, hopeful, nonviolent, insisting always in the vision of peace. In the trials of this life, let me always turn to you crucified, and find mercy and new life. Strengthen me in the Way of the cross as I pour out my life, like you, for my suffering sisters and brothers.

O Good Jesus, hear me.

Jesus of the poor, Jesus of the Sermon on the Mount, Jesus of nonviolence, Jesus of women, Jesus of the homeless, Jesus of the marginalized; Jesus healer of the sick, liberator of prisoners and oppressed peoples, preacher of good news, peacemaker, peaceful resister, servant, and friend—be with

me. Hear my longings, my heartsounds, my cry for justice
and peace. May your reign be realized here and now, on
earth as it is in heaven.

Within Thy Wounds, Hide me.

Lead me into the world of the poor where you continue to
suffer; to live poor, one with you; to serve you and love you
in their eyes; and to speak the truth of your justice. With you
in Central and South America, in Africa, India, Asia, the
Middle East, on the streets of North America, in the womb,
on death row, wherever people live, suffer and die, let me be
there, at the service of Love. Do with me what you will.

Permit Me not to be Separated from Thee.

Never for a moment allow me to stray from you, Christ, and
from your Gospel Way of life. Be ever at my side and let me
know it. Let me be ever at your side, together always, never
alone, never forsaken, never abandoned. Though I walk in
the shadow of death, may your presence always protect me
and be my peace. Let me live in the Spirit of your resurrection. Let me walk in the Spirit of nonviolent love. Let me
know always your victory over death and war.

From the Wicked Foe, Defend me.

From apathy, from thoughtlessness and carelessness; from
first-world comfort and murder and nuclear crime; from hatred and death penalties; from ego and arrogance, selfishness
and pride; from riches and honor; from violence and systemic injustice; from fear and doubt; from achievement and

ambition and success—Christ, defend me! Be my shield. Be my rock. Be my nonviolent resister.

At the Hour of my Death, Call me.

Keep me faithful all my life—living fully, serving everyone, loving all peoples, reconciling all sides, standing with the victims of violence, promoting nonviolent social change, breathing your Spirit of love and peace. In my hour of death, in this very moment, call me to your presence that I may see you face to face to make my home with you. May my passing be the fulfillment of a life of love, a celebration of peace for humanity and your greater glory.

Bid me come to Thee that with Thy Saints, I may praise Thee, forever and ever,

In union with the apostles, the saints and martyrs, with Mary and Joseph, Clare and Francis, Dorothy Day and Peter Maurin, Martin Luther King, Jr., and Gandhi, Thomas Merton and Franz Jaegerstaetter, Etty Hillesum and Horace McKenna, Rutilio Grande and Oscar Romero, Ita Ford and Maura Clarke, Dorothy Kazel and Jean Donovan, with all those who love you and each other, that I may sing your praise and share in the banquet of your table in the fullness of your beloved community of peace forever.

Amen. Alleluia.

18.
A Day to Remember:
Memorial Day, 1989

The key to understanding Jesus' last hours is his plea, "Remember Me!" He wanted us to remember him, to keep his memory alive in our own hearts. To practice "right memory," as the Buddhists say.

It could be said that we have lost our memory, that we have lost our minds by allowing war, violence, nuclear weapons, prejudice, and greed to run rampant in our hearts and our world. "Re-member me," Jesus says. "Put me back together in my people who are divided, broken, apart, torn asunder, cut in two."

Memory. A spiritual gift. To let the memory of Jesus live in me so as to live in others. To remember how the Spirit of Jesus has lived in me, moved in me, moved in us all, touching and changing our lives.

Our little community has left inner-city Washington, D.C., for a long weekend retreat in the mountains of Western Maryland. It is Memorial Day weekend, a time when the country marks the memory of those who have died in its wars by celebrating those wars as the glory days of the past. It is a false memory, a large-scale betrayal of the dead who live now in the light of God's reign, awake to the truth of nonviolence.

We too are here to try our hand at remembering, hopefully at true memory, to re-gather our spirit, the Spirit of God among us, to breathe easier in that Spirit.

Outside the weather has cast a fog upon the green fields and mountains. A light rain falls. It is hard to see far into the distance.

Inside, in a little cottage, we are trying to see into the distant past, into the unforeseen future, into the reality of the present moment. We stayed up late last night singing spiritual songs and songs of protest, three of us playing guitars. This morning, waffles, orange juice and Bible study. Then, faith-sharing, a sharing of our life histories, the memory of our recent past, the memory of Christ alive in us during these days of national amnesia. Three days of what St. Ignatius called "spiritual conversation."

Each community member takes a turn, baring his soul before his brothers. The good times and the bad, the hopes and the joys, the pain and the tensions. Then the brothers respond: with affirmation, with reaction, with insight, offering a new direction, some light, a word of guidance. In the process, community is born. People are facing the reality of life together, lived in the memory of Jesus, at peace in the Spirit of God among us.

My turn comes, a sharing of gratitude for all the support and friendship, a sharing of the struggle to serve the homeless and to stand for peace, a sharing of my life as a young Jesuit, a sharing of my weakness and sin, a sharing of my hope in God and God's reign breaking forth in our midst. The response? An outpouring of gratitude, affirmation and support—as a Jesuit, a Christian, a human being—as well as a slight brotherly chastisement: you are too judgmental, too narrow-minded. I am being shaped by the community into the image of Christ, remembered in community as the Human One.

Then, Eucharist! A celebration of song and silence, word and reconciliation, blessing and healing. With water, we sign ourselves and pray for one another. With bread and wine, we remember the Human One, and return to our spiritual center. With hands on each other's shoulders sitting in a circle, we bow our heads and pray for God's blessing. And we receive one, with gratitude.

Dinner, late night discussions, a late morning sleep, prayer together, quiet walks, more faith-sharing, more discussions—so it goes. A community is reborn because it is remembering. Memorial days that celebrate life. Days to be remembered.

Later. The sun is shining. The sky is as clear and as brightly blue as any sky could be. The sixty-five-degree weather and cool breeze now call forth a new spirit, a refreshing spirit of new life, new hope, and new possibilities. A new day is born. Easter occurs again. And we remember: God loves us and calls us to be signs of love in our broken world. Our hearts turn to God with joy.

On such a day, I know I belong in the Company of Jesus because I experience his presence, his life, his spirit in that company, here and now, among these people, in this place, in this time and right memory. What would Jesus say? I think the Spirit of Jesus speaks clearly: "Amen. I am with you. Be with me. Come. Follow." Simple words for complex people trying to be simple disciples. A people of faith trying to recall that first call, to hear it again, and to say "Yes" with a greater devotion and more steadfast action than ever before. The memory of the past enlivening the present to be more faithful in the future.

For years now I have lived and walked in the Company, laughing, crying, struggling, listening, and speaking out—all to be faithful to the vision, to the Memory of the One whose name I take. I take this moment to look back, in full memory. Years of struggle every step of the way. All the ups and downs and highs and lows and valleys and peaks. All the graces and fallings from grace. All the many days and faces and struggles and places. And I have discovered that in the nonviolent struggle for life, in the transformation of one's heart and soul, one experiences life. Perhaps this is what resurrection is all about.

This past year's journey through life! So many adventures, good days, hard times, dark moments, and the breakthroughs of light, community and revelation, so many days when the vision of another world, the reign of God, became clearer to see as it broke forth in the life around me.

The homeless! The daily suffering of Christ crucified, beaten, despised, cursed, ignored. The injustice of life on the streets—the apartheid, the death penalty that is homelessness. All the pressing issues of the day come together before our eyes. I see the streets of Washington, D.C., a few blocks from the White House, become a sort of death row, a new apartheid. People are evicted, they sleep on heating grates or in boxes, and some freeze to death. Drug sellers with their walkie-talkies stalk the streets like Salvadoran death squads or Filipino vigilantes. The sufferings of women with children in the makeshift shelters resemble the dislocated lives of Nicaraguan women or Ethiopian families. And everyone feels the effect of a nuclear bomb already detonated in their lives. Our lust for nuclear war lies behind all this suffering.

Over the course of these years, life has smiled on me, and beckoned me forward, to be a sign of life for others, to resist death so that all may know the fullness of life. The Voice of Life speaks to me— and I rejoice. In these words, I take heart for the journey ahead.

"Come, then, my beloved, my lovely one. To you, I reveal the glories of the future, a world yet to be born which is already here. A world of love and happiness, peace and joy, compassion and justice. My world, then, offered for you.

"You have walked these days and I fill you with my grace for I love you. I love you as I love every human being on the planet, unconditionally, without limit, forgiving everything, longing to see you at peace. I give brothers and sisters, the huge family of humanity to be your own new sister and brother in the new creation I am making. I give you many days to come, to pursue with me the love which is my community, the justice and peace which is my hope. All these things I give you.

"I am with you every day through all time. I am with you now as I have been with you then, in your younger days, in the immediate days to come and in the years ahead. I will take you to places you never dreamed of; introduce you to people suffering and struggling in ways that will seem unimaginable to you; and reveal new things to you that will leave you speechless, silent, dumbfounded. I will pour out my grace upon you as you choose to be more faithful to the Way of Life I taught. You will go where you would rather not go, and you will suffer and be rejected and you will die and everything will appear to have been in vain. You will feel hopeless, as though your life has been a failure, but I will use your life and your love to transform not only your heart, but the whole of humanity.

"You are invited to set your face with me towards Jerusalem, to go to the cross, to take up the risk of nonviolent resistance to death and oppression. I have done it; I am with you and call you to that same fate, the fate of the poor. I call you to stand with the poor, to join them in their nonviolent struggle for liberation, to speak the truth that needs to be spoken publicly. In that struggle, your very life will be required of you. But do not be afraid, for I am with you.

"Then, through the power of resurrection, you will learn what it means to be a person of truth and love; you will learn what it means to be a peacemaker; you will learn what it means to be my follower. For I will take you by the hand and lead you into my dwelling place, and I shall call you My Son, and you shall live there forever with me and with all my other sons and daughters, every other human being. All these things shall happen, for I am the Alpha and the Omega, the One who creates, redeems and sanctifies. I am the Peace you seek, the truth you long for, the love you so desire. You shall see me face to face, and you shall know joy, for behold, I call you by name to be my companion."

19.
God Is Our Only Security:
Psalm 33, Praise Be to God

Rejoice in God, O you righteous!
Praise befits the upright.
Sing to God a new song,
For the word of God is upright;
and all God's work is done in faithfulness.
God loves righteousness and justice;
the earth is full of the steadfast love of God.
God brings the counsel of the nations to naught.
Blessed is the nation whose God is the Sovereign.
God looks down from heaven, and sees all humankind.
A ruler is not saved by a great army;
a warrior is not delivered by great strength.
The war horse is a vain hope for victory,
and by its great might it cannot save.
The eye of God is on those who fear God,
on those who hope in God's steadfast love,
that God may deliver their soul from death,
and keep them alive in famine.
Our soul waits for God
who is our help and shield.

Indeed, our heart is glad in God,
because we trust in God's holy name.
Let your steadfast love, O God, be upon us,
even as we hope in you.
                Psalm 33: 1, 3-5, 10, 12-13, 16-22

It has become a familiar scene. My friends and I enter the lobby of Riverside Research Institute, the Star-Wars think tank on 42nd Street in New York City. We sit down, block the main entrance, and break into song. "We're gonna lay down our sword and shield, down by the Riverside; We ain't going to study war no more." The singing might be a bit ragged around the edges, but it has spirit.

The police are called. The vans line up outside. A lieutenant confers with the building supervisor or whoever issued the complaint. We await arrest.

Just then, someone usually stands up, opens the Scriptures and begins to read. "Rejoice in God, O you righteous! Praise befits the upright. Sing to God a new song!" For several years running, whether on the birthday of Martin Luther King, Jr., or the anniversary of the bombing of Nagasaki, it has been Psalm 33.

I can recall several occasions when I have turned to this poem, whether in trouble with friends or in solitude. The words spell out for me the calling, the message, the spirit of our movement and moment. It is an exhortation to persevere in hope and trust as we practice nonviolence. It is the same message announced by the earliest Jewish community in its day of trial and trouble: "Our God reigns. Not the gods of this present age; not the powers of this world. Our God reigns."

The Word today is the same, with only minor changes regarding the latest false god. "Our God reigns," we find ourselves proclaiming. "Not the nuclear weapon; not Star-Wars; not the MX; not the Trident submarine or the Trident II missile. Neither the Soviet idols nor the American idols. Our God reigns, and wants us to disarm and live in peace together."

Throughout the so-called enthronement psalms of Scripture (47, 93-99, and I would include 33), we hear the same message: "Sing a new song: Our God reigns!" It is a song that was sung with exhilaration, and packed with political power. Such a new song among a persecuted community sung in public no doubt landed them in even greater trouble.

Psalm 33, like the enthronement psalms, is addressed not to the ruling authorities or military forces so much as to the believing community. The upright, the believers, are urged to sing a new song, because it is true that our God reigns, that our God sees what is going on in the world, that our God loves us and protects us and still calls us to be loving people in the world.

Scripture scholar Erhard Gerstenberger gives a noteworthy introduction to our text:

Psalm 33 is a type of petitionary hymn of the early Jewish community, drawing on ancient mythological traditions as well as historical experiences. In a situation when all the odds are against the chances of survival, a local community defies all threats by singing aloud its praises to God. It thus strives to keep alive, in worship, the hope for justice and equity and humaneness under adverse circumstances.

Psalm 33 is a hymn for the beloved community of peacemakers which speaks directly to that community, calling each member to praise God. It explains why the community should praise God—because God is the creator of the world and God loves justice and God is sovereign over all the nations and their forces of death and violence. Finally, the psalm articulates on behalf of the community a confession of hope and trust in God. The whole psalm builds to a climax in its final verse, a simple, one-sentence petition of prayer: "Let your steadfast love, O God, be upon us, even as we hope in you."

Sing a new song? To make such a request in times like ours could easily generate innumerable threnodies. The psalm exhorts us to praise God, and implies that we should do so with joy and verve. But who can sing a new song to God knowing the daily tragedies and misguided course of the world? If we truly understood the sins of our nation, the sufferings we inflict on the poor, the oppression with which we comply, the intentions of our government, the schemes of the Riverside Research Institute, how can we sing a new song to God?

The psalmist is clear. We can sing a new song because despite our ineptitude and sinfulness, God is still God. God is just and loving. That, we are told, is reason enough for innumerable new songs of praise.

A song of hope sung these days is something new indeed. Psalm 33 is, in other words, a song of hope. Scripture scholar Walter Brueggemann says of Psalm 33, "The ones who can 'read creation,' who can discern in its good order the loyalty of Yahweh, are the ones who can live hope-filled lives. Not to be able to 'read creation' is to live hopeless lives; not to know the real name of the Creator; not to be able to trust in the Creator for justice is to be hopeless.... Psalm 33 is a profound assertion about God, but also a bold announcement about true faith in Israel."

Psalm 33 has roots in the pagan literature of Egypt and Babylon. The Jewish community co-opted the pagan insight into the creative power of the word and the Israelites perceived that word to be personal, dependable, loving, and faithful, fulfilling all the potential of the created universe through themselves as God's chosen people.

The believers are supposed to praise God and sing a new song, we are told in verses 4 and 5, because "the word of God is upright; and all God's work is done in faithfulness. God loves righteousness and justice; the earth is full of the steadfast love of God." The God of justice and faithful love was being just when creating the world. Creation took place because God is a God of justice. The world is full of God's love and God is faithful to that love and justice and this reality is worth singing about and proclaiming anew.

The combination of God's word and action is emphasized here: God merely breathes a word, and the heavenly hosts are created (vv. 6-7). The first hearers of the psalm would have grasped the touch of humor and pride in these lines, for they put to shame in a very simple image the false gods of the Egyptians and Babylonians. God's word is powerful and that word always bears fruit in action which is just and loving.

"Blessed is the nation whose God is the Sovereign," the poet writes. In other words, "Blessed are those who trust only in God, solely in God; they will be blessed by God with the gifts of life because they do not rely on the false gods of death, and their deceptive weapons and armies."

God looks over the earth and sees all humanity, we read in verses 13 through 15. God knows our systemic infidelities; God takes note of our idolatries. And God still remains faithful to the justice and love in creation.

Such expressions have strong political overtones. This psalm, like all the psalms, is filled with social/political images, such as: justice; the nations of the world; God as sovereign over the world; God as enthroned; God observing the unjust deeds of humanity. But in verses 17 and 18 the writer gets specific, almost Isaiahan in explicit, political analysis:

> A ruler is not saved by a great army;
> a warrior is not delivered by great strength.
> The war horse is a vain hope for victory,
> and by its great might it cannot save.

Specifically, the word for "warrior" translates as a "mighty man" or a "professional soldier" or "military leader." The "war horse" referred to "the mounted cavalry of the king" but would have symbolized military power as a whole. The most formidable weapon of that time, we are told, was unreliable. The word used is *seker*, meaning "a lie, a deceptive hope." Such military force goes against the purpose of God; it can not help but do otherwise, since its primary purpose is to kill. Such verses issue a strong political judgment, and ultimately a call for nonviolence that would have been just as scandalous then as it is today.

These images referred to the destructive forces of the time, the weapons and methods of ancient warfare. They pale in comparison with the military, nuclear realities of today.

A new translation might read as follows:

> A US president or South African ruler or Filipino general or
> Latin American dictator is not saved by a great army, by
> thousands of troops, by death squads, by invading forces.

A soldier in the Contras, a Salvadoran death-squad assassin, an officer on a US battleship in the Persian Gulf, none is protected by the great power of military might.

A nuclear bomb, a Trident Submarine, an MX, Cruise, or Trident II missile, each is a lie, a deceptive hope for victory. By their great might, they can save no one from violence and death; rather, they bring violence and death to all.

As one commentator summed up, "In the poet's view, to be a nation 'under God' means abandoning trust in military arms." Such a message, we might say, is Franciscan and Gandhian, the message preached by Dorothy Day and Martin Luther King, Jr., the message of nonviolence taught by Jesus.

God is sovereign over all, the poet continues. God's eye is on those who fear God, who stand in awe of God, who hope in God's steadfast love. God sees and delivers Her people from untimely death and famine, the two most prominent afflictions of societal infidelity, the consequences of military violence and oppression. Verse 19 could be even better translated, "To rescue them from Death, to preserve their lives from the Hungry One." God will save those who do not trust in the devouring violence of the military machine. These examples of extreme urgency under the most brutal oppression illustrate the truth that God can deliver and preserve God's faithful ones in *any* circumstance. Therefore, trust in God.

The message is clear: God is not on the side of those who rely on their own power. God always defends those who love and worship God, who place all their hope in God's assistance, and in patience wait for God's good favor, even when death threatens their lives.

The community of believers must hold complete confidence in this God as it resists the force of military might. It is a political statement, encouraging the community to trust in God and resist the deadly forces that roam the world, even though those forces appear to be invincible.

Verses 20-21 issue a confession: "We wait for this sovereign, this all powerful God, who is our help and shield; who defends us in this political world."

Then, community members declare to each other and to the world: "We are glad because we trust in God's holy name."

Finally, they offer a simple, heartfelt prayer of trust: "Let your steadfast love, O Sovereign, be upon us, even as we hope in you." The community offers this prayer because the believers live out their belief in a God of justice and peace. They confront the lie of military power, the systemic power of murder that holds the world hostage. The prayer gathers up the theme of the psalm, God's faithfulness to God's word and God's power to uphold and bless God's people. The whole psalm expresses complete confidence in God. The community of believers need not be anxious, because God's authority is not in doubt and will not be challenged. Their security in God alone is well grounded and this indeed is a cause for rejoicing.

The political implications of Psalm 33 are not unique. Many other psalms are explicitly political in their praise of God. Elsewhere, we read such reminders: "God abhors those who are bloodthirsty and deceitful." (5:6) "Let the nations know that they are only human!" (9:20) "Some boast of chariots, and some of horses; but we boast of the name of the Sovereign, our God." (20:7-8) "Dominion belongs to God who rules over the nations." (22:28) "God sits enthroned as ruler forever." (29:10) "God broke the flashing arrows, the shield, the sword, and the weapons of war.... All the warriors were unable to use their hands. At your rebuke, O God of Jacob, both rider and horse lay stunned." (76:3,5,6) "All the gods of the nations are idols, but God made the heavens." (96:5) "God does not delight in the strength of the horse, nor take pleasure in the might of a human being, but God takes pleasure in those who fear God, in those who hope in God's steadfast love.... God makes peace in your borders...." (147:10,11,14)

Such a word is just as new and dangerous for us today as it was for the early communities. One theologian told me recently that these psalms can not be said in our time as they might have been originally proclaimed. "If you go into downtown Washington, D.C. and truly say, 'God reigns,' " he said, "they'll call the police to get you." However, the risk of such a proclamation, I believe, is precisely what is needed today. These psalms were meant to be taken seriously, and thus to be proclaimed with the same wild enthusiasm of the early Jewish community. Our mission, like that struggling community's, is to announce first to each other that we are called to believe with all our hearts that God does in fact reign and that all these false gods of our present day and age are nothing but pretenders to the throne. They are not God; *our God reigns!*

Walter Brueggemann puts it this way, in reference to such psalms: "Praise is a bold, political act." The worship of God in communal hymns like Psalm 33 reminds me that the psalms are political and prophetic, public testimonies of the truth, declarations of allegiance to God, pronouncements against the idols of the age, and calls for resistance to evil.

Can we have a worship that is politically responsible, in an age of mad consumerism, violent addictions, and the nuclear nightmare? The rhythm and blues of the believing, resisting community through the ages, from the early Jewish community to the civil rights movement, reveal that we can and still do and should continue to go deeper into true praise of God. Psalm 33, and the new song of worship it calls for, inspire us to enact our faith through the politically risky, public task of obedience to God, not allegiance to worldly powers.

When Psalm 33, like all the Scripture, is read from the context of risky discipleship in action, it takes on an urgency and a power that can be shocking and deeply empowering, and ultimately tremendously consoling. Psalms such as this should be read to one another as we seek to embody God's word in our nonviolent actions for disarmament and justice. The Word in the context of risk—our own bodies on the line—is quickly unleashed, and manages to touch our hardened hearts at a deep level. When recited by the believing community as it stands before Riverside Research (or the Pentagon or the Concord Naval Weapons Station in California or similar places), the exhortation and instruction of such communal hymns come alive. Relying on God rather than weapons and violence is practiced by the believing community as it resists such weapons and idols of death. The Word in that setting of nonviolent resistance can be a challenging witness, and a consoling reminder of our identity.

When we go to the Riverside Research Institute or the Pentagon and demonstrate nonviolently, we are trying to enact the words of this psalm. We try to live out the teaching that God is greater than all these entities of death. We trust in God and we rejoice that others trust in God as well. We are trying to enact and live out the hymn as the psalmist urged so that all might live.

As we enact our faith and offer a word of peace in places like Riverside Research, we must keep telling each other the story of what we believe—even as we resist and act to change the disbelief and its deadly consequences around us. We have to help each other believe because, given the pressures of our culture, it is hard for us to believe that we can rely solely on God. The majority of us Christians today are afraid of the consequences of trusting in God alone for our security. We do not want to give up our idols and false securities. We trust in ourselves, our plans, our money, our possessions, our rulers, our weapons, and not in God and God's word of love.

But God demands a living faith from us. We are called to place all our trust, all our security in God, in good times and in bad, in life and in death. The psalmist recognized the need to keep that vision alive in the community; we must struggle to do the same with each other as we make peace in our world.

When we do these things, when we celebrate life and creation and justice and God's faithful care over us, we are indeed singing a new song. And we have cause for great rejoicing, and for offering a heartfelt prayer of trust to God.

"Let your steadfast love, O God, be upon us, even as we hope in you." Amen.

20.
Start From Solitude:
A Gethsemani Journal

Truly I have set my soul in silence and peace.

Psalm 130:2

December 1989

The 1980s transformed my life. Perhaps I should say, God, moving in the Spirit of the times, has transformed me. In any case, I find myself in a drastically different mindset now as I embark on the 1990s and look to the 2000s. With such sobering thoughts, I've come to the Trappists in Kentucky looking for silence. I want to set my soul in peace, to close out a decade—the 1980s—with hopes and prayers for the 1990s, that a world of peace might become a reality, that I might be part of the transforming Spirit sweeping the world.

I moved to California this fall, to begin theology studies at the Jesuit School of Theology in Berkeley. I landed here in the snow-covered backlands of Kentucky, at the Trappist monastery of Gethsemani, straight from vigils and demonstrations in the San Francisco Bay Area against the US war in El Salvador. With the brutal November 16, 1989, murders of my six Jesuit friends and brothers, their cook and her daughter in El Salvador, I was thrown into a whirlwind of nonviolent action. We spoke out clearly, peacefully, truthfully:

"Not one more bullet for the death-squad government of El Salvador!" We knelt down in front of the Federal Building in San Francisco to make our statement, and were carted off to jail. We carried coffins onto the nearby grounds of the Concord Naval Weapons Station, from where all US bombs and military supplies are shipped to El Salvador. We were arrested, booked, and jailed.

Now, I'm in silence. The silence is everywhere: the guesthouse, the church, the hillside. All is silence. I have entered another world, for a time of retreat.

It is Advent. A light snow falls over the knolls and pine trees on the Abbey grounds. The monks continue their vigils and vespers, singing the psalms of praise and hope.

The Trappist monastery of Gethsemani has been drastically remodeled and refurbished since the days of Thomas Merton. Though it does not look as it did during Merton's day—what with a new church, a new guesthouse, a new infirmary, and other repairs—the spirit of contemplative prayer still pervades the place. About seventy monks, including two novices, live and work here. The Merton quote on the brochure sets the tone: the monastic milieu offers a place apart "to entertain silence in the heart and listen for the voice of God—to pray for your own discovery." Communing with God requires a measure of solitude, a stillness and emptiness, a waiting on and attending to the Spirit, it continues. Such a stillness can be found here.

"The contemplative life must provide an area, a space of liberty, of silence, in which possibilities are allowed to surface and new choices—beyond routine choice—become manifest," Merton writes. "It should create a new experience of time.... one's own time, but not dominated by one's own ego and its demands; hence, open to others, compassionate time." I have come to enter into this compassionate time, to listen to the silence of God.

One of the monks who met me at the airport is about to celebrate his fiftieth anniversary in the monastery. His face glows from a spirit of joy. It gives away the story: he has looked upon the face of God, and lived. One of the few people I've ever met who look, act and radiate an experience of God. This brother has already died and now lives in Christ. One of those rare people with Christian eyes.

This evening, I met Brother Patrick, who invited me to come and visit Gethsemani. A live wire, full of fun and laughter. I am learning something from the monks already, something about being a human being. A sense of love and joy.

At Vespers, the overwhelming sense of it all, being here at last! Outside, the weather is cold, cloudy; snow lies everywhere. And my unexpected reaction: Merton was right. Places such as these hold the country together by the seams, as he wrote his first evening here in 1941. If I had come here ten years ago, fresh out of college, eager to give my life over to God, I might have signed right up.

This morning, after Vigils at 3:15 a.m., and 5:45 Lauds and Mass, I rested. Then, a long walk in the snow, first through the cemetery, then out to the road, across the field, up a hill, through the trees, to a grove where a statue of Jesus in agony as at Gethsemani stands in the silence of the white forest cathedral.

So I'm here to listen and to enter into the silence, solitude, love and peace of God, to be intimate with God through the vigils, walks, rest, reading, conversation, and silent prayer. A time to lose myself in the silence and to find God there.

Upon my arrival, Brother Patrick gave me a book for my retreat, Bernard Tyrrell's *Christointegration: The Transforming Love of Jesus Christ*. The first sentence reads: "Is an intimate, loving relationship with Jesus Christ possible and desirable today?"

I put the book down and marvel at providence. Brother Patrick said it came in the mail today, and he thought it might be helpful for me. It's as if he had been reading my journal notes. Yes, that is the question for me: Can I, in the midst of nonviolent action for an end to US military aid to El Salvador and the nuclear arms race, enter into the transforming love of God, as Jesus did?

Already, I am filled with joy and gratitude, overwhelmed at God's graceful presence here and the transforming love of Jesus Christ which I know has already touched me in the simplest, human ways.

A reading from Philippians, during Vespers, sets the tone for my time of silence.

Rejoice in the Lord always. I say it again, rejoice!.... The Lord is near. Dismiss all anxiety from your minds. Present your needs to God in every form of prayer and in petitions full of gratitude. Then God's own peace, which is beyond all understanding, will stand guard over your hearts and minds, in Christ Jesus. Your thought should be wholly directed to all that is true, all that deserves respect, all that is honest, pure, admirable, decent, virtuous, or worthy of praise. Live according to what you have learned and accepted.... Then will the God of Peace be with you. (4:4-9)

Around 5:10 p.m., it occurred to me that I had visited Merton's grave, but that I had not offered a prayer there. So, out the door into the cold night air, I took off for the cemetery, through the snow, along the edge of the church, up to the large pine tree and Merton's grave underneath it. A simple white cross, like all the Trappist graves, except his with a Christmas wreath around it. Merton is buried at the edge of the cemetery, next to the bell tower of the church.

I looked around, saw no one, and began the prayer that I had prepared. "Tom, please pray for me that I be a witness for peace and an apostle of nonviolence." With that, the huge church bells started ringing and I nearly fell off my feet from the loudness of it.

I regained my senses, and took that as a sign that my prayer was heard.

It's been ecstasy for two days now. Nothing visionary, just pure peace and silence. The consolation is the pure joy and peace and downright happiness of being here—and knowing well that Christ-God loves me so much. In that awareness, which one rediscovers unwittingly in monasteries, I am happy. I find joy. As I write this, I know these things. It is nothing that I have done. It is a gift. I know this. God has looked down on me and smiled. Indeed, God is with me and takes joy in being with me. God loves me and loves loving me, as God loves everyone. It is existential, not just pious rhetoric. I am unable to express what's happening. It's all very human and very simple. I am at peace, still, like the snow on the ground or the birds in the trees. Given my life and track record, this can only happen when I drop everything and flee to the monastery.

This evening, after Compline, I sat in my room and read the texts on God's love for us all (Isaiah 43; 2 Cor. 4:7-10; and 2 Cor. 5). It was very consoling. A deep, deep peace, such that I cannot will, came upon me. I pondered the day the Salvadoran Jesuits were assassinated, when some of us visited the Salvadoran Consul General in San Francisco. Reliving that encounter in mind—the words I spoke implicating the Salvadoran government in the murders, and his attempt to strike me in response—I imagined Jesus with us, his hand resting on my shoulder throughout the confrontation. Jesus looked at me and said, "I love you," and I responded, "I love you, too, Lord. I surrender myself completely to you, and offer you my life and soul. Take, Lord, receive. Here I am. Speak, your servant is listening." Through the Scriptures, I heard the voice of God say "Do not be afraid, for I love you. I have called you and chosen you. You are precious in my sight."

I am consoled by the kindness, generosity and hospitality, the laughter and contagious joy of Brother Patrick. He reveals the true spirit of a Christian monk. Here is someone close to God, someone *mundo corde*.

At moments, I stop and break down in tears over these things, overwhelmed by God's intimate love, the gifts given to me, the transformation that comes over me, the peace granted to my poor soul. The monastery continues to be a blessing for me.

The Gospel at Mass this morning. "Behold, I am the handmaid of the Lord. Be it done to me according to Your will." Let my attitude be the same.

Two cups of coffee at 4 a.m. and I was wide awake, ready to go. Prayer and peace in the snow all day.

A two-hour walk, across the road, past the barn and the cow pastures, by the frozen lake, through the woods and up the knob to the old firetower, immortalized in the biography of Merton, as a prospective hermitage. I was nearly at the top, looking out over hundreds of miles of rolling Kentucky hills, when my fear of heights overcame me and I turned back down. It was too rickety, and missing too many floorboards. A long peaceful walk in winter.

I'm sitting on St. Joseph's Hill, overlooking miles of snow-covered Kentucky hills, the sun blazing down upon me. It feels like paradise. One goes to Gethsemani not to escape or forget the world, but to draw strength from the grace of contemplation and creation in order to live in the world in a spirit of compassion, nonviolent love, and mercy. One goes to Gethsemani to remember what life is all about: becoming fully human, seeking God, entering into love and compassion for all creation.

I thought as I sat on that hill, that I would like God to come and unite my heart with God; to break the false self which tries to control God. My prayer: to do God's will and thus to be united with God and all humanity, now and forever.

I prayed for the grace to become a saint, a true disciple, an apostle of nonviolence, a peacemaker. And I felt filled with confidence that my prayer would be answered. I was filled with the faith that one day I shall be in the communion of the saints in heaven with God, face to face, and that I can share in that communion now with all those who make peace and seek justice.

After dinner and Compline, a walk in the night. Ten degrees below outside, and a million stars in the sky.

Today is the 141st anniversary of the founding of Gethsemani. Last night, a one-hour meditation on the words of Jesus in the Gospel of John: "Anyone who loves me will be true to my Word and my God will love that person, too. To such human beings, we will both come and actually live inside their souls." (14:23) Today, after Vigils at 3:15 and morning Mass, a reading from Psalm 90 and the Song of Songs filled me again with the consolation of God's love for me and for us all. Yes, though I am unworthy and one of the greatest of sinners, still God deigns to love me and shower me with affection and love. I confess my sins to Almighty God, my Mother and Father, and to the whole world, and I praise God for God's mercy and love. This spirit moved me deeply to pray for peace and an increase of love in the world.

After breakfast, one of the monks took me on a long walking tour of the monastery. Through the church, outside to the cemetery, back inside into the large "chapter" room where the monks hold conferences, down the stark, white brick hallways, past the courtyard, into the kitchen and the dining room, beyond the mailboxes and finally to the scriptorium, where nowadays magazines and periodicals are kept for leisure reading. Outside again, we walked to the library building where pottery, music, and other studios encourage the creativity of the monks. We visited the upstairs library, and saw the vault where Merton escaped to read and write in perfect silence during the 1940s and 1950s, long before he had a hermitage of his own. Afterwards, we visited the barns and the kitchen factories where the cheese and fruitcakes are prepared and shipped. We returned to the guesthouse through the basement tunnels.

At one point, the monk hinted that most of his life is spent processing cheese. While I am impressed with this truly communist society, and the day-to-day labor of the monks, I must confess some questions about the whole cheese-making and fruit-cake business. I understand their philosophy: they support themselves, rather than rely solely on donations. But it makes one wonder. If the monastery were a sanctuary for Salvadoran refugees, took in homeless people, and was more blatantly against war and injustice, perhaps I would not have so many doubts. The monastic stability, prayer, and obedience are powerful witnesses in our culture. But one gets the impression they may have gone overboard. My hunch is that Merton would still have much to say about the whole "business" ("Cheeses for Jesus") of monastic life. I am reminded, too, of theologian and activist Jim Douglass' insight that in our nuclear culture, perhaps the new monastery is the prison cell where nonviolent resisters are sentenced for their civil disobedience.

But I am certainly edified by the monks. And I can hardly question the splinter in their eye without examining the "two-by-four" in the eye of the North American Jesuits: we have huge retreat houses and properties sitting on thousands of acres across the country that could be put to the service of the poor and the struggle for justice.

I prayed for about twenty minutes in the church balcony, over the Song of Songs and God's great love for me, all the many gifts and blessings given to me without my deserving them, all offered freely and unconditionally. I reflected on the rightness of my calling as a Jesuit—as the setting of my struggle to be more human—not a Trappist. I do feel a need to work for peace and justice in the world, more like Daniel Berrigan and the late Horace McKenna, than Dom Fox and the Gethsemani Trappists. I love the rest and prayer and silence and solitude of this place, but God calls me to speak a word of truth in a spirit of active love to the world.

Afterwards, I walked in the guesthouse garden, on this, the fourth day of snow, four inches by now, around the stations of the cross and then up the cemetery to pray at Merton's grave. I prayed there for all my friends in the peace movement, and all those laboring for peace and justice around the world. I thanked God with great gratitude for the life of Thomas Merton and praised God for Merton's life and example, thinking that I wouldn't have come this far (literally and figuratively) without the witness of Merton, as well as those in his company—Dorothy Day, Martin King, Franz Jaegerstaetter, Gandhi. Then, I asked Merton to intercede for me, (as he had asked St. Therese of Lisieux to intercede for him) that I be faithful all my life, an apostle of nonviolence and peace, a true disciple of Jesus, a witness to the resurrection, a good Jesuit, a writer for the cause of justice, that God might use me if God wants to; that my life might give greater glory to God; that someday I may join Merton and the saints and martyrs in praising God forever, face to face with God. A good prayer. I believe it was heard.

It's bitter cold out now and still snowing. One week from today, I shall be on my way back to California, and another state of mind— work, activism, classes. The important thing is to enjoy walking and sitting and resting in the presence of God, the peace of God, and the love of God. That's what I thought, on the church balcony this after- noon: how *good* it is to dwell in God's love, to be still and "know that I am God." So rarely do people do that. So rarely do I do it.

Dear God, I pray that you come and love me and speak to me and be present to me in the best way, in whatever way you can and you want. I pray you bowl me over with your word and your love. I pray that you transform me, that you help me to be less hardhearted and more open to your loving presence in every human being. I do want to surrender myself completely to you, God. That's why I started this life of adventure in the first place. I place all my trust in you. All is yours, take and receive. I know that I have not placed all my trust in you, but rather in myself, in my ego, in my own idols. I pray that you help me through all this and transform my blindness and sinfulness, and shatter the idols that I bow before so that I may depend solely on you. I am weak, broken and sinful—and I remember this. Yet you love me. Let me then, enter into your love wholeheartedly, and love you in return. Let me be like the saints, who loved you most completely; I know I have not done anything to deserve your love. So, thank you for this great gift. I praise you and I love you, God. AMEN.

A tape of Merton giving a conference on prayer during the 1960s was played to the retreatants during lunch. Merton spoke of Guigo and St. Bernard and the importance of truth in a theology of love. First thing we have to do, Merton said, is to confront our own falsity. Otherwise, we will go along on all kinds of truths but we will not grasp them and we will not love others because we will not have accepted the truth of ourselves, our own falsity, the truth of our own nothingness. My morning meditation in a nutshell.

Now I sit on a frozen folding chair under the statue of St. Joseph on the hill across the monastery, looking out at the valley, mulling over these insights.

What does it mean to speak of the resurrection of Thomas Merton, as a saintly and prophetic follower of the risen Jesus in the twentieth century? Is Merton, like Day and King and Romero, asleep in the Lord, waiting for the Day of the Lord? Or, are their spirits active now, in prayer, for the coming of justice and mercy here on earth, as well as doing the work of God in the next world? Who can say? Perhaps, these are the wrong questions. Perhaps, it is important simply to bow to their memory, to the committed lives they left behind as examples to us all, and to commit ourselves to the same zealous life of nonviolence, truth-telling, and peacemaking.

After None prayers in the afternoon, I came inside and began to read Bernard Tyrrell's book, *Christointegration*. I'm stunned once again at the Providence of this gift. It speaks exactly to where I am, about responding to the transforming love of Jesus, with chapters about Christ as healer, liberator, brother, friend, beloved, lover, and abiding presence. Tyrrell records a charming tale about Karl Rahner, who said once to a theologian, "You're actually only really dealing with Jesus when you throw your arms around him and realize right down to the bottom of your being that this is something that you can still do today." A simple, trusting love in Jesus from such an intellect.

At this point, I put the book down and in my running contemplation with Christ, threw open my arms and embraced Christ, saying "I love you." Consolation through and through.

Such an image! For the first two years of my Jesuit life, while I was in the Pennsylvania Novitiate, my meditation focused on an embrace and walk with Christ, as my older brother, along the Sea of Galilee. God coming to me as my brother and friend. A touching image, and true to life.

I continued the prayer tonight and decided to see what Christ looks like. I pulled back to look on the face of Christ in my mind's eye, and there I saw my brother Jesus looking like me! The shock surprised me. I had imagined myself embracing Christ who looks like me; that I'm embracing myself, but actually Christ. To see myself as Christ, as Christ living in me, and to embrace and love myself, the Christ within me, all so that I can love Christ present in every human being on earth, especially the poor and oppressed. Total integration, with Christ and the true self. Christointegration.

Tyrrell writes that an intimate love relationship with Jesus Christ molds our perceptions of life; colors the way we respond to situations and others; makes faith, hope, and love the deepest realities in our daily living; gives us confidence in the victory of life over the powers of death; gives deeper meaning and value to all our other friendships; and gives a unique vision of life and eternity. "I believe that it is part of the charism of a follower of Saint Ignatius to fall deeply in love with Jesus Christ," he concludes.

What happened in my prayer this afternoon was an inner experience of peacemaking and reconciliation. Christ made peace within myself; through Christ, I made peace with myself, and was reconciled to myself, and to Christ, and the world. The fruit of love and grace.

Later. In prayer, I embraced Christ again and heard the words of mission, "I want you to transform others with my love." I stopped and slowly realized that I was being sent forth to a life of transforming love. To transform the spirit of everyone, including the official at the Salvadoran Consulate on the day of the Jesuit assassinations, from fear and hostility to love and repentant forgiveness: that Christ might live in me and transform others with his love acting through me. My response? "Let your will be done, Lord. Let it be done according to your wish. I am willing to be transformed by your love so that you might transform others by your love through me."

Needless to say, this is an invitation to conversion, to become Christ, to become John Dear, to become the person Christ wants me to be. Christ is working in me. I have resisted this transformation, and now I pray, Lord—please transform me into the loving person you want me to be. Make me a channel of peace for the whole world.

I have lost all sense of time and don't know whether I'm coming or going. Being here is like stepping into eternity. All at once, you are transported into heaven, with the communion of saints, praising God. The songs and psalms are wonderful. This does not mean that I have forgotten the work of peace and justice for the poor that is so pressing. Nor that I have forgotten the masses who die from malnutrition each day, the thousands who kill or are killed each day in war. But the peace of this prayerfulness is strengthening.

The psalms are so powerful. Some are downright violent, of course. And some of the monks' prayers are like none I've ever heard before—all about death and destruction. There's no beating around the bush: reality is being dealt with here head on, in all its mundane brutality and glory.

The closing song at the end of Compline, which is sung in the dark every evening, as a prayer of protection to Our Lady of Gethsemani, is the most touching. Slow, meditative, full of love and trust.

Funny how I'm not at all caught up in the mad rush of Christmas, in the commercialism which plagues the nation. The church is stark; the air is bitter cold. An advent wreath is the only clue that we might be near Christmas. The sanctuary is poor, poor, poor, and thus all the more meaningful. Christmas is stripped to the bare bones and all that's left for us is to ponder the mystery of the Incarnation, which we do.

During lunch, a tape of a monk speaking on the practice of meditation was played. "Conversion is to the spiritual life what revolution is to political life. We all know the best revolutions are peaceful, when people embrace positive social change." Keep saying your mantra; move towards the Light of God, every morning and evening, he advocated. Turn away from violence and turn towards the light of God, he advised. "Meditation helps us to see as God sees."

I had the chance to speak with one of the monks at length, on the difficulties of monastic life. "The world is here," he said. "We are dealing with the essential questions of life. Perhaps one of our greatest services is to help those who are seeking to do God's will to help them find their place in the struggle for peace and justice."

At lunch, we listened to a tape of Merton speaking on Sufism. "To be a mystic is the greatest fulfillment in life," Merton quoted the Sufis. "Mystics have a certainty of God and a desire for God, but no way of explaining God to others. Because of this, mystics will spend their lives being told by others that they are wasting their time searching for God."

I thought: when my false, egoistic self is wiped away and I am my true self, then I am one with Christ, one with love, one with peace, one with the Great Spirit of the earth and the universe and the heavens and history and this is what resurrection is and what the spiritual life is all about. Perhaps this is the search of the mystic.

As I was finishing dinner tonight, Brother Patrick came by to tell me the sad news that President Bush ordered the US military to invade Panama, leaving hundreds of civilians dead and much of the capital destroyed. I am deeply saddened by the imperial might of our nation, its lethal policies towards our sisters and brothers to the south. How far we are from the simple command to "Love thy neighbor." I mourn for the dead of Panama, and for the loss of our loving spirit as a people.

Sitting with the Lord and allowing his transforming love to work freely in me; being filled with God's love for me—I find strength and hope, even despite this dreadful news.

"The one who tries to lose his life in a calculated way will get smashed by Reality," writes Jim Douglass in *Lightning East to West*. "It is that ultimate degree of losing any control over Reality which can lay the foundation for a growth in truth.... Gandhi compared the individual to a drop, and the energy within her to an ocean, that ocean of energy which is humanity, Self and God. Gandhi wrote: 'If we shatter the chains of egotism and melt into the ocean of humanity, we share its majesty. To feel that we are something is to set up a barrier between God and ourselves; to cease feeling that we are something is to become one with God. A drop in the ocean partakes of the greatness of its parent, although it is unconscious of it. But it is dried up as soon as it enters upon an existence independent of the ocean.'

"The kingdom of Reality," Douglass continues, "will be like lightning striking in the east and flashing far into the west when that hidden, latent energy of the Unconscious Self which is God and humanity has been opened by sacrifice, and allowed to surface into a conscious flash of truth, a force of oneness manifested in a spiritual chain reaction of which we already have examples: the effect of Jesus as Christ on the empire which crucified him, the power of Gandhi as soul force over the empire which jailed him and the warring factions which killed him. Lightning east to west will be the widening practical realization in an end-time of the meaning of Jesus' and Gandhi's revolutions, and the consequent, surfacing truth-force and love-force of a finally conscious oneness, a progressive re-uniting of individual psyches in an expression of inconceivable energy."

To lose myself in God as a drop becomes one with the ocean. To enter the truth-force, the love-force, the lightning fire of our nonviolent God—this pursuit of a lifetime, this struggle to be a human being is worth any sacrifice.

Deep waters, and I am grateful for them.

My prayer, to be lost in the infinite love of Christ-God, and feeling on the edge of it. Over and over in my mind: Love, love, love.

After Compline, I sat in my room under a pile of blankets, and called upon the Spirit, formally; then, imagined Christ present before me, saying: "I love you. Relax. Everything's fine. Do not worry. Do not be afraid. All will be well. I have plans for you. I've been with you in the past and will continue to be with you. I want you to enter more fully into my love. To trust me as you have before. To follow me on the peaceful road to peace." I sat in this love, resting in that peace and reality and present moment as best I could. Christ is integrating me, and I am experiencing the achievement of my inner unity (which Gandhi and Merton wrote about so passionately), more than ever. Such is grace.

Nothing happened, and yet, everything happened. It was very real, and normal and natural and not overly exciting and all very good. A quiet peace and silence.

I'm touched by Merton's witness of solitude, retreating to a hermitage in the midst of the hectic war years of the Sixties. An intriguing, curious act. Could I do that someday—live as a hermit, in solitude, prayer, peace, and reflection? Do I have the inner resources, the spiritual strength to enter into that solitude? Am I that united in my soul, in my inner life? Do I truly love myself so as to give my life to the world that way? Is it even possible for me, for short periods of time, to go deep into that solitude (given that such a life may not be what I am called to do) so as to be more fully aware when I am actively working in the vineyard? What did Merton discover in the long loneliness of his Kentucky hermitage? Did he find the inner unity which breeds peace? From all accounts, he did.

Christmas Eve, 1989

A good night's sleep, but I was late for both Vigils and Lauds. I showered, ate breakfast, read my spiritual reading, and then sat and thought for a while, soaking in the peace.

Later, Mass with a forceful homily. I heard God trying to say: "Don't try to bargain with me, calling attention to your formal prayer. Get lost in my love and set your gaze on me—all the time. This is what I want from you: your constant love."

It happened again. I went out to Merton's grave and said my prayer to God. "Through Merton's intercession, let me reach my true self, achieve inner unity, evangelize for your greater glory, enter into your love, and be a witness for peace and an apostle of nonviolence to the whole world." Just then, the bells rang, right at that moment. I nearly fell over from fear, and then I laughed and thanked God.

A good hour-long walk across the roadway into the snowy woods. Very quiet. Deer tracks everywhere in the snow. A frozen lake as the image of peace. A beautiful walk with God in the solitude of my heart and the Kentucky snow.

Christmas Day, 1989

O blessed day! What a marvel—the incarnation of God as a human being! And more: God is born into total poverty and homeless-

ness, into the life of an oppressed people, refugees, on the outskirts
of a brutal empire. God slips into the life of suffering humanity. God
chooses sides, and sides with the marginalized. This is indeed good
news for the poor.

After last night's dinner and prayers, I slept from 7:30 p.m. until
10:00 p.m. as recommended by the monks. Then, a very long
Christmas vigil and Mass. Fifteen readings and fifteen songs—I
nearly passed out from exhaustion. I retired to bed at 1:30 a.m. It's
now 8:30 in the morning and I feel much better.

I've been contemplating the words of St. Ignatius of Antioch,
one of the first Christian martyrs. "I am yearning for death with the
passion of a lover.... All the ends of the earth, all the kingdoms of
the world would be of no profit to me; so far as I am concerned, to
die in Jesus Christ is better than to be monarch of earth's widest
bounds. He who died for us is all I seek; He who rose again for us is
my whole desire."

A quiet Christmas day of prayer and meditation, based on
Isaiah's poetic words of justice and vocation. The blessing continues. The solitude, the silence, the community of pray-ers—these are
great gifts. I pray now with a half smile, like the figures at Polonau-
ruwa which struck Merton. "Everything is emptiness and everything
is compassion." I am entering upon the hidden wholeness, the hidden ground of love, emptiness, compassion, and mercy. Christ, in a
word.

It has been snowing all day.

Praying in perfect calm, peace and silence, sitting in the presence
and absence of God, in a Buddhist meditation. Afterwards, a long
walk in the sun and the melting snow. I came upon the little her-

mitage where Merton lived alone his last few years in the Sixties. I was overwhelmed with a sense of standing on holy ground, the dwelling place of a saint and true contemplative. Across the fields and the road, out towards Dom Frederick's Lake, I ended up sitting on an old stump for hours looking at the countryside, the birds, the sun and the glorious surroundings of nature.

According to our culture, prayer is totally useless. There are no results, and we should not expect results from prayer. This is very difficult for all of us who are socialized into capitalist America.

Prayer is not supposed to make us peaceful or holy or anything. We simply sit with God and accept God's love and listen to God and the silence of God's love. In the eyes of the culture, this is a useless exercise.

We need to shatter the traditional image of the saint by becoming a new kind of holy people. Generous, kind, always friendly and out-going and at the service of others, but politically dangerous! Seeking justice, speaking the truth, practicing nonviolence, fighting war and injustice, defending the poor. These Gospel things make for holiness. They can only be sustained through a life of prayer.

I went for a long walk west, through a herd of cows who watched my every step. Walking along through the fields, I encountered Brother Paul, the poet monk. I asked where he was going and he said he was off to spend his weekly day of recollection in a hermitage on one of the hills. I asked him to pray for me as we parted and he continued on his way across a field towards the woods. I sat under a tree and watched him walk for a mile, over snow covered hills, until he disappeared into the woods. And I was thinking of God's sorrow and the horrors and sadness of the world, and I thought, "Go, Brother Monk, and pray for the world. The world does not care that you disappear into the woods. The world says your life is wasted, your days are useless, your prayer is pointless. But you know better." Given the world, I think the monk is onto something.

Such a person knows about the real world, the world of trees and hills and the sky and birds and lakes and deer and cattle. I love this nature and, as I looked about me over the miles of rolling, snow-covered hills and forests, I was filled with gratitude for the gift of creation. I recalled a tale from the life of Dorothy Day, how one day, while baby-sitting with her grandchildren, she said, "Today, let's go kiss the earth." I have never done such a thing, I thought. So, with great reverence, I kissed the ground and I kissed a tree. I want to be at peace with the earth, even if everyone is hellbent on the destruction of the planet, I want still to side with Mother Earth, truly my Mother. To be on the side of Creation, like the monk.

As I approached the cemetery, to pray at Merton's grave for the close of the day, the bells began chiming, and I smiled.

Dear God, I am grateful and thankful for these days of grace, silence and peace, for looking closer toward your Face, to that day when in joy I shall see you face to face. Thank you for looking at me face to face. Send me forth now to see you in the face of all people, especially in the poor and oppressed, in the marginalized and enemies of this nation. Send me forth to be a sign of peace and nonviolent love to the world, to be a reconciling presence among people. Fill my heart with your peace all the days of my life, and I shall be a peacemaker. Amen.

Part Four:
The Practice of Nonviolence

When we are really honest with ourselves, we must admit that our lives are all that really belong to us. So, it is how we use our lives that determines what kind of persons we are. It is my deepest belief that only by giving our lives do we find life. I am convinced that the truest act of courage, the strongest act of humanity is to sacrifice ourselves for others in a totally nonviolent struggle for justice. To be human is to suffer for others. God help us to be human.

Cesar Chavez

I have not the shadow of a doubt that any man or woman can achieve what I have, if he or she would make the same effort and cultivate the same hope and faith.... Those who are attracted to nonviolence, should, according to their ability and opportunity, join the experiment.

Mohandas Gandhi

You say you don't want anything to happen to me. I'd prefer it that way myself—but I don't see that we have control over the forces of madness; and if you choose to enter into other people's suffering, or love others, you at least have to consent in some way to the possible consequences.

Ita Ford

21

The Road to El Paisnal:
A Pilgrimage to El Salvador

July 1985

The road from Aguilares to El Paisnal in El Salvador, twenty-six miles north of the capital, is dirty and desolate. On the way to El Paisnal—the smaller of the two towns, it has only a church and two dozen small homes—the fields extend for miles on either side. Only the massive volcano of Guasapa can be seen, looming behind.

At 5:55 p.m. on March 12, 1977, Father Rutilio Grande, a Jesuit pastor, concluded an evening Mass in Aguilares and began the short drive down this road to his birthplace, El Paisnal, to celebrate Mass there. Accompanied by several children and an older farmer, Rutilio was about half way there when, in the middle of that isolated stretch, his jeep was fired on by machine guns from behind. The jeep turned over and Rutilio, the older farmer and a young boy lay dead, victims of Salvadoran death squads. He was the first priest to be thus assassinated. The boy's and the farmer's names were added to an already long martyrology of poor Salvadorans.

Rutilio Grande had been assigned by his Jesuit superiors to be the parish priest for two rural parishes. Previously, he had taught theology in the Catholic seminary in downtown San Salvador, the capital of El Salvador. As he settled down to his parish duties, he discovered that most of his parishioners were peasant farmers, just barely surviving. They were uneducated and poor, yet extremely faithful and devout Catholics. As he befriended these people, he realized that the local political leaders had been preventing them from establishing adequate schools, farming systems, homes, and villages. Rutilio organized the people to speak up and demand certain basic rights for themselves. He said God wanted everyone to have enough food, decent homes, good land, and good schools. As he joined the people in demonstrating peacefully for their rights, he was targeted by the soldiers and death squads of the political leaders. They decided to kill Rutilio to set an example for the people, so that the people would not organize themselves and make further demands.

And so, Father Rutilio Grande was executed.

Since that day, over 75,000 Salvadoran peasants, farmers, human-rights workers and churchworkers have been killed at the hands of the government death squads. They have been killed because they threatened to change society, to make it more just and more peaceful. They were killed because they spoke out against the killings. They were killed because they were active in their churches, most of them Catholics, trying to take seriously the biblical words of love and justice. Among those brutally murdered, as all the world knows, were Archbishop Oscar Romero and four North American churchwomen, Ita Ford, Maura Clarke, Dorothy Kazel and Jean Donovan, all of whom had been serving the poor. Years after the death of Rutilio Grande, North American Christians and Catholics are just beginning to look to this servant of the poor, this instrument of peace, and ask, "What can we gain from his life and death?"

To probe this question, I took up, with another Jesuit, a prayerful walk from Aguilares to El Paisnal one Friday afternoon in the summer of 1985. I had come to El Salvador at the invitation of the Jesuit Refugee Service and the Catholic Archdiocese of San Salvador to be an international observer in a new camp for the displaced victims of the war.

Aguilares was quiet. People were sitting in the park; soldiers were strolling about, machine guns in hand. We slipped out of town and began down the dirt road. It was hot, over 100 degrees, and tension was in the air.

There is no shrine to Rutilio Grande along that dusty road. In fact, there is nothing along that road. That stretch of dirt road is as dangerous today as it was in 1977, and so it remains abandoned and desolate.

Not far off, US helicopters circled around the Guasapa volcano. We could hear machine-gun fire and we knew that children, women, and some men were living there. We saw bombers flying and every now and then that terrifying thud of a bomb shook the ground, killing someone. We knew the bombs and planes were supplied by the US government, as was the training for the pilots and the soldiers, all at the cost of some one and a half million dollars a day to US taxpayers for the death-squad government of El Salvador. But we kept walking, thinking of Rutilio Grande, praying for peace.

We came to El Paisnal. We entered the small church and prayed at the altar where Rutilio is buried with his companions. We saw the one-room house where he lived. Before starting our journey back, we stopped into one of the homes to buy something to drink. There, five men stood, guerrillas armed with machine guns. They looked as though they had been living in the jungle for days and were just stopping into a store for food. We exchanged greetings and started back to Aguilares. It was only a little while before we realized we were being watched and followed.

When we returned to Aguilares to catch a bus back to San Salvador, the reality of our pilgrimage dawned on me: we had crossed some imaginary line between two enemies—the death squad armies of the Salvadoran government, backed by the Pentagon and US administrations (such military support has been ineffectively and pusillanimously denounced by the US Catholic Bishops and other religious leaders), and the revolutionaries, camped out in the jungles. Our walk in memory of Rutilio had taken us across a borderline and back again, and it struck me that this was a fitting way to remember him, the man of peace, who went from place to place, from enemy to enemy, breaking bread, praying, speaking about justice and the sufferings of the poor, and trying somehow to reconcile people, to be a Christian symbol of reconciliation.

Had not this been the glory of Rutilio Grande? He had refused to run or hide, but stayed and went forward. Rutilio remained in the thick of violence and insisted on justice and nonviolent love, just as Jesus had done. Rutilio suffered the consequences for such loving insistence; he was shot dead. One must assume, however, given his life, that God has seen to the resurrection of this Christian. His spirit seemed to flourish in the hearts of many in 1977 and thereafter. Indeed his spirit flourished with us as we walked that road on that sweltering day from one armed camp to another, both sides intent on killing one another. Like the two disciples walking the road to Emmaus, we came to a deep awareness in our hearts that God was with us and that God was with those who live and die for peace and justice. What happened to us that day on the road to El Paisnal has happened to Christians throughout El Salvador since the murder of Rutilio Grande. The martyrdom of those seeking justice has set many hearts on fire. One word to describe this energizing, life-giving spirit that takes over one's heart in such new ways is—resurrection.

In the mid-1970s, when Oscar Romero was appointed Archbishop of San Salvador, most of the people of the country were deeply disappointed. The people of the country, ninety-five percent of them living in dire poverty, had hoped for someone who would take a strong, prophetic stand, demanding justice on behalf of those in need. But Romero had always remained far removed from the people, and had never spoken up strongly on behalf of the peasant peoples. However, throughout Romero's transition, he remained in close contact with Rutilio Grande, who had been a close friend for years.

The moment Romero heard the news that Grande had been assassinated, he traveled north to claim the body and to preside at a Mass for the dead. With Grande's death, he began to speak out against the government, realizing that the government was behind the injustices which the poor and their spokespersons suffered. He excommunicated the people who killed the priest and his companions, closed down the school in Aguilares for three days and sent the students home to reflect on the meaning of Grande's life. He announced that, until the government brought answers to Grande's death, no member of the church hierarchy or the clergy would attend any civil ceremony, and, in open defiance to the government ban on all public gatherings, he ordered all the churches to cancel their Sunday services so that the entire country could participate in person or by radio in a special memorial Mass at the Cathedral in San Salvador. Indeed, Grande's death sparked Oscar Romero to speak up for the basic human rights of all the Salvadoran poor, and to demand an end to the killings, a demand that ensured a similar fate for the archbishop three years later.

Rutilio Grande, according to his biographers, once told a group of poor farmworkers, "God is not somewhere up in the clouds, lying in a hammock! God is here with us, building a reign of justice on earth." A month before his death, Rutilio preached at an outdoor Mass, and condemned the murder of the poor, and called for people to love one another:

> The code of the reign of God is love, the key word which sums up all the ethical codes of humanity: love, without boundary lines, exalted and offered in Jesus. It is the love of sisters and brothers, which breaks down every sort of barrier and boundary and which must overcome hatred itself. We do not hate anyone; we love even [those who act like] Cain. The Christian has no enemies, even these Cains.... I'm quite aware that very soon the Bible and the Gospel will not be allowed to cross our borders. We will get only the bindings because all the pages are subversive. And I think that if Jesus Himself came across the border at Chalatenango, they would not let him in. They would accuse the Human-God of being a rabble-rouser, a foreign Jew, one who confused the people with exotic and foreign ideas, ideas against democracy—that is, against the wealthy minority, that clan of Cains! Without any doubt, they would crucify him again. God forbid that I be one of the crucifiers!....It is dangerous to be a Christian in our world. It is almost illegal to be a Catholic in our world, where the very preaching of the Gospel is subversive.

Rutilio did not betray or deny Jesus; he was faithful. In all this faithfulness, I cannot help but ponder the resurrection of Rutilio Grande. He offers us a model for our discipleship, for walking in the footsteps of Jesus. He invites us all to speak out against US military aid for war in El Salvador and to take a stand for peace on behalf of the suffering people. Perhaps we too will be given the gift to walk forward in faith—fearless and nonviolent—in the name of Love and Truth, reconciling those around us, transforming violence into peace and justice for and with the poor. This is my hope as I remember the death of a peacemaker, a justice-seeker, and a friend of the poor. May we go on, with that same courage, in memory of Rutilio, in memory of Jesus.

22

Accompanying the Returning Peoples: El Salvador Revisited

August 1988

On August 15, 1988, Bishop Thomas Gumbleton and I flew to El Salvador to join other US churchworkers in accompanying some 2000 refugees as they returned from Honduras to their home villages in El Salvador. Last October, some 4000 Salvadoran refugees left Honduras to return home, a move unprecedented in Central American history. The military forces, the governing authorities and the US Embassy have all opposed such repatriation efforts; but the determination of the people, and the support of international and Salvadoran religious communities, have enabled the refugees to return home. After two weeks back in El Salvador, I am deeply moved by the struggle of these poor people. Something new is happening in Central America, something profound, something momentous. Yet it is something as old as the Scriptures.

Fifteen North Americans journeyed to Honduras to accompany the people into El Salvador, while fifteen of us went to El Salvador to meet and help receive them at the border. Returning to El Salvador felt like going home.

On August 13, while we were in Houston preparing for the trip, the refugees left Mesa Grande, the Honduran refugee camp, a few days earlier than planned, taking whatever possessions they had—a chicken, an extra shirt, a Bible. The Salvadoran armed forces have militarized the repopulated areas of previous journeys, and they were beginning to realize that more people wanted to return, so they are trying desperately to prevent it. When the refugees reached the Salvadoran/Honduran border, they were stopped. The refugees demanded that they be allowed to enter without being searched, and that the "internationals" or North American solidarity people be allowed to accompany them, and that the caravan of Salvadorans and internationals from the Salvadoran side be allowed to receive them. Despite the sweltering heat and lack of adequate food and water supplies, the refugees decided unanimously to wait right there until such demands were met. Eventually, they were allowed to pass through, but the "internationals" were not allowed to enter El Salvador. It was a moment of tremendous emotion and danger, someone said later. At the exact moment of crossing into El Salvador, a woman gave birth to a child in one of the buses. Lutheran Bishop Medardo Gomez later told us, "That was a message from God."

After being held up for several more days near the border, the refugees were permitted to pass into the two designated towns in the province of Chalatenango where they wanted to relocate. Some 4000 refugees remain behind in Mesa Grande, but many are thinking of returning this fall or next year.

While this was happening, more than thirty busloads of food and supplies and supportive Salvadorans, internationals and North American churchworkers tried to go to the border to welcome the newly arriving refugees. They were all stopped about twenty-five miles south of the border on a road in Chalatenango. Military soldiers with trucks, machine guns, helicopters, and a tank prevented such a demonstration of solidarity from occurring. To continue the solidarity, the people decided to camp our right there on that country road in front of the military in the sweltering heat. Five long days of hanging out by the buses followed.

In an effort to scatter and intimidate the people, the military began to harass them. In the late hours of the first night, at 4 a.m., while everyone was asleep in the buses, the military set up a loud-speaker system and began blaring out the sounds of a high-pitched siren followed by simulated machine-gun fire. Such scare tactics were repeated regularly.

Our particular delegation, which included several sisters and priests, came at the invitation of the refugees, and went up on Tuesday, August 16, to be with the immobile caravan. One woman, one of the leaders of the returning people, told us, "We are strong. Those soldiers are our brothers and sisters. The people who want to repopulate are also our brothers and sisters. So we will not leave here. It is unjust to force us to go back. We will stay and apply moral pressure." Her words expressed the power of this large-scale act of nonviolent resistance: poor people confronting the forces of death and repression.

We walked around and met many courageous people. The scene was particularly poignant for me because that was the stretch of road where I had been stopped three years earlier when I was traveling by myself north to visit the sisters who live and work in Chalatenango. Our bus was stopped, and we were ordered out and searched. I was the only North American on board, and I was scared. Now, three years later, our delegation joined in a prayer service right there on the road side with the soldiers watching. So began a long, beautiful afternoon of song, speeches, applause, Scripture readings and cheers which overcame the simulated machine-gun fire and sirens. Bishop Gumbleton read from the book of Ezekiel:

> Mountains of Israel, you will grow branches and bear fruit for my people, who will soon return.... I shall multiply the people who live on you. The cities will be lived in again and the ruins rebuilt.... I shall repopulate you as you were before; I shall make you more prosperous than you were before, and so you will learn that I am Yahweh.... I mean to display the holiness of my great name, which has been profaned among the nations.... And the nations will learn that I am Yahweh—it is the Lord Yahweh who speaks—when I display my holiness for your sake before their eyes. Then I am going to take you from among the nations and gather you together from all the foreign countries, and bring you home to your own land. I shall pour clean water over you and you will be cleansed.... I shall put my spirit in you and make you keep my laws and sincerely respect my observances. You will live in the land which I gave your ancestors. You shall be my people and I will be your God. (Ezekiel 36:8-11; 23-28)

One of the ways in which the Salvadoran government could disrupt the repatriation movement was to challenge our presence as supporters. The government proclaimed through the newspapers that our religious delegation was a group of "communists" and "reds" who were trying to "manipulate" the refugees. The headlines on the day of our journey to Chalatenango announced the possibility of all foreigners (meaning religious solidarity people) being expelled from the country. In order to challenge such false accusations, we decided to hold a press conference in San Salvador. Surprisingly, our stand was broadcast and published widely throughout the country.

On behalf of the group, Bishop Gumbleton repudiated the attacks made against us, and said *they* were in reality the threat to the repopulated people. "If the Salvadoran government is acting in good faith, why are they unwilling to allow an international, religious presence to bear witness to the repatriation/repopulation effort?" he asked. He called on the Salvadoran government: "1) to halt its attacks against the Salvadoran people who wish to return to the land they know and love; 2) to allow full access to these communities by national and international church and humanitarian agencies; and 3) to respect the right of these communities to receive humanitarian aid, in accord with the recent Central American peace plan, Esquipulus II."

When one of the reporters asked our thoughts about "democracy" in El Salvador, one of the sisters in our group replied that since food and other supplies are not allowed to reach incoming refugees, "what kind of 'democracy' really existed in El Salvador?"

One companion stated that it was an insult to the refugees to say that we manipulated them. Indeed, the whole accusation of manipulation could only have originated in the US Embassy. Its overtones were clearly racist and patronizing.

In truth, the US government is manipulating the Salvadoran government and the Salvadoran press. One gets the impression that El Salvador, like so many other places in the third world, is simply viewed by the US government as a colony of the United States.

Our remaining days in the Land of the Savior were filled with meetings with church leaders and workers, trips to the countryside, and dialogues with the suffering people themselves. Although we were never allowed to meet the refugees who had just arrived, we met with others who had gone through similar experiences of displacement and resettlement. One woman in a small village told stories of the constant military harassment this summer and how she was kidnapped and raped by soldiers. One village that we briefly visited had just been turned into a veritable military camp. Twelve people had been arrested and disappeared a week before. The sight of two very sick, malnourished children in the face of heavily armed soldiers who were eating the villagers' only food was overwhelming. This captured in one scene the suffering of third-world children everywhere.

One evening we visited the chapel where Romero was shot and killed. With Tom Gumbleton presiding, we celebrated with bread and wine the memory of Jesus at that altar, and spoke of Romero's witness. Across the road stands the little hermitage where Romero lived. Romero often said that if he was killed, his blood would be the seed of liberty, that he would then rise in the people. The priestly robes that he wore when he was killed at the altar now hang in a glass case for all to see. The robes are covered with his blood, the blood of a martyr, a saint, a Christian. Truly, a startling sight.

The heroic, prophetic Lutheran Bishop, Medardo Gomez, considered by many to be the spiritual successor of Oscar Romero and victim of constant death threats, told us, "Our church is bleeding from many years of crucifixion and what keeps us in high spirits is the hope of Jesus' resurrection. Our church is an active participant in this cycle of life and death and resurrection." Later he said, "I never understood the Word of God which reads, 'Happy are those who are persecuted and called all kinds of things....Rejoice, and be glad.' I never understood what it meant to find joy in persecution. Now, we're persecuted and one feels joyful. The joy comes in being accused of doing something evil, when in reality we are doing something good in God's name. When this happens, God gives real joy. This is the activity of the Spirit of God."

Jesuit theologian Jon Sobrino told our group that one thing we should learn from the Salvadorans is that they are stubborn in their pursuit of justice and peace; they are survivors. "It's not easy to go on and on with the revolutionary work of the Gospel. It's easy to do it for a year or five years, but then one wants to stop. Be open to being stubborn, like the Salvadoran people," he urged. "Do not give up the struggle for justice."

It is clear to me that the situation in El Salvador is worse than ever and the suffering people are stronger than ever. The US government continues to send tons of military aid to the brutal Salvadoran government and that means poor people continue to be arrested, bombed, tortured, and killed. The political party ARENA is calling for "total war," not just "low intensity war." This means they want several hundred thousand more people killed. From their perspective, the 75,000 killed since 1980 are just the beginning of the bloodbath they have in mind.

Yet despite all this continued violence and death, there are signs of hope and faith in action. The Calle Real refugee camp run by the Archdiocese of San Salvador, where I worked three years ago, is closing. Our delegation attended the final party, where there was much dancing and celebrating, and a few tears. Sr. Margaret Jane Kling, some Salvadoran friends and I had a happy reunion. People are returning to their villages, and that is a tremendous sign in the face of overwhelming evil. In the face of great danger, the people are strong in faith. They are walking forward.

The repatriation efforts are, ultimately, one of the most dramatic events in Central American history, perhaps world history. As one of the base community priests said, "Repatriation is one of the greatest examples of nonviolence—people facing the greatest difficulties with the conviction of truth and faith in God." Although these events get no coverage in the US media, they are one of the most significant happenings in the world today. (The Salvadoran and US governments know this very well; that is why they are working so hard to stop it and the international support it gets.) Indeed, these "Going Home" campaigns are reminiscent of the civil rights movement in our own country. The standoff on the road to Chalatenango reminded me of scenes from Selma, Alabama. They sing Central American versions of the movement song, "Ain't Gonna Let Nobody Turn Me Round." With such courage acted out in dramatic movements of nonviolent resistance, their victory—their right to live in peace—has already been assured and granted. The simple acts of nonviolent resistance, similar to the works of Martin Luther King, Jr., and Dorothy Day, are daily played out in El Salvador and Central America, and this is a cause of great wonder and encouragement for us all.

The poor of El Salvador are teaching us about nonviolence and resistance.

Now back in Washington, D.C., I am struck between the similarities of the suffering Salvadoran people and the strife of the homeless poor. The sufferings of the homeless are intense, and like the poor of El Salvador, I am convinced that God is with them. My struggle and hope is to be with the poor and thus with God and to participate in God's liberating work of nonviolent love that begins in the world of suffering and pain. A visit to El Salvador makes this clear. Our God is alive and working in the hearts of the poor, giving them the strength to stand up to the forces of evil in order to create a new world. With God on their side, there ain't nobody gonna turn them around.

23

Send Bread, Not Bombs:
Conversations with the Secretary of the Army

Prior to going to Central America to live and work in a refugee camp in 1985, I met with the Secretary of the Army in his office at the Pentagon. He is a friend of my father's, and had heard that I would be going to Central America. He invited me to share my views on Central America with him. I accepted the invitation.

I was escorted by several guards through a network of Pentagon hallways, flags, plaques, and war memorabilia before I finally arrived at the large waiting room outside the Secretary's office. His lobby was filled with paintings of war scenes from the American revolution. When I was finally introduced to him, I told him I was very concerned about what US policy was doing to the poor of Central America.

I asked him to do what he could to stop US intervention throughout Central America, to take a strong personal stand against the militarization which kills the poor. I suggested that he seek nonviolent resolutions to the differences he had with the people of Central America. I told him about the Pledge of Resistance campaign, the pledge of some 80,000 North Americans to speak out against US military intervention in Nicaragua, El Salvador, Honduras, and

Guatemala, and commit nonviolent civil disobedience should the US wage a full-scale war on Nicaragua.

The Secretary listened, but he did not like what he heard.

Very politely, he stated that these were legitimate concerns and that I had every right to express them, but that the need to protect American security and to protect the Americas from Soviet interests were too pressing. His responsibility, he said, was to keep that region "free from the Soviets."

I concluded by asking him to reflect on my questions as he made those decisions, to remember the lives of the poor, and to do the right thing which would be the nonviolent thing.

He inquired about my life and offered to meet with me again after I returned from Central America. I told him I would, and as a sign of goodwill toward him as a person, I offered him a gift: a copy of the poster used at the Sojourners' Peace Pentecost gathering a few days before. In bold yellow letters, it read: "All life is sacred. Choose life!" (Deut. 30:19)

I left for El Salvador the next day, where I lived and worked for two months in the Calle Real refugee camp. There I witnessed the daily bombings of Guasapa mountain and heard regular machine gun fire. I traveled to Guatemala and met with Christians ministering to the poor, native peoples living high up in the mountains who were victims of murder, massacres, and injustice. In Nicaragua, I stayed in a poor village near the Honduran border, and heard stories of the Contra war waged against a terribly poor and peaceable people.

When I returned, I met with the Secretary again, and shared with him what I heard and saw in Central America. I told him about my work in the refugee camp, the daily bombings nearby, and what the refugees were like. I recounted the episodes with Salvadoran soldiers who questioned me and described the large letters "US" on their uniforms and weapons. I explained for him the barren site where the four North American churchwomen were killed in December 1980. I relayed to him what I heard over and over again from the poor people of Central America: "Please tell you government: We don't need weapons, or guns, or bombs, but food, houses, bread to eat. We are not Communists. We are not Russians. We are simple people trying to eat. Stop killing us. We have too many orphans. Please send bread and not bombs."

Then, I reported my impression of Guatemala and how I learned first hand that the United States is intimately involved in supporting a government which is systematically killing its own people. Finally, I chronicled my visit to Nicaragua: my solidarity with Father Miguel D'Escoto and his thirty-day fast for peace and an end to US support for the Contras; my encounter with a woman whose son was kidnapped by the Contras; the story of the Contra attack which left eight mothers dead in Estelli just as I arrived. Lastly, I told him of my visit to the Honduran border and how I was struck by the absolute poverty in which the people live, how they are being killed daily, how they all asked that the United States please stop its war against them.

I stressed that if we sent food, aid, and medicine and stopped bombing, militarizing, and threatening the people of those countries, then we would build up friendships and allies. "It appears to me," I said, "that by pushing the people up against a wall in their search for justice and food, the United States is forcing the peoples of Central America to turn to guerrilla warfare, to violent revolution, and to the Soviets for aid. If we stop killing people, work for dialogue, and offer food, then they will see us as friends and we will not have anything to fear."

With that, the Secretary replied, "Well, I have some questions for you." He asked, "What should the US do about the Soviet tanks that are already in Nicaragua, about the Cuban presence in Central America, and the rebels everywhere?" He offered a quick answer: there is nothing we can do but wage a war "to stop communism," to get them to do what we want. He said that he did not believe that by offering food and aid, that the chances for building democracy would improve. I responded to each charge, but had the terrible feeling that he had no idea what he was talking about. He had never been to Nicaragua, and had only visited US military bases in El Salvador and Honduras for a few hours. He did not know the suffering people, their poverty, or their desire for peace. He did not know what he was doing.

"I cannot stop you from saying the things you want," he declared. "We live in a free country. But being in a position of responsibility, I will not do what you want me to do. I have a responsibility to clear up the mess in Central America, and I intend to do what I can, even though it may take twenty or thirty years."

We continued back and forth until it was obvious that we were going nowhere. After half an hour, I concluded, "This saddens me very much. As a minister of the Gospel and in the name of the poor people who are getting killed in Central America because of the US military, please reconsider."

"I wish you'd reconsider," he retorted. "We need good Catholics like you to be chaplains in the Army."

I did not know how to explain to him that Catholicism for me was a commitment of nonviolence in discipleship to Jesus that demanded a lifelong struggle against war and injustice. I could never be a chaplain in an army.

I gave him a copy of a report released by a church group calling for more humane policies towards Central Americans, along with a small picture of the crucifixion of a Nicaraguan campesino by a Solentiname artist.

His thinking, like most uncritical North Americans, is childish, I thought as I left. It was almost as if the Secretary of the Army were saying, "But they have their tanks down there, so why can't we have our tanks down there?" Indeed, that was what he said.

On the way home from the Pentagon, I thought of Thomas Merton's essay on Adolf Eichmann, the Nazi death camp supervisor who was found perfectly "sane" at his war-crimes trial, and Merton's insight that we Americans have drifted into those same insane, murky waters. Merton wrote:

> We equate sanity with a sense of justice, with humaneness, with prudence, with a capacity to love and understand other people. We rely on the sane people of the world to preserve it from barbarism, madness, destruction. Now it begins to dawn on us that it is precisely the *sane* ones who are the most dangerous.... It is the sane ones, the well-adapted ones, who can, without qualms and without nausea, aim the missiles and press the buttons that will initiate the great festival of destruction, that they, the *sane* ones, have prepared.

My friend, the Secretary, is a very pleasant person: warm, friendly, engaging, and by all North American appearances, very "sane." But Merton is right: it is precisely this "sanity" in our society which is organizing the murder of innocent people in Central America and elsewhere in our world, as well as the possible destruction of the entire world. What America calls "sane" is precisely the insanity that has led to the arms race and to intervention and murder in Central America. This so-called "sanity" pervades both the Secretary and myself and all Americans. The duty of the Christian, as Merton saw, is to act against this prevailing wind of so-called "sanity" with all one's heart, soul, mind and strength, and to lead others away from it as well, so that life may be preserved.

As Daniel Berrigan has written, Jesus' whole message can be summed up in four words: "Repent! Be made sane." After my conversations with the Secretary of the Army, I am convinced: it is a message we Americans need to hear.

July 19, 1989

On this the tenth anniversary of the Nicaragua revolution, several hundred people crowded into the basement of St. Aloysius' Church for a prayer service of celebration and remembrance. It was not a celebration of war, or violent revolution; rather, a celebration of the spirit which tries to bring justice for the poor in Nicaragua and which invites us to reconciliation. Five Nicaraguans and five North Americans carried candles to the altar, and there, lit each other's candles. Then, a procession of fifty children—Nicaraguan boys and girls and North American kids from our neighborhood, black, white, and Hispanic—carried balloons and gifts to the altar. We broke into song. We prayed for peace and reconciliation between our governments. We prayed for an end to the fighting, for the poor of Nicaragua and the United States. And we pledged to pursue peace between our nations, so that peace might indeed become God's gift to us.

24

We Do Not Live By Bread Alone:
A Fast of Repentance

January 15–February 5, 1990

On the morning of November 16, 1989, I was sitting at my desk in the hills of Berkeley, California, writing a letter to a friend who was considering entering the Jesuits. The Society of Jesus is committed to working for justice and standing with the poor, I wrote, but few Jesuits live up to our calling. Just then, someone knocked at the door. "Did you hear the news? Six Jesuits, their cook and her daughter have been assassinated in El Salvador. Ignacio Ellacuria, Ignacio Martin Barro, Joaquin Lopez, Amando Lopez, Juan Moreno, Segundo Montes, and Elba and Celina Ramos."

I was stunned, as we all were.

Before I had time to think, we were on our way to the Salvadoran consulate in downtown San Francisco for a prayer service and demonstration. Later that day, at the afternoon Mass, as the congregation began singing "The Lord hears the cry of the poor," I broke down and wept. I had known and admired the martyred Jesuits from my trips to El Salvador. Their courageous example and commitment were inspiring, and the loss was painful.

As the months went on, Jesuits and friends in the Bay Area mobilized forces for peaceful public demonstrations against all US military aid to El Salvador. Letters were written and calls were made to government officials. Open forums and prayer services were held. Many Jesuits were arrested for nonviolent civil disobedience for the first time. Similar witnesses occurred around the country.

But the situation in El Salvador only worsened. After the president of El Salvador declared that the murderers would be captured and imprisoned (something which had never happened, despite the 75,000 people killed since 1980), the president called for an increase in military aid. The war raged on. Congress and the public showed little sign of wanting to stop the military intervention into that poor country.

What should one do? How does one respond in faith to this continuing crisis? What would Jesus do?

The Gospel of Matthew records an episode where the disciples were unable to cure a boy possessed by a demon. Jesus grew upset at their lack of faith. "What an unbelieving and perverse lot you are!" he exclaimed. After he cured the boy, the disciples approached Jesus with the question, "Why could we not expel the demon?" "Because you have so little faith," Jesus replied. "I assure you, if you had faith the size of a mustard seed, you would be able to say to this mountain, 'Move from here to there,' and it would move. Nothing would be impossible for you. This kind does not leave but by prayer and fasting." (Mt.17:14-21)

Some days, moving a mountain from here to there appears easier than stopping US military aid to a third-world nation like El Salvador. For Jesus, this work of peacemaking and justice, of stopping the demon of militarism from ravaging the poor, is a matter of faith. The question we began asking ourselves was, "Do we have enough faith to cast out the demon of militarism? Do we believe in the power God has given us to do what is right?"

We decided to fast and pray so that the demon of US militarism would no longer kill the poor of El Salvador.

On January 15, 1990, the birthday of Martin Luther King, Jr., in the tradition of Mohandas Gandhi, Dorothy Day and Cesar Chavez—two Salvadoran women, a diocesan priest from Berkeley, another Jesuit, and I began a twenty-one-day fast for peace in El Salvador. Our goals were twofold: as North Americans, and in the name of the North American churches, we would publicly repent through the old-fashioned biblical method of fasting for the sin of US military aid to El Salvador. Also, we would call upon all Christians and people of faith to speak out for an end to US military aid to the death-squad government of El Salvador.

Embarking on a twenty-one-day fast for peace in El Salvador was like stepping out of a lifeboat onto the water and walking toward a beckoning hand. We stepped out of the boat to walk on water not knowing the outcome, knowing only the darkness and mystery of the event and the invitation to walk. But we were not alone. As the community of fasters around us grew daily, we experienced renewed strength. In San Francisco, over 100 people of faith joined us in our prayer and fasting, in one form or another. In over twenty-five cities across the nation, from Boston and Syracuse to New Orleans and Chicago, people fasted and prayed together for an end to US military intervention.

Gandhi declared that at certain times, fasting is a duty. These times, we reflected, certainly call for extended prayer and fasting by many people in repentance for our violence towards the Salvadoran people.

It was an easy decision to begin the fast. Like many others, I had been shocked and saddened as the US government sent billions of dollars worth of guns and bombs to El Salvador, $1.5 million a day for weapons of death, throughout the 1980s. I had watched helplessly as the death-squad government of El Salvador systematically murdered poor farmers, children and churchworkers with these weapons of death bought with US money. In 1985, I lived in El Salvador, and witnessed the sufferings of the Salvadoran people and the brutality of the US presence there. I saw with my own eyes the daily bombings of the countryside. I saw young Salvadoran soldiers with machine guns, wearing uniforms that said "United States," harass the poor; and I was questioned by those soldiers because of my work with the Jesuits in El Salvador. I knew that US policies and military hardware were the major factors in the continued oppression and murder of the poor, of my sisters and brothers in faith. In this context, deciding to fast in repentance was, therefore, a logical—even "normal"—response.

Those who fasted had been working for years to end US military aid to El Salvador. We had spoken out at churches and school groups across the country, written extensively and met with Congressional leaders. We had demonstrated for an end to US military aid at the Pentagon and the Federal Buildings in San Francisco and Los Angeles, at the Concord Naval Weapons Station where the bombs are shipped to El Salvador and at the US Capitol where Congress was set to vote on continued military aid. I had been arrested at all those places for nonviolent civil disobedience, in an effort to awaken the conscience of the nation. Yet, the situation in El Salvador remained worse than ever.

We were shocked to hear Mr. Bush and a group of congressional representatives declare shortly after the massacre that because the

Salvadoran president had admitted that the Salvadoran army killed the Jesuits, now everything was all right and military aid could continue. This line of thinking broke every rule of human logic, yet unfortunately, remained consistent with the (disabled) mentality of imperialism.

The New York Times subsequently reported that a US military advisor knew in advance about the murder of my brother Jesuits. This terrible news, too, was not surprising; the US has been helping the Salvadoran armed forces commit murder for years.

And so, we began to pray and fast. We kept vigil at the Federal Building in downtown San Francisco every day at noon for one hour and held open, public prayer services every day at the Catholic Cathedral and a nearby Lutheran church. Our message was simple: "We cannot let our government get away with murder any longer. Now is the time to cut off all military aid to El Salvador. We should not be associating with such a brutal, fascist regime that pretends to democracy."

We fasted in a spirit of love, hope, and peace, to call attention, not to ourselves, but to continued US military aid. We called upon US leaders to send bread, clothing, and medical supplies to the suffering people of El Salvador and Central America who live in such desperate poverty. We envisioned the dream of Martin Luther King, Jr., which we invoked at the beginning of our fast, to be a reality for all people, including the Salvadoran people.

Fasting is a very simple process, I discovered. You simply refrain from eating, drink a tremendous amount of water, get plenty of sleep, and say many prayers. Life slows down, like a film in slow motion. You enter a new time, and there, you find peace and calm. Your emotions settle down, and everything is reduced to the basics. After a few days, you lose your desire for food, and your disposal system shuts down. Inside, your spirit is liberated and begins to soar. It's as if one's soul is cleansed and everything becomes a little clearer. It became a time of grace, as if I had been in a room of darkness, but now I walked in the light.

Mohandas Gandhi, Dick Gregory, Mitch Snyder, Dorothy Day, and Cesar Chavez are probably the most famous fasters of our time. Gandhi was a notorious faster. He was so beloved by the masses that when he started a fast to the death for an end to violence, the violence stopped. People did not want him to die. In 1933, Gandhi fasted for twenty-one days so that the Hindus would abolish untouchability. "The fast was an uninterrupted twenty-one days' prayer whose effect I can feel even now," he reported months later. "All fasting, if it is a spiritual act, is an intense prayer or a preparation for it.... My fast was a prayer of a soul in agony.... But the mere fast of the body is nothing without the will behind it. It must be a genuine confession of the inner fast, an irrepressible longing to express truth and nothing but truth. Therefore, those only are privileged to fast for the cause of truth, who have worked for it and who have love in them even for opponents, who are free from animal passion and who have abjured earthly possessions and ambitions.... Fasting must come from the depths of one's soul."

The fast proceeded in a quiet, unnoticed way. After a few press interviews and the public prayer vigils, there were long hours of silence by myself and together with my friends. After a while, I lost interest in reading or writing and just wanted to rest. Several days were particularly difficult, when all I could do was think of food (especially pizza).

We undertook the fast in the biblical, Christian and Gandhian spirit of love and truth-telling. We were trying to touch the souls of those we loved, people of faith, not only in the San Francisco Bay area, but throughout the country. Through our little entrance into redemptive, suffering love, we hoped that the Spirit of God would be able to sway the will of the people toward peace. Perhaps it was pretentious. We kept sorting out our motives. But in the end, with a constant reminder of the US-backed killings in El Salvador, it always felt like the right thing to do. We began to experience hope and joy.

The principal participants were two Salvadoran women, Gloria and Adela, who provided the inspiration for our communal witness. Gloria had fled from El Salvador six years earlier and had been working since then on behalf of her people. She founded the Central American Refugee Committee, one of the leading organizations of Salvadorans working to support Salvadorans in the United States. "I am fasting to call on the North American people to end their military aid to my country," she said when we began. "There are problems here in North America, with the homeless, with the poor, with people with AIDS who have no place to live. The money for war in El Salvador should be used for these people."

Adela fled to the US at the height of the violence in late 1989, leaving behind three little children. Years ago, her two brothers were tortured and killed; then her own husband. At one point, she herself was captured and brutally tortured for several days. After she was released, she joined an organization of women working for peace in El Salvador, and her name was again added to the death list. When she heard about the fast, not long after she arrived in the US for the first time, she quickly volunteered to join in so as to experience "a greater spiritual solidarity" with the suffering people of El Salvador.

Besides Steve Kelly, another Jesuit scholastic, also fasting was Bill O'Donnell, pastor of St. Joseph the Worker Church in Berkeley. Bill has long been a folk hero on the West Coast, involved in issues of justice for years. He has been under intense pressure from church hierarchs to slow down and keep quiet. But Bill O'Donnell knows his Gospel. He wants to remain faithful to the Way of peace. "Fasting makes me confront my own hypocrisy, duplicity, and blindness and clarifies so clearly my government's proclivity to violence, its arrogance, its greed," he told one reporter. "The fast minimizes my cynicism and bitterness. In its place, it gives me hope that change can happen. It gives me heart to struggle against those people who are killing innocent people."

The day before we ended the fast, Adela was able to speak on the phone for the first time to her children in El Salvador. She wept as she told us that throughout their conversation, she could hear bombings in the background. "Mommy, we are so afraid," her children said. Then, she begged us quietly, "Please, keep doing what you can to end the war."

We closed the fast with a 7 a.m. Eucharist in a packed church. Gloria spoke. "Every day, there is more bad news from El Salvador," she began. "We feel deeply pained, but we still have hope. We always have hope. We have more hope now than ever. We need to continue these works of peace and justice so that one day my people, the people of El Salvador, can live in peace and justice."

We will never know whether or not the fast was "effective." But the fast may have helped promote a spirit which will one day abolish military aid to El Salvador and elsewhere, and which will help us all undergo a conversion of heart towards real justice for all the world's poor. We clung to the truthfulness of the fast as a simple act of prayer and hope in God. We did our best, turned to God, and were filled with hope that our prayer would be heard.

Hope in a time of violent despair. That, indeed, is a great accomplishment. Something like moving a mountain.

25

St. Valentine's Day:
For the Love of God

February 14, 1990

One wintry morning, on the train tracks at the Naval Weapons Station in Concord, California, some one hundred and fifty people of faith gathered for Eucharist. Two or three times a week, bombs are shipped from the Concord Naval Weapons Station to nearby Navy yards and then on to the Philippines, El Salvador, and elsewhere. Whenever we gather for prayer on those train tracks, the shipments are automatically stopped. On this particular day, we prayed and sang; we heard the Word of God. We broke bread and shared the cup in remembrance of Jesus. Then, we acted in a spirit of nonviolent love. We walked onto the base. It was, after all, St. Valentine's Day.

George Murphy, S.J., rector of the Jesuit Community at the nearby school of theology, gave a simple homily. "This is a day to celebrate love, love for our sisters and brothers in El Salvador, the Philippines and in all those places labeled as the enemy by our government, as well as love for our brothers and sisters in the military who must hate doing what they are asked to do. We are here to celebrate God's love for the poor, and God's love for justice and peace. We are here in the cold to call for an end to these arms shipments; to ask that these trains send gifts of peace; that the military aid of bombs and bullets be transformed into gifts of bread and medical supplies. On this day of love, we hope that God's love will soon be triumphant."

"Make us bold in the works of peace," we prayed after communion. "Give us your spirit that we might love one another. Help us to remember the apostles and martyrs who stood in a spirit of nonviolent love, especially the martyrs of El Salvador. Help us likewise to speak a word of love to all those trapped in the world of war."

In the center of our gathering, placed along the tracks, were eight handmade, black coffins, symbolizing the six murdered Salvadoran Jesuits and their two women co-workers. We picked the coffins up and walked slowly down the road to the main entrance of the weapons base. Some twenty-eight of us carried the coffins across the line onto the base. We set them down and then knelt in silence. A line of twenty Marines with machine guns stood at attention in front of us, while various police officers and county sheriffs conferred. After a short while, we took turns asking that the work of the base be stopped. A pediatrician told about her visits to El Salvador to treat the victims of the US bombing attacks and pleaded that the shipments from Concord come to an end. The actor Ed Asner, who had flown up from Los Angeles to join us, said he was present to add his voice to the growing movement opposing the US wars around the world.

In a short time, we were arrested, handcuffed, brought to the local precinct, and jailed. We were fingerprinted, questioned, booked, and finally released. Eventually, the charges were dropped.

One journalist later wrote that Valentine's Day on the tracks at Concord signaled a new beginning for the church. "On this clear day—the day to celebrate love—you could see the outlines of a new religious community taking shape—an ecumenical, intercultural, even international worshiping and witnessing community of faith."

Such a new community is emerging, and the fact that it is growing out of a common urgent concern at a place like Concord gives one hope for the future of the churches—and the world.

Concord has a history, and it is bloody. Ninety percent of all bombs used in the Vietnam war were shipped from Concord. Nowadays, the weapons are shipped to the Philippines, El Salvador, Guatemala, Honduras, Israel, Korea and elsewhere. Missionaries in El Salvador, on numerous occasions throughout the 1980s and early 1990s, have found shrapnel and fragments of bombs with the name "Concord" written on them.

But Concord is most well known for September 1, 1987. On that day, veteran and anti-war activist Brian Willson sat on the train tracks to block a train carrying bombs destined for Central America. He was deliberately run over and lost both legs in the process. The whole world watched in horror as the scene was replayed on the evening news. Brian's survival was a miracle, but even more miraculous was his spirit of forgiving, nonviolent love which continued to blossom after he was injured. Today, Brian Willson continues to speak out against weapons shipments and call for the transformation of our society.

Ever since that fateful day, people have camped out on the tracks, keeping permanent vigil and blocking every weapons train that tries to pass. Their message is stunning in its simplicity: "It is time to stop shipping bombs to the third world for the purpose of mass murder. Enough is enough. We cannot allow the death industry to continue. Not in our names."

Those keeping vigil challenge the people of Concord and North America to recognize the evil that is prepared in the weapons industry. As a nation, we have not begun to reflect on the sinfulness of our military and naval bases—at home and abroad. When we do grasp the horror of this evil, we will not be able to remain silent. We will have to respond in a loud public outcry against the business of death. We will be compelled to change. We will repent and put away our evil intentions.

On that day, the Concord Naval Weapons Station and all such places will be transformed into centers of peace, into transitional housing for the homeless and refugees, and international outreach stations which ship food and medical supplies to those in need.

There are moments before any act of nonviolent, civil disobedience when I feel afraid, sometimes terror stricken. I am afraid of the violence that might be done to me, afraid of jail, afraid of the transformation that I know will happen in me. But the fear fades with every experiment in nonviolence, with every step of contemplative peacemaking that I am able to take.

In the process of our trying to transform Concord, these actions have transformed me, deepened the Spirit of peace within me, and purified my heart. With every action at Concord, I am transformed along with the people of the weapons base. The process of loving transformation affects everyone.

Transforming the world, we are slowly learning, means transforming ourselves. We ourselves have to walk the road of transformation, the narrow way of nonviolence, into the places where death, violence, and injustice reign supreme. Then, our transforming, nonviolent spirits, insisting on justice and peace, will catch on and transform the business of death into a reign of life. That transforming spirit will return and touch our own hearts, transforming them into pools of love and peace. On that day, we will enter the reign of God. The God of life, the God of love, the God of peace will reign supreme on earth as God does in heaven. It will happen because we walked the road of nonviolence and embraced the transforming love of God.

26.
The Resurrection of Ignacio Ellacuria

July 1990

Five years ago, I traveled to El Salvador with four other Jesuits to spend a summer living and working in a church-run refugee camp out in the countryside. Before embarking on our immersion into the Salvadoran struggle for justice, we spent a day with Ignacio Ellacuria, S.J., the liberation theologian and president of the Jesuit University in San Salvador.

I was deeply impressed by his passion for justice and peace, his great hope that the war would end, his determination that all US military aid to El Salvador would be cut off, and his vision of a new society for the Salvadoran poor.

"We are dedicated to proclaiming the reign of God, a reign of justice and peace," Ellacuria told us. "Tell everyone to work for an end to US military aid and to promote dialogue between all sides in this war," he said. "Tell the Jesuits of Georgetown University that as long as they support the US State Department's war in El Salvador and military aid, that they are living in mortal sin. Those policies are killing our people."

His words were sharp and to the point, and I will never forget them.

That evening, we joined his community for a long meal filled with stories, laughter, and sharings. They took turns telling us about each bombing attack on their house. I remember Ellacuria showing me where a bullet chipped the chair I was sitting in, when the military opened fire one night while they were at table. They laughed recalling how one bomb pushed one of their beds across the room while the Jesuit in it remained asleep.

With deep hope and love, they encouraged me to do what I could for justice and peace in El Salvador and the United States.

Ignacio Ellacuria and those Jesuits showed me what it meant to be a Christian.

Five years later, after countless demonstrations, arrests, speeches, heated discussions, fasts, prayer services, fact-finding trips, TV interviews, conversations with US military and Congressional leaders, and letter-writing campaigns, I went back to El Salvador.

This time, I went to Ellacuria's grave, and the graves of the other Jesuit martyrs. They are buried together in the Romero Chapel at the Jesuit University, next to the little house where they were massacred. The words over their name plates are from the Jesuit mission documents: "We do not work for justice and peace without paying a price."

I saw the many Bibles and religious books shot full of bullets on that terrible night. I saw the picture of Archbishop Romero which hung in their home; a bullet had been shot in Romero's heart. I saw bullet holes on the walls and bloodstains at the doorstep. Everywhere I saw the story of the martyred people of El Salvador.

I saw these things and I was overcome once more with grief.

But outside, on the front lawn where their bodies were discovered along with the remains of Elba and Celina Ramos, their cook and her daughter, a garden of roses has been planted.

As I walked around and examined those red roses, I met a gardener. He smiled and greeted me, then went back to work, cleaning the garden.

Later, I learned that he was Elba's husband, Celina's father. He has worked in the rose garden every day since Easter.

It dawned on me: I was visiting an empty tomb.

Luke's question came to mind: "Why do you seek the living among the dead?" "The ones you seek are not here," I heard the gardener say. "They have been raised, like the Risen One. Go out to the countryside, and there you will find them, among the poor."

I went to Chalatenango.

Way up in the north, among the green hills near Honduras; past military troops, machine guns, tanks, fortresses and US helicopters; in the village of Coral de Piedro, which was bombed by US warships last February, where four children and one adult were killed, some three thousand poor farmworkers came together from the surrounding areas to celebrate the life and witness of Ignacio Ellacuria.

On July 22, 1990, they renamed their village "IGNACIO EL-LACURIA COMUNIDAD." Jesuits, churchworkers, and human-rights activists from all over El Salvador, along with many international supporters, joined them in a special Mass for peace and justice.

"We will continue to speak the truth and work for peace and justice in El Salvador, like Ignacio Ellacuria did," the Jesuit provincial, Chema Tojeria, said in his homily.

Afterwards, the eating and drinking, the folk music and dancing, lasted long into the night. I saw it with my own eyes: the Salvadoran poor were celebrating.

I heard the good news from them. The suffering people of El Salvador would not be put down. Death would not have the last word. God's Peace would reign in their lives. Alleluia would be their song.

I witnessed something astonishing. Ellacuria was rising in the hearts of the Salvadoran people, inspiring them to continue their struggle for peace. All the martyrs were rising—the other Jesuits, Elba and Celina, the four churchwomen, the 75,000 massacred poor, Monsignor Romero, Jesus.

There was dancing and singing. Life reigned in the midst of death. The poor were celebrating a victory: truth, temporarily crushed, was rising in their hearts.

Peace be with you, they said. The one you seek has gone ahead of you. He is risen. Let us rejoice and be glad.

Part Five:
The Struggle for Nonviolence

I shall die, but that is all I shall do for death.

Edna St. Vincent Millay

Mercy is subversive activity.

Jon Sobrino

Those who would give light must endure burning.

Philippine prisoner

27.
Seventy Times Seven:
Life on Death Row

The scribes and Pharisees brought a woman along who had
been caught committing adultery; and making her stand there
in full view of everybody, they said to Jesus, "Master, this
woman was caught in the very act of committing adultery,
and Moses has ordered us in the Law to condemn women
like this to death by stoning. What have you to say?" They
asked him this as a test, looking for something to use against
him. But Jesus bent down and started writing on the ground
with his finger. As they persisted with their question, he
looked up and said, "If there is one of you who has not
sinned, let him be the first to throw a stone at her." Then he
bent down and wrote on the ground again. When they heard
this, they went away one by one. (John 8:3-9)

The Gospel explains it all. Capital punishment was the rule of the
land. Everyone was in on it. Death held final sway over the poor and
the rebellious. If Jesus was to speak for love of life, at some point he
had to speak against their love of death.

The religious men of his time brought to Jesus a woman whom
they were going to stone to death, legally, for committing the crime

of adultery. Her male companion, who also would have committed the adultery, was not to be killed; he was not even brought forward. When Jesus was pressed for his opinion, as they were about to stone her, he began to trace on the ground.

What he traced there has boggled the thoughtful for centuries. But it is not so much what he traced that matters but the fact that he stopped to trace on the ground at all. His calm, childlike response must have taken the scribes and Pharisees totally by surprise. It changed the center of their attention, from their fury and anger to his scribbling on the ground. Once they were listening and trying to figure out what he was doing, then he proceeded to give an answer, knowing they could hear it and a life might be saved.

"Let the one without sin cast the first stone."

Jesus not only condemned the death penalty, he poetically chastised the scribes and Pharisees for considering themselves sinless and able to pass judgment on others. Jesus' words made them realize their own sinfulness and filled them with shame.

His words should have the same impact on us today.

A few miles south of Atlanta, Georgia, just off the main interstate highway, past the McDonald's, across the street from a 200-year-old cemetery, lies the Georgia Diagnostic and Classification Center, otherwise known as death row. The grounds are maintained as well as those of an elite country club. After a half-mile of travel, past the blue lake on the right, tall white towers appear in the distance, connected by white walls and chain fences that enclose a mammoth, white, windowless building. Up close, the scene is unusual and disturbing in the extreme. It immediately reminded me of Dachau.

In 1981 when I visited Dachau, the infamous Nazi concentration camp, I could not help noticing that it was situated in a typical, suburban German town. Behind all the green trees loomed a large compound cornered by tall, imposing towers, which in their heyday had been guarded by soldiers twenty-four hours a day. At Dachau business as usual meant death as usual. Suburban German life proceeded normally.

It is the same in Georgia and across the United States at every death row. Killing takes place inside these massive structures as a matter of routine; outside, the routine of daily life proceeds as usual. Currently, some 125 people live on Georgia's death row, waiting to be killed, legally, by their government. More than 2,500 people sit on death rows in thirty-seven states around the country. More than 5,000 people have been executed in the United States in this century; over 150 people have been put to death since 1977.

From atop a five-story white tower a voice yelled down, "What are you doing here?"

"I've come to visit a friend," I shouted back, straining to be heard.

After thirty minutes of negotiations, interviews at various security checkpoints, and a maze of long hallways and cell doors, I came upon the visitation room. I had come to Jackson, Georgia, to visit my friend, Billy Neal Moore, who had been on death row for almost fifteen years.

Billy grew up in a poor Georgia family, married early, fathered a son, enlisted in the Army, and saw his marriage break up. He had always struggled financially. One day, after he and a friend named George Curtis had been drinking, they planned to rob the home of George's uncle. After running from the scene with George, Billy returned alone to the home of the elderly uncle. The uncle approached Billy, apparently shot at him and missed, and then hit Billy's leg with the handle of a shotgun. In a panic, Billy shot and killed him with the gun. On July 17, 1974, after waiving trial by jury, Billy was sentenced to death.

Billy was granted a stay of execution in 1978. A few years later he was baptized in a prison bathtub, resulting in Billy's feeling "for the first time in my life an experience of total acceptance and love. God's love cut through and washed the scales from my heart," he reflected afterward.

In 1984, Billy was granted a second stay, just seven hours before his scheduled execution. Petitions on Billy's behalf included pleas for clemency from six relatives of the man Billy murdered. During his first six years in prison, Billy was never allowed outside; now, he is allowed outside briefly twice a week. Over the years Billy has corresponded with more than 100 people from across the country and the world. He acts as a counselor and convener of prayer groups on death row. The courts will make a final decision regarding his life by the end of the year.

Billy and I have become good friends during the years that I have known him. From the time I received his first letter, after I had written to offer a word of friendship and consolation, I have been struck by his faith. He wrote: "Your letter was appreciated and I do thank you, but know that the Lord Jesus Christ is in full control of my life."

We spent two and a half hours sharing, praying, laughing, and talking about the future during our visit. Over these past years, Billy's insights, reflections, and prayers have touched me like the letters of Paul, who Christians tend to forget was a notorious murderer before he converted to Christ and became an apostle for the faith (Acts 7:58; 8:3; 9:1-2, 21; 22:3-5, 19-20; 26:9-11). Billy has become a person of the Spirit and the Word, of nonviolence and love, an apostle of Christ for many of us.

Ironically, Billy Neal Moore, a death-row inmate, has become a teacher and model of Christian nonviolence for me. He prays with the strength of knowing that Someone is listening. Rarely have I encountered such faith. "Here, on death row," he once wrote to me, "I try to live a Christian life in ways that will get others to desire the life of Christ.

"My whole life has become a vow of nonviolence, as much as I can live," he continued. "The greatest wars and battles are in each of us and it's only by the Holy Spirit that we can maintain peace...." "I want to be nonviolent, so I respond kindly and respectfully to the guards and other prisoners," he told me on a recent visit. "I know God forgives me," he says. Like others on death row, Billy has come to realize that God always sides with the victim, the victim of any violence.

"If churches really knew that the death penalty was adverse to Jesus Christ, then they wouldn't support it," he writes. "So many Christians accept the salvation and forgiveness of God for themselves, yet for the people on death row there is no forgiveness at all, only death.

"People have to be reminded about the times when they did something wrong and realized it and changed," he wrote to me recently. "They have to see that change is possible and can happen with a person on death row. Christ is the Changing Agent in us all. If it can happen with them, why can't it happen with inmates on death row? The loving Spirit of Christ, that Changing Agent, is at work in us all." No one should be killed, he concludes. We should all be given the chance to change, the chance to live.

Capital punishment is a sign of the deep sickness in our culture. Our culture is addicted to violence and is desperately ill. The plagues of abortion, war, racism, sexism, consumerism, apartheid, torture, and nuclear weapons are all signs of that illness in the world. The death penalty, like these other signs of society gone awry, is immoral, unethical, un-Christian, and evil.

Contrary to what its supporters claim, capital punishment—as many studies have shown—does not deter people from committing violent crime. Rather, it is used by the powerful to maintain the illusion that violent crime is under control and being disposed of. In reality, capital punishment "disposes of" the poor, primarily the black poor. Rich people who commit murder can hire lawyers to get them off death row. The poor are the ones who are killed on death row, and the government spends millions of dollars killing them. As Billy told me, "Since I've been on death row, the government has spent more than $1 million preparing for my death. If I had just a fraction of that money originally, I wouldn't be here. That's what I was looking for when I was young."

The death penalty is racist. According to the National Coalition to Abolish the Death Penalty, in a six-year period in Georgia, thirty-nine percent of capital murder cases involved white victims, yet eighty-four percent of the death sentences imposed were in those cases with white victims. During that same period, black defendants were charged with twenty-three percent of murders of white victims, yet blacks received forty-six percent of the death sentences imposed in those cases. Black defendants charged with killing white victims were eleven times more likely to be sentenced to death. Such discrimination exists not only in Georgia but everywhere the death penalty is used. Ninety percent of those on death row are there for killing white people, although each year almost half the homicide victims are black.

The death penalty is a slow form of torture, culminating in murder—the premeditated, meticulously legal killing of a human being by another human being—and by the entire society.

Capital punishment, like all violence, is inconsistent and illogical. In this case, society justifies capital punishment to set an "example" for those who kill. Approximately 20,000 people are murdered each year in this country, and 4,000 are convicted of murdering others. Several hundred face death row.

As Christians we must recognize in every human being the presence of God. The Scripture is explicit about this: God is in each one of us. We are all children of God, all redeemable. Particularly, Christ comes to us in the distressing disguise of the poor, in our enemies, in the unborn, in prisoners. Followers of Jesus are therefore a pro-life people who side with any victim of violence, always resist death, and promote human life for all through steadfast mercy and compassion.

The challenge for us today is to take seriously Jesus' words on death, sin, and forgiveness. The challenge is to hear the voice of God in the death-row inmate saying, "Killing is wrong. Christians should not kill."

Our word is a word of forgiveness and life. We are asked to forgive and offer hospitality to the murderer, as Ananias was asked to accept Saul—the notorious murderer—into his house, where Saul became the beloved apostle Paul (Acts 9:10-19). Unfortunately, as Martin Luther King, Jr., observed, "Capital punishment is society's final statement that we will not forgive."

Jesus' retort to capital punishment speaks to our common sinfulness. *"Let the one without sin...."* challenges those of us who think we are not sinful. In reality, all people are sinners. This is part of our original sin. Even if we have not actually killed someone physically, as Billy Neal Moore has, we are guilty of participating in and supporting a system that has murdered thousands, indeed millions, of people in more than 100 wars during this century.

From God's perspective, we are all guilty. Not one of us is without sin. Like the crowd wanting to stone the adulterous woman, we should simply walk away from the idea of killing someone on death row, ashamed of ourselves. Jesus breaks the limits set by society on how much we are allowed to forgive. Jesus forgives everyone.

Capital punishment is as legal today as it was 2,000 years ago when Jesus was legally executed. Today we have the choice to stand with the executed, as Jesus did and Paul learned to, or with the executioners, as Pilate and Herod did.

For followers of Jesus, the only consistent ethic is the nonviolent ethic of the cross, the way of life that chooses to side with victims of injustice. Jesus taught his followers that true discipleship for him means not only not inflicting the penalty of death on others, but risking the death penalty for oneself. The symbol of discipleship in the early community became the cross, which translates today into the electric chair.

The nonviolent ethic of the cross is a way of loving our enemies and all those whom the state condemns to death—the poor, the unborn, those on death row. We are to offer the healing hand of redemption to everyone, including those who the state says can no longer be redeemed.

We have to question—peacefully, respectfully, nonviolently — the people who have the power to kill others. Jesus questioned those who held the stones in their hands. We are asked to do the same, to confront the people who enforce this policy of death with the words, "Let the one without sin be the first to throw the switch."

The photos of cheering crowds at the places of executions are signs that our society lacks the desire to rise above such barbarism and violence. As long as people cheer and mock the murder of any human being, as long as they pay for it with their tax dollars, as long as they continue to do business as usual while the government executes people in prisons across the country, the killing and brutality will never end.

To me, Billy and everyone else on death row, like the homeless and the hungry, represent Christ present and suffering in our world today. We are invited to a radical forgiveness and healing, to forgive as God forgives, to allow others to live. We are called to forgive seventy times seven times; and not just those everyday small annoyances which others do to us, but even cold-blooded murder—even the murder of our loved ones. We are called to forgive the murderer as Christ forgives the murderer, as Christ forgives us. We are called to be reconciled with those who have injured us (Mt. 5:43-45) and to pray for forgiveness for our sins "as we forgive those who have sinned against us." (Mt. 6:12)

While we must offer sympathy and support for the victims of violent crime and their families, we must also offer the compassion of Christ to those on death row, and prevent their murder. Those who die on death row will stand someday in paradise with the risen Christ, who was briefly on death row, briefly entombed. On that day, Christ will ask of us: "Why didn't you work to stop these homicides? When you electrocuted or gassed or lethally injected that death-row inmate, you did it to me."

Billy Neal Moore and others on death row hope and pray, like Christ in Gethsemani, that we will all undergo a change of heart and with God, choose life.

August 1990

In an unusual and historic decision, the Georgia Board of Pardon and Parole has commuted the death sentence of Billy Neal Moore to life imprisonment! Those of us in Georgia during those days consider this action nothing less than a miracle of God.

On Tuesday, August 21, 1990, just thirty hours before Billy Moore was scheduled to be executed on the Jackson, Georgia, death row, the five-member panel heard testimony from Moore's family, members of the religious community, and the victim's family, before concluding with a unanimous decision for clemency.

Sarah Farmer, niece of Fredger Stapleton, who was shot and killed by Billy Neal Moore some sixteen years before, pleaded on behalf of her family that Moore not be killed. With tears in her eyes, she recalled that shortly after the killing, a crying and repentant Moore had told her how sorry he was. Her plea was one of the most moving testimonies of forgiveness and nonviolence most of us gathered in support had ever witnessed.

When the clemency decision was announced in the crowded Atlanta courtroom, we began singing "Amazing Grace."

"We have prayed for this for a long time," said Norma Gripper, Moore's sister, "and this shows that if you are steadfast, your prayers will be answered."

Billy's scheduled execution drew appeals for mercy from thousands of people, including Mother Teresa and Jesse Jackson. Lawyers from around the country volunteered their services. As the execution date approached, some of his friends and family gathered for prayer services in Georgia. On the Sunday before the scheduled Wednesday execution, a gathering was held at St. Peter Claver's

church in Macon, Georgia, to pray for the members of the board of
Pardon and Parole, that they be granted the wisdom and compassion
to issue clemency.

Meanwhile, on the same evening, Billy was conducting a prayer
service for his brothers on death row. They were praying for a peaceful solution to the crisis in the Persian Gulf.

Earlier that day, Billy had sent a message for our Macon prayer
gathering. He suggested that if we wanted the Board to be merciful,
then we should try in the next two days to be as merciful as we could
to each other and all those we encountered. He asked us to pray for a
deep spirit of forgiveness in our own hearts, so that every trace of
anger, hatred, hostility, and fear would vanish. In this spirit of nonviolent love, he said, God would move in us. Our prayer would be
rooted in a lived authenticity. He wanted us to be like Christ, practicing unconditional love and forgiveness. If you want to do something
for me, he said, forgive all those who have offended you. Reconcile
with everyone as Christ would have you do, he said.

In this spirit, Billy was sure that God would step in and work a
miracle of mercy and forgiveness.

On Monday, the Georgia Supreme Court denied a last-minute legal plea for a stay of execution. That plea would be presented to the
US Supreme Court the next morning, but Billy's lawyers told us
there was no hope for a stay of execution from the Supreme Court.

In that spirit of painful anticipation and prayer, a handful of us
gathered for an early morning Mass outside the prison gates in the
Georgia countryside the day before the scheduled execution. Afterwards, we received permission to visit with Billy on death row.

Billy walked into the visiting area in great spirits, smiling,
laughing, telling us not to be discouraged, trusting in God's power to
confound the powerful and reveal mercy. Instead of discussing his

last meal and his burial arrangements, as we were prepared, Billy led us in prayer and in a lively discussion about what he would do when he was released from prison! We joined hands and prayed for the Board members, for all those on death row, and for peace in the world.

Suddenly, one of the guards walked in and announced that the US Supreme Court had intervened and granted a thirty-day stay of execution. We were overjoyed. Billy would not be electrocuted. Deep down, however, I said to myself, "I'm very grateful, God, but we have been praying for *clemency*. We want Billy off death row!" I looked up and saw Billy smile. He turned to us and said, "This is just the beginning."

The guards ordered us to leave, since Billy was no longer scheduled for execution. We decided to drive to Atlanta to meet our friends and Billy's family who were scheduled to testify at the clemency hearing.

When we arrived in Atlanta, we learned to our surprise that the Board of Pardon and Paroles had decided to go ahead with its clemency hearing. We walked in just as it began, and saw the Stapleton family enter, and Sarah Farmer plead for Billy's life. Many in the courtroom wept at their beautiful display of forgiveness. They witnessed to us all the true meaning of Christianity—unconditional love, boundless mercy. Several ministers spoke of their first visits with Billy, how they had gone to visit him in order to minister to him, but quickly found themselves being ministered to by Billy.

An hour later, Wayne Snow, chairman of the board, announced that they had granted clemency, and that Billy's sentence was commuted to life. He would be released in several years. We were overwhelmed by the decision. We had prayed and prayed for such an outcome, and lo! it was given to us. We all agreed: God had worked a miracle in our midst. Only God could move the US Supreme Court and the Georgia Board of Pardon and Paroles in such a day, in such an age. It was one of the most profound experiences of God's presence working among us that we had ever witnessed.

It was a week to remember.

I left Georgia renewed with the power of prayer, the importance of non-stop, deliberate, focused prayer offered in a spirit of mercy and nonviolent love, on behalf of the poor, on behalf of justice. Billy taught us this lesson. He has been praying for years, and trusting that his prayer had been heard. For him, it was a matter of awaiting the revelation of God's hand. His attitude was, "Don't act as if God hasn't heard your prayer. God has heard you; trust God's response."

We were all struck by the confidence and assurance with which Billy faced his execution. He always maintained that he would not be executed, even up until the day before the scheduled horror. From our point of view, after countless conversations with lawyers, police officers, government officials and anti-death penalty activists, the situation looked very grim, to say the least. Unlike Billy, we were not convinced. But Billy asked us to pray and believe, and so we did. His challenge was straight from the Gospel, "Where is your faith?"

We found such confidence terribly challenging. One of his friends and supporters had lost her sister-in-law that same week after a painful battle with cancer. She, too, had prayed and hoped that she would live. But indeed, she died, after an agony of pain. Why had Billy been spared? We do not know. But we would agree that his prayer, his faith, the community of love that was formed around him—these factors were significant, albeit mysterious.

Finally, we concluded that, though many in the world are at war with each other, God is active in our midst, and waiting for us to turn to God and beg for pardon. God is awake, not asleep, we agreed. God longs for us to practice that focused, unconditional mercy and love which Billy urged for us. God has granted us all clemency and is waiting for us to grant each other clemency.

While our friend Billy looks forward to the day of liberation, there are thousands of other men and women sitting on death rows across our country. Very few of them had the support structure and loving friendships that Billy had. Few on Georgia's death row know any other people besides their guards, their fellow death-row inmates and the handful of dedicated Georgia Christians who minister to them with love and friendship.

The task before us is to reach out in similar fashion to befriend as many death row inmates as we can; to flood every death row with visitors; to offer friendship, love, and mercy; and to inspire a change of heart in our country that will touch every Board of Pardon and Parole, every governor, and every leader until the death penalty is abolished once and for all.

Billy believes such a day is possible. After this miracle in Georgia, I believe as well.

28.
The Epiphany of a Teacher Dying Young

There is a scene in Robert Bolt's play, *A Man for All Seasons*, in which Thomas More tries to persuade the young ambitious Richard Rich not to pursue a career in the government. Instead, More asks, "Why not be a teacher? You'd be a fine teacher. Perhaps even a great one."

"And if I was, who would know it?" Rich responds.

"You, your students, your friends and God. Not a bad public that," replied More.

It is a scene touching and profound, for Richard Rich, like the rich young man of the Gospels, turns away, unable to choose the simple life. The rest was history.

On the Feast of the Epiphany, in the suburbs of Scranton, Pennsylvania, a thirty-year-old high-school English teacher died from a sudden and agonizing bout with cancer. Mark Clarke taught the literature of Melville, Hawthorne, Hemingway, Fitzgerald, and O'Connor to the young women and men of a Jesuit high school in Scranton for seven years. Before coming to Washington, D.C., I had also taught there. Last week, I dropped everything and drove up for his funeral.

Mark was one of the few who took Thomas More's advice and in a short time became a great teacher, although this was known only by his students, his friends, and God. He was renowned among this circle of students and friends for his questioning spirit and his diligent search for truth. Over the years, he became greatly loved and admired by his students and colleagues on the faculty. But it was only in his death that we realized he was among the truly great.

The Book of Wisdom speaks of people like the young Mark Clarke:

> The just person, though he die before his time, will find rest. Length of days is not what makes age honorable, nor number of years the true measure of life; understanding, this is humanity's gray hairs; untarnished life, this is ripe old age. He has sought to please God, so God has loved him.... Coming to perfection in so short a while, he achieved long life; his soul being pleasing to the Lord, God has taken him quickly.... (Wisdom 4:7-14)

Mark was a kind of Mr. Chips character, playing the absent-minded professor, wearing his ever present tweed jacket, looking a bit disheveled, books and papers coming out everywhere, students following him. A piercing intellect, a searching soul, our own young Socrates, he was a balm for the spirit and a fresh breeze for one's mind. He was humble and intelligent, and we are grateful just to have been his friend. He was that rare spirit who could teach people because he himself so wanted to learn from others. He taught people, in short, to grow in spirit.

A few years ago, he had been invited to join the newly elected Governor Casey's staff in Harrisburg, but instead, he elected to remain true to his vocation of teaching, to pursue the humble path of wisdom and to share that wisdom with the young and humble. He knew what he was doing. He took the likes of Thomas More seriously.

In his suffering, a great spirit of love was revealed. The bravery and love and faith he demonstrated became an epiphany for those who knew him—family, friends, fellow teachers, students—one of those rare moments in a lifetime. After his death, long lines filed past his coffin to pay last respects. On a cold, icy, dreary day, a mournful crowd packed a neighborhood church to be at his funeral.

I only knew Mark briefly, during two hectic years. He lightened the burden of teaching for me by his jokes and advice. We would often discuss late into the night the issues and questions of the world. Last summer he took several students to the Soviet Union as his contribution for peace in the world. It was his way of loving his enemies, of revealing the truth that we are no longer enemies, that in fact, we are all one. While there, he became ill, but even in the hospital, he reached out and in doing so taught a lesson. He consoled a sick child, by giving the child his treasured baseball cap. The giving of the gift made a deep impression on the American students who watched.

He started to teach again last fall, but slowly became ill. At first, he was diagnosed with hepatitis, but by Thanksgiving, his doctors realized that he had cancer and that it had spread to every corner of his body. Mark was in great pain, indeed, a terrible agony. He received hundreds of cards from students and former students and many wanted to visit him, but he was in too much pain. He would lie in bed in silence, with his family around him. But through it all, he never wavered in faith or doubted for a moment God's presence with him. He maintained a deep belief in God. He died conscious, in agony, with his family present.

One evening during the last weeks of his suffering, family members and friends were standing outside his hospital room asking each other, "Where is God in the midst of Mark's pain?" They didn't know that Mark had awakened and heard them. When they entered his room, he pointed to his heart, and told them that God was with him, in his suffering.

Those who were blessed to know Mark Clarke have come to realize that throughout his illness he continued to teach us. His final lesson was the class of a lifetime. He taught us how to die well. He lived in his dying because he showed great love and revealed the suffering Christ to us. In Mark's death, God taught us, the circle of Mark's friends and students, a great lesson. Mark's suffering love revealed the power of the cross, and now he shares in Christ's resurrection.

We stand in awe and with renewed courage that such a one has gone before us. He was unknown to the world, neither a famous leader nor entertainer, neither rich nor powerful. He was a humble teacher, filled with a wisdom that is out of this world. He was a brief shining moment in our lives, offering us a lesson for the rest of our lives.

We mourn and grieve for Mark; our grief is deep, but we are renewed, born again by his witness of love, to make our lives an epiphany for God. Would that the whole world knew Mark Clarke; his wisdom would help us all grow wise in spirit and truth. The example of his life has marked the circle of his friends and students forever. Perhaps his legend may have a ripple effect, influencing more and more people. This is our hope as we remember Mark, who remembered Christ, the humble teacher of truth.

May he rest in peace. May his story be told wide and far. May we be worthy of the lesson of his life.

29

Land of the Brokenhearted:
A Philippines Journal

For the poor around the world, the reality of life is much the same. It is a daily struggle against death. That struggle is nearly always a losing battle. Poverty, hunger, homelessness, bombs falling from the sky, internal refugees, political prisoners, death squads, military troops with their machine guns at every corner, disease, the disappearance of prophetic people, the murder of churchworkers and farmers, ecological disasters, consumerism and its fallout, the ever-present US imperial forces—the list goes on.

From my own experience with the homeless on the killing streets of Washington, D.C., and New York City, to my work in a refugee camp in a bomb ravaged village of El Salvador, to visits in war-torn Israel, Egypt, Ireland, Guatemala, and Nicaragua, I thought I was prepared to enter that reality of life and death which the poor struggle through in the Philippines. I was wrong.

The unjust suffering and violence waged against the poor of the third world—the majority of the world—is heartbreaking. Life among the poor of the Philippines (ninety percent of its 60 million people), is a day-to-day struggle to survive against a system gone mad.

The Philippines is a living disaster, a victim of violence, injustice and US imperialism. Now more than ever, under the regime of world-famous Cory Aquino, that life and death struggle for justice and peace is harder than ever. The revolutionary energy of nonviolence unleashed in the people power event of February 1986 fizzled out after a few weeks. It never got beyond Manila in the first place. In the end, there was no revolution, only a change of characters. The stage, set, and costumes remained. So did the plot. In fact, the repression from the Aquino government is worse than ever, worse than the worst days of Marcos, according to churchworkers throughout the country. "A whole way of life is being destroyed," one priest told me. "An entire people are being crushed." The realization that Aquino would not solve the pressing problems of poverty and hunger has left the masses in despair. The Philippines is a land of broken promises, broken dreams, broken hearts, broken spirits, and broken bodies.

And yet, and yet, there is a spirit of hope and faith that one encounters among the victims of violence and oppression. It is a faith, one senses, that if unleashed, could be a lightning force for transformation, for nonviolent change that could oversweep the world. The people possess a revolutionary faith. They are learning the bitter lesson not to place their hope in governments and presidents, but in God alone. As they struggle with God to proclaim God's kingdom of justice, they are beginning to sense that God is with them, quietly, but firmly. God is present among the poor, oppressed peoples of the world who take the future into their own hands by living nonviolently in a spirit of community, calling for justice and peace. The Christ of hope walks the countryside of the Philippines, sparking a permanent spirit of nonviolent revolution in the broken hearts of the poor who have found courage to demand justice.

I journeyed into that broken land to listen to the voices who cry out for justice and peace, to the churchworkers, women, farmers, urban poor, refugees, prisoners, and nonviolent activists committed to creating a new world out of the shell of the old. They are no longer confronting the horrors of the Marcos dictatorship. Now, they are struggling against the Aquino era. For the poor, for the starving, the brutalized masses, there is, I learned, no difference.

My travels took me far and wide, from Manila to Bacolod on the island of Negros, in a jeepney down south, then by foot along dirt paths, through streams and mud, past many battalions of Filipino soldiers, vigilante death squads, CIA agents, and guerrilla revolutionaries, to a little mountain village of twenty huts, called Cantomanyog. I visited a dozen such villages and met with their base Christian communities, as well as with Pax Christi groups in the urban slums of Cebu City, the rural hills outside of Kabankalan and the garbage dump slums of Manila. I saw the oppressive reality of the US Naval Base at Subic Bay. But there was something special about Cantomanyog, something bold and daring. They live in the most brutalized region in all the Philippines. Yet, they call themselves a "zone of peace."

A zone of peace! My working-class neighborhood in Oakland, California, has been declared both a drug-free zone and a nuclear-free zone. But a "zone of peace"? What would a "zone of peace" situated in the heart of a war zone look like? I asked myself. In a land ravaged by war, injustice, hunger, and poverty, what does it mean to live in peace? In a world where the rich get richer and the poor die, where the permanent war against the poor has been called "peace," what could it mean to declare oneself a "zone of peace"?

Cantomanyog is not reachable by any modern means of transportation. Only a vigorous walk along mud paths and over rickety bridges will take the pilgrim into a countryside all but forgotten by the modern world. Unfortunately, the only outsiders who know about Cantomanyog are CIA agents, US military advisors, and Philippine soldiers who are engaged in an all-out war against the poor. It is in that forgotten land that the people have formed a community to say No to war in the hope that a peace based on justice may someday prevail. The local pastor told us, "The issue here is *survival*. We are fighting against the powers and principalities, the forces of death."

In 1989, 300 children died from hunger as the result of the US-organized bombing raid, "Operation Thunderbolt." Some 35,000 people were evacuated from their bamboo huts throughout the island of Negros because of those bombings. Many village leaders and farmers were killed by the military forces, the vigilantes, or the guerrillas. The people of Cantomanyog began to ask themselves, "Why is this war happening here?" They met on Christmas Day, 1989, and decided then and there to issue a statement calling for peace. Their simple declaration was delivered to both the Armed Forces of the Philippines and the New People's Army.

"We want to avoid or prevent conflicts in our place between the military power of the Communist Party and the Armed Forces," their statement began. "This decision means that there will be no firearms allowed inside Cantomanyog, the zone of peace. This will help us improve our means of livelihood and our lives as a whole."

In February 1990, 300 Christians from all over Negros made a pilgrimage in what they called a "peace caravan" to the village of Cantomanyog. Their week-long journey was to culminate in a celebration declaring Cantomanyog a zone of peace. They came close to turning back on several occasions. Soldiers and death-squad vigilantes threatened them along the way. On the last day, 300 soldiers and vigilantes blocked their path as they were about to enter the village. But their nonviolent persistence bore fruit. On February 16,

1990, during a worship service and Eucharist, Natividad Epalan, a community leader holding her two-year-old child, read a statement declaring the village of Cantomanyog to be the first "zone of peace" in the Philippines.

"Our village is open to everyone whose intentions are good," she read. "We wish to be free from the danger of weapons of war and death...therefore, whoever enters this zone of peace should not bring any guns with them."

A wave of joy and peace swept over the Cantomanyog residents. Many wept. Unarmed, protected only by the hand of God, they returned home to their small bamboo huts. Their declaration for peace stirred the hearts of Filipinos everywhere. Their willingness to risk their lives in a nonviolent stand for peace gave others hope that someday the war might indeed end and the poverty be eliminated.

The zones of peace were originally conceived by Bishop Antonio Fortich. Recognized internationally as the "Oscar Romero of the Philippines," Fortich himself is a walking peace zone. A bishop of the largest city on the island of Negros for twenty-five years, he became a voice for peace and justice for the poor only within the last decade. As government soldiers murdered the poor of his diocese, he began to speak out. He adopted a steadfastly nonviolent approach in his call for justice for the poor and an end to the repression. The more he criticized the military and the Marcos regime, the more death threats he received. He called the Philippines a "social volcano" ready to explode. Loved by the poor and marginalized, Fortich became the object of intense animosity from wealthy landowners and military officers who had once been his friends. In 1985, the Cathedral rectory where he lived was burned to the ground.

Like Archbishop Romero of El Salvador, he began taking in hundreds of refugees from the war-torn countryside into the diocesan seminary. When the new Aquino government continued the repression, he stepped up his criticism. He denounced the government's total war policy and the presence of the US bases, and called for peaceful negotiations, an immediate cease-fire throughout the Philippines, and land reform. In response, the courtyard of the seminary building where he now stayed was bombed while he slept. Today, the bullet-riddled walls of that courtyard testify to the danger that he still faces. In July 1989, his name topped a widely publicized death list of twenty-four priests, sisters, base community leaders, and farmers. Worldwide pressure organized by Amnesty International may have helped prevent the massacre of these churchworkers.

A firm proponent of nonviolence and a person of great warmth and humor, Bishop Fortich was subsequently nominated for the Nobel Peace Prize for his effort to create the peace zones. Despite constant harassment and death threats, he remains a strong person of faith. After years of hierarchical silence, Bishop Fortich has become a true disciple of Jesus. He has taken the risk of the cross, staked his life on the pursuit of peace rooted in justice, and tasted the Spirit of resurrection in the process.

"Peace will be truly realized," he said, "if there is real conversion of the heart. The zones of peace, although a small step, can help that conversion happen. It is like a mustard seed. It will bear good fruit, not only on Negros—but throughout the Philippines and the world.

"I have learned over the years that justice must be planted first before there will be peace," Fortich told me the night I arrived in Bacolod. "Peace is the flower of justice. I have also learned that it is not easy to work for peace. It is very risky. Thanks be to God, I have never been hurt in those incidents, but they have given me courage to continue to speak out for justice and peace. I still have fear. This mission for peace, for justice for the poor, is very, very risky. But every day, I get from the suffering poor more courage to continue the struggle. My hope is in the people," he concluded, "and in their constant hope for justice and peace, in their hope that one day, they will have a decent life, food, homes, work, and peace for each other. We always have hope because the poor have hope."

Nearly all Filipinos hope that one day soon the military and imperial might of the United States will leave the Philippines. For nearly every Filipino, the US military bases represent the unsaid truth that the Philippines is still a colony of the United States. Nowhere is this colonial force clearer than in Olongapo, the home of the US Naval Base in Subic Bay.

Much like San Francisco, Subic Bay is one of the most beautiful ocean inlets in the world. Altogether, five US military installations are located in the Philippines, occupying more than 192,000 acres (an area larger than the state of Massachusetts). Sixteen thousand US troops and hundreds of US civilians are stationed on those bases, and some 65,000 Filipinos work there. The Subic Naval Base was originally installed by Spanish colonial power, but when the Philippines became a US colony in 1901, the US took over Subic.

Olongapo is an open wound of poverty and oppression, a wound that is attacked every day. Life on the streets of Olongapo is a dead end. Over 20,000 Filipino women and children are trapped in a downward spiral of prostitution and drug-dealing for the US troops. This "hospitality industry" operates behind a front of countless bars. The tragedy of this nightmare has included the transmission of AIDS from US sailors to Filipinos.

In the midst of this dark night, a handful of former prostitutes and drug-addicts have begun to reach out to those still caught in the trap. The Buklod night care center offers counseling to women, while the PREDA Foundation ("Prevent and Rehabilitate Drug Abusers"), run by Irish Columban missionary Shay Cullen and a dedicated staff of social workers, provides a loving atmosphere to help children get off the streets and into school. They are able to reach only a handful of the thousands who suffer and die on Olongapo's streets. But this outreach is the only hope for these women and children, as long as the US bases remain. In the process of reaching out, Cullen has also become one of the most outspoken critics of the US bases.

"The situation of the Philippines is similar to the historical, political, economic, and religious situation that Jesus of Nazareth found himself in," Cullen observed when I visited the PREDA center. "It's really the same chess game. The script is the same. A foreign power dominates the masses of people who live in poverty and oppression. The elites have sold out to the bribes of the foreign power. The clergy, like the Pharisees, do not care about the suffering masses but instead are caught up in their rituals. The guerrillas [the NPA] are no different than the zealots who tried to overthrow the Romans. Meanwhile, the prostitutes, the crippled, the children, and the poor are abused, crushed, and pushed aside.

"How did Jesus respond to this situation?" Cullen asked. "How would he respond to the situation here in Subic Bay? Jesus looked at the woman caught in adultery, and his first response was compassion. He then convinced the authorities not to inflict death. Prostitution shows up throughout the Gospels, and always Jesus shows great understanding and compassion. But, he gets sick and tired of the attitudes of the elites and the religious bigots. He confronts them and criticizes their hypocrisy. Taking such a prophetic stance in such a hopeless situation—in a province of the Roman Empire simmering with revolution—could only result in crucifixion. Jesus took his stand and accepted the risks. Our situation here in Olongapo is the same. We have to speak out against the US bases while we offer our compassion to the suffering poor, the prostitutes, and the children.

"Tell the people of the United States to come and stand with us in solidarity," Cullen urged, "to stand with us in nonviolent resistance to the forces of evil that are crushing the life out of the poor and the hungry. Tell them that the forces of evil here have their roots in the United States. The hope for true liberation here in the Philippines, for freedom from hunger and the politics of hunger, is that Christians in the United States will stand up and confront the forces of evil in the body politic in the United States, just as Jesus confronted the whitened sepulchers of his day. We expect Christians in the United States to stand up and be counted for Christ's sake.

"If the mothers of the US sailors knew what their sons were doing here, they would force their sons to resign from the Navy and the Air Force," Cullen concluded. "The sailors never write home about what they do here. The US naval base corrupts these young men, not to mention the harm it does to the Filipino people, especially to the women, and to the land."

Given the easing of tensions between East and West, the charade of the US bases in the Philippines has become very clear: the US is simply protecting its economic control over the millions of poor people who suffer and die so that the US economy can thrive in wealth. Though the US claims the bases are maintained to protect the Philippines, in reality, the US warships and military personnel protect US business interests in the Philippines and throughout the Pacific rim. McDonald's, 7-Eleven, Shakey's, and Caltex gas stations can be found throughout the Philippines. US businesses in the Philippines send billions of dollars back to the US each year, and those companies want the money to keep flowing. The US bases insure US dominance over the Philippines, and thus protect those businesses from being taken over by a Filipino government which would turn that money over to social programs for the poor.

Though the US claims to keep the bases to protect Filipinos, most Filipinos feel less secure with the bases because they have made the Philippines the target for nuclear war. The US stores nuclear weapons in the hills surrounding Subic Bay. Soviet officials have told the Philippine ambassador that Soviet nuclear missiles are aimed at the Philippines because of US nuclear missiles in Subic Bay. The US "neither confirms nor denies the presence of nuclear weapons in Subic." The Aquino government's constitution called for a nuclear-free Philippines, yet, nuclear bunkers can be seen plainly from any hill around Subic Bay. "The continuation of the US bases in the Philippines means an ever greater threat to peace," Shay Cullen states. Indeed, the only real threat to the Philippines is the United States.

The idols of nuclear weapons, US imperialism and materialism are upheld at the expense of the poor. Poverty, hunger, homelessness, disease, drug addiction, and illiteracy could be eliminated in a short time with the money and energy used to maintain those bases. "The people of the Philippines are being sacrificed for the US military," the Church Coalition for Human Rights in the Philippines has stated. "Land needed to produce food is used for target practice. Philippine women and children are trapped in a web of prostitution which satisfies the desires of US servicemen. At the same time, US aid given to hold onto the bases continues to strengthen the Philippine military. The military in turn protects the privileged wealthy class against the starving masses who struggle just to survive each day in poverty and oppression."

Through the bases, the US has been able to bankroll, organize and carry out the Aquino government's policy of "total war" against the New People's Army, which means that every Filipino outside of Manila is suspect. The millions of rural poor who live in desperate poverty have become the targets of the US-planned "low intensity conflict." As in El Salvador, the people are the enemy. US tax dollars have provided eighty percent of the helicopters, automatic weapons and other equipment used by the Philippine military in this war against the poor. Bombing operations have forced the evacuation of thousands of civilians, and killed thousands of church leaders, farmers, human-rights lawyers, and trade unionists who advocate human rights, land reform, higher wages, and a removal of the US bases.

After a short while in Olongapo, it became very clear to me that the US bases have to go. The US bases threaten peace; destroy the environment; corrupt the lives of the sailors; destroy the lives of the women and children of Olongapo; spread AIDS, drugs and addiction; keep the Filipino people oppressed and colonized; do not solve the reality of poverty; endanger the people of the US as well by continuing the global military policy of first-strike capability and nuclear insecurity; promote sexism and racism and the assumption that women and Filipinos are somehow less human than US servicemen; and serve no useful purpose except to ensure the economic growth of wealthy US businesses. The US should withdraw its bases as soon as possible, work to help relieve the Philippines' staggering $29 billion debt, which has crippled their economy, and provide food to help stave off the widespread starvation. At the same time, the US should eliminate its military role in the Western Pacific and demobilize all its forces in that area.

Even in light of these realities, the US bases are only a symbol, albeit a deadly symbol, a symbol that kills. As one priest told us, culture is the key. Poverty, hunger, and the sickness which is the US culture now pervade the poor of the Philippines. The bases are a sign of a germ that has infected everyone in the Philippines. Even if the bases are removed some day, the low-intensity conflict, the hunger, the poverty, the Filipino dream of US consumerism will remain unless society is completely restructured. Attacking these root problems will require a radical transformation, conversion of every level of human existence. A first step towards this conversion will be the closing of the US bases.*

As I walked through the streets of Olongapo, one of the teenagers from the PREDA center turned to me and said, "I hope Olongapo will live on its own one day. Tell your people to remove the bases and just let us live in peace. They exploit people. Let us live in peace."

As more and more people start to challenge the presence of the bases and the Aquino policies, the government steps up the repression. For those who do speak out, the future looks grim. One person who began to pay with the price of his own freedom is Jaime Tadeo, national chairperson of the Philippine Farmers' movement. On May 10, 1990, agents claiming to be with the Department of Agrarian Reform entered the movement headquarters asking for Tadeo. When he came out to greet them, they arrested him. They were from the Na-

---

* The eruption of Mt. Pinatubo on June 9, 1991, forced the closure of Clark Air Force Base, but despite popular efforts calling for its removal, the Subic Naval Base is still operating. If the US is ever forced to leave Subic Bay, it will use Palau for its military operations. For further information, read *Resisting the Serpent,* by Bob Aldridge and Ched Myers.

tional Bureau of Investigation. Unfairly sentenced to eighteen years, Tadeo has been imprisoned since that illegal arrest.

As the imprisoned Nelson Mandela was for South Africans, the imprisoned Jaime Tadeo has become a living symbol of the Filipino poor who struggle for a new life rooted in justice and peace. Tadeo is respected nationally and internationally as a charismatic and deeply religious leader of organized farmers who advocate genuine agrarian reform in a country still entrenched in feudalism and colonialism. Seventy percent of the Filipinos are farmers. "Land reform is God's tenth commandment," he told me when I visited him in prison. "Thou shalt not covet thy neighbor's goods: that includes land."

Tadeo had been persecuted under the Marcos regime for his outspoken stand, but it was his criticism of the Aquino regime that finally landed him in prison. After Cory Aquino came to power, she invited Tadeo to join a national committee to write the new constitution. As the brutal measures of the Aquino regime multiplied, and as the number of arrests, disappearances, bombings, and assassinations increased, Tadeo spoke out even more boldly. He criticized the presence of the US bases, much to the anger of the US Embassy, and maintained his call for land reform. His subsequent imprisonment on trumped-up charges represents a new step in the US-backed program of low-intensity conflict. All those who organize the poor in a demand for social justice will now be silenced, one way or another.

The Philippine National Penitentiary, south of Manila, where Tadeo is imprisoned, is a medieval prison built for 200 people but currently warehousing some 800 men, most of them because of their work for social change. Tadeo reminded me of Cesar Chavez. He manifests the same humble, spiritual commitment to justice. "The passion, death, and resurrection of Christ is the story of the Filipino people," he told me. "Right now, we are experiencing that passion and crucifixion. But one day, we will experience the resurrection. The suffering and martyrdom of our people will strengthen and increase the people's movement," he declared with a smile. "We will inherit the kingdom of justice.

"I talk with the other inmates about creating a new society where there will be no prisons for the poor like this one," he continued, "but instead, a society where land, education and jobs will be available to all people."

Although he faces many years of suffering in prison, his spirit, like that of the oppressed peoples of the Philippines, remains strong. "Haven't we said that to be incarcerated is all part of the sacrifice for the struggle?" he wrote to his friends shortly after his arrest. "How can one be free without first being imprisoned? How can one resurrect without first dying? My imprisonment is but a prelude to another chapter in the struggle of the poor of the Philippines."

This spirit of dedication and commitment is the same spirit I encountered among the suffering peoples of El Salvador, Guatemala, and Nicaragua. In a refugee camp in El Salvador, men and women who had lost their families, homes, and land, told me through their tears that God was with them and that one day, they hoped to live in a just society where war and hunger no longer exist.

In one of the most forsaken, terrorized villages on the island of Negros, I discovered that same powerful spirit of hope. Church-workers and base-community members have been waging a war against poverty and injustice on Negros for years. Now, however, the low intensity conflict, the "total war policy" of Cory Aquino, has reached them in full force.

One evening, I crouched into a crowded bamboo hut for a base community meeting, one of the hundreds of thousands of Christian cells that make up the body of Christ, the church of the poor, throughout the third world. Many were starving and all were malnourished. One pregnant mother of eight children had not eaten for several days. They had no work, except for an occasional day in the field planting sugar cane. They did not make enough to survive; the landlords took all the profits of their labor.

A "military detachment" of soldiers, committed to Cory Aquino's "total war" policy, was stationed on either side of the village. As we read from the Gospel of John and began to share our reflections, sixteen guerrilla soldiers passed through the area and looked in on us.

We were in the middle of a war zone.

At that moment, the group broke into song. The simplicity of the lyrics, the terrible poverty and hunger, the hard bamboo of the floor, and their warm hospitality hit me all at once in that moment, a *kairos* moment for me. They sang: *"We are the church. We are the church. We are the community of peace and love."*

Such simple words, so unassuming, and yet so revolutionary! All at once, the truth hit me hard: We in the first world, in the United States, think the world revolves around us. How quick we are to conclude that we are the center of the world. How quick we are to say that the center of the church lies in Rome and more so, in the US. How quick first-world church officials are to say that they have the first and last word about Christian life today. In our arrogance, we think we have a monopoly even on God.

Yet as the poor of the Philippines know, reality is much different. The center of the church, the center of reality lies in the midst of the poorest of the poor of the world, among the marginalized, persecuted and oppressed, the victims of first-world violence, the ones who continue to suffer but refuse to give up the faithful, nonviolent struggle for justice. They are victims of US violence, military violence, vigilante violence, revolutionary violence, institutionalized violence—and yet, they are the locus of Christ's peace. They reveal the justice of God. They are the church. They show us the meaning of peace. They illustrate a vision of what it means to be human. They demonstrate what a community of love is: in the midst of war, in a situation of absolute poverty and hunger, they share whatever they have with each other in a spirit of hope that God will see them through this injustice. It is just this manifestation of selfless love which marks the presence of God among them. God is with them because they are the oppressed of the earth. Their faith, hope, and love is alive.

The Philippines! Such a sad tale of oppression, injustice, victimization, hopes betrayed, murder, international terrorism. Marcos has come and gone, along with a nonviolent battle for freedom that caught the breath of the world. But, the blood flow continues, along with the hunger, the burial of children in cardboard boxes, the poverty, the suffering. The world turned and looked at the Philippines for four days in February 1986, and then turned away. Since then, CIA and US military officials have orchestrated a well-planned, Nazi-like laboratory of war and terror. The low-intensity conflict waged with Cory Aquino's full approval by the US and their hired death squads aims to keep the poor poor, divided and at each other's throats so that the economic robbery of global politics can continue. Through it all, the U.S. culture brainwashes the Filipino people with empty dreams of Marlboro country, Disneyland, Coke and blue jeans. In so many ways, Filipinos forsake their own lives and find themselves under the spell of Legion, the evil spirit sheltered in the Pentagon and on Madison Avenue.

The Philippines has become another El Salvador and the United States is to blame. Like so many other third-world victims, the Philippines lies on the side of the road bleeding and dying like the brutalized man in the parable of the Good Samaritan. In this case, the US is the international bully that robbed and beat up the Philippines. For the suffering Filipinos, there is no international Good Samaritan to come to their aid. The message I heard over and over again in the Philippines was heartbreaking: "We are starving. Life is harder than ever. We want rice. Do what you can to stop the persecution, the war, the US control, so that we can grow food and live in peace." The political reality was summed up in the slip of noted activist Karl Gaspar, who kept referring to Mrs. Aquino as Mrs. Marcos.

After walking through the war-torn countryside of Negros, witnessing the bombings of poor villages, hearing the horror stories of military raids and vigilante, death-squad atrocities, the tales of the internal refugees, and the violence done to those who call for the removal of the US bases in Olongapo, after seeing the hidden world of the suffering, urban poor in Cebu and Manila, and looking upon the imperial presence of the US bases in Olongapo, I realized that the US sponsored low-intensity conflict has now reached frightening proportions. Every right-wing, fanatical group has been armed to pit Filipino against Filipino in order that they do not unite to oppose US domination. "The US wants to create chaos in the Philippines to maintain its market," one Filipino sister told us. Another sister put it more directly: "Tell the US we do not want your help if all you can give us is war and weapons and poverty. Shape up your own lives."

In recent decades, many of us have begun to see the world through the paradigm of war and peace. But now, as the poor of the third world are telling us, it is time to see the world through the paradigm of oppression and liberation. We need to understand that war *is* oppression, that low-intensity conflict, the nuclear-arms race, and US military bases mean hunger, poverty, homelessness, misery, and death for the poor of the third world. Likewise, peace *is* liberation. The reign of peace—real nuclear disarmament and cessation of bombings and military aid and death squads—will mean liberation for the poor. It will mean food, clothing, adequate housing, healthcare, education, and freedom for those who have suffered for so long. This work of liberation is what the peacemakers of the third world are engaged in. A journey to the Philippines is a pilgrimage into the paradigm shift itself.

Walking through the poorest slums of Manila, amid the trash, urine, feces, dogs, shacks, dead fish, rocks, mud, streams, rivers, smog, and noise, I felt defeated. How can people live in such squalor and misery? I asked myself. The answer was devastating: they do not. They die—by the thousands, by the millions. Children die every day. Teenagers, women, men—all die before their time. Such is poverty, as Jon Sobrino says, "an early and unjust death."

Yet there *is* hope. Voices of sanity *do* cry in the wilderness of the Philippines. Though the US uses the Philippines as a laboratory for war, oppression, and death, the struggling poor themselves are turning it into a laboratory for peace, liberation and life. Bishop Fortich, Jaime Tadeo, Karl Gaspar, the many priests and sisters, the thousands of base-community members, the women, prisoners, farmers, and children—all live the daily struggle for justice and peace, and articulate a vision of that day when the reign of God will be realized in food for the hungry, housing for the poor, clothing, medicine and education for the young, and disarmament and peace for all. One day, the Philippines will be free of US imperialism, its deadly bombs and cultural hegemony. One day, the Filipino people will wake from their nightmare and a revolution of the spirit will be realized.

May God grant the struggling people of the Philippines courage and strength for the road ahead. May they continue to speak and resist, and know the risen Christ in the struggle. And may the people of North America, especially we in the USA, stand with them.

Part Six:
The Wisdom of Nonviolence

The question is not, do we go to church; the question is, have we been converted. The crux of Christianity is not whether or not we give donations to popular charities but whether or not we are really committed to the poor.

Joan Chittister

The real job is to lay the groundwork for a deep change of heart on the part of the whole nation so that one day it can really go through the metanoia we need for a peaceful world.

Thomas Merton

The soul of peacemaking is simply the will to give one's life.

Daniel Berrigan

of the Gospel of John makes clear, Christians co-opted that political statement as a sign of allegiance and discipleship to Jesus Christ. In other words, when a person was baptized, that person declared publicly that Jesus Christ was "My Lord and my God." The political statement of baptism ensured martyrdom, for it declared that the emperor was not who he said he was; and furthermore, there was Someone else who was more powerful, Godlike even. Such a strong proclamation provoked the fury and wrath of the empire. Capital punishment followed shortly thereafter. Thus, becoming a Christian and being baptized were taken very seriously by those who were attracted to "the Way." Christian faith was taken seriously, too, by the ruling authorities, since it was seen, rightly, as a revolutionary threat to their reign of terror and oppression. If everyone in the empire announced allegiance to this "Christ," there would be nothing left for Caesar. The imperial forces recognized the threat of revolution from miles away, and used the force of death to stop the movement from gaining momentum. Thus, one did not go lightly to the waters of baptism. Baptism was a subversive act. Baptism was a road to death.

For believers, baptism was something else as well. It was an entrance into resurrection, into the new life of Jesus Christ, and his way of nonviolence. Baptism in the early church was used to symbolize entrance into a community of nonviolence led by the spirit of Jesus. To his followers, Jesus was the Anointed One of God, the Christ. A nonviolent resister whose fame had spread far and wide, he had been murdered by the military, political, and religious forces of his day for his nonviolent resistance to injustice. In this spirit of resurrection, his community of disciples took up where he left off, preaching a word of repentance, forgiveness, nonviolent love, and justice for the poor. By baptizing a new member into the community, the community itself continued to make a political statement to society at large: they found salvation in God through Jesus—not through obedience to the Roman emperor and his local toadies.

The symbol of baptism itself was co-opted from the Roman military, which used a similar rite to mark entrance into what I would call the community of violence, oppression, and idolatry. In his book, *Doors to the Sacred*, Joseph Martos writes that the origin of the sacraments, and particularly baptism, manifested overtly political overtones:

> The term *sacrament* comes from the Latin word *sacramentum*. In pre-Christian times a *sacramentum* was a pledge of money or property which was deposited in a temple by parties to a lawsuit or contract, and which was forfeited by the one who lost the suit or broke the contract. It later came to mean an oath of allegiance made by soldiers to their commander and the gods of Rome. In either case, the *sacramentum* involved a religious ceremony in a sacred place.

> Christian writers in the second century A.D. borrowed the term and used it to talk to their Roman contemporaries about the ceremony of Christian initiation. They explained that baptism was something like the *sacramentum* administered to new recruits—it was a ritual through which people began a new life of service of God.[1]

The sacrament of baptism developed from those early roots of the Christian community as described in the Acts of the Apostles. Certainly, the symbolic ritual of entering military life—the symbol of all that was evil, the imperial force that killed the Christ—was co-opted to signal a new lifestyle in a reign of nonviolence and peace. Through the ritual of baptism, the new community member joined a more powerful side which still required the laying down of one's life, but for the noble cause of justice and mercy. The newly baptized Christian was missioned to be a sign of nonviolence to a world of imperial violence.

Today, in Christian communities across the United States, we have strayed far from the political, public statement of discipleship which was made in the early practice of baptism. We have lost any understanding of the consequence of baptism. Baptism today—and the recognition of one's own baptism—is far from subversive. This crisis occurs because the North American church is in danger of losing its own identity—its very soul—in the culture. Grace has become very cheap, as Bonhoeffer feared.

Very few in the United States today will be killed for accepting allegiance to Christ through baptism, since, unfortunately, most Americans consider themselves and the culture "Christian." We live, indeed, in a post-Christian era. However, in the third world, martyrdom is still a daily reality. To declare against the ARENA party in El Salvador in favor of the Gospel of Jesus and the community of Christians that serves the poor, is to risk assassination. In El Salvador, the Philippines, and South Africa and other war-torn, third-world countries, the blood of martyrs is redefining what it means to be a Christian, and thus, what it means to be a human being. That blood—the great ecumenical reconciler—is bearing fruit in a new understanding of our common discipleship. The blood of modern day martyrs—from Franz Jaegerstaetter and Martin Luther King, Jr., to Oscar Romero and Jean Donovan to Ignacio Ellacuria and Ignacio Martin Barro—speaks to us about the meaning of baptism, and its paradigmatic quality of entrance into the human community of peace.

The sacraments of the church could be thought of as instruments of grace in our lives which propel us into the politically dangerous, publicly daring mission of active nonviolence and resistance to evil, the work of justice and peace which is at the heart of our faith lives. As paradigms, the sacraments of the church are unique. Sacramental theologian James Empereur, S.J., cites four paradigmatic qualities of the sacraments: they are explicitly clear expressions of God's grace; they are personal encounters with God; they are ritualized climactic moments in the life of the individual and community; and they are public and recognized.[2] Sacraments, in this light, are signs of God's graciousness in the world for all people, signs of God's nonviolent love and justice, and thus, signs of our love and justice towards one another. Baptism, ideally, symbolically, is the paradigm of welcome entrance into the human family, into the unity that all human beings share as sisters and brothers. Confirmation becomes then a symbol of all human commitment. (If young people were confirmed between the ages of 18 and 21, the sacrament could help them embrace the countercultural calling of the Gospel that was given at baptism, just at the moment when the culture calls us to begin the lifelong quest for money.) The sacrament of reconciliation is a paradigm of all human reconciliation, between God, individuals, societies and all humanity. Eucharist represents the sacramentality of every meal, of every human sharing as an impetus for justice and love. Marriage can be seen as a paradigm of every human encounter, every human friendship. Ordination symbolizes human responsibility and public leadership on behalf of the community. Anointing is the paradigm of all care for the ill and deprived.

Given the dark times in which we live, it may be beneficial to reflect on the paradigmatic, public dimension of the sacrament of baptism. Besides being a ritual acted out in a public ceremony, what does baptism say to the world? What does it mean to say that in baptism, we find a model of entrance into the human community? In other words, what is the political significance of baptism? How is it that today, people kill one another or plan nuclear war against millions of people and still consider themselves baptized Christians? How can we return to the root meaning of our symbol?

The sacrament of baptism symbolizes the incorporation of a human being into the human community. The Rite of Christian Initiation (R.C.I.A.) upholds the ideal of the Christian community, and states at the same time that all humanity is good and salvific. In Christian initiation, we are called to accept ourselves as we are and yet strive for the ideal of being human. Conversion is a process, not a thing to achieve, we are reminded. And yet, in the baptism of an adult, the new Christian marks a new beginning—discipleship to the Christ of the Gospels. The community celebrates its own ongoing conversion by welcoming a new member.

Simply put, baptism celebrates the human person's entrance into full humanity, the person's conversion and ongoing conversion and thus the conversion of the human community into the fullness of what it means to be human. Baptism is the sign of a person's entering into the question, "What does it mean to be human?" and the Christian community's constant recognition of the question for itself. Community is necessary for salvation, and baptism ritualizes our entrance into the human community and thus our salvation. As a public statement, it has profound potential.

Two concrete examples may shed light on the question. The first occurred several years ago in New York City at the Catholic Worker house where Dorothy Day labored for many years. There, one Easter eve, a young woman who had lived and worked among poor church communities in El Salvador and among the homeless of New York City stood up and was baptized. The Christian community of the Catholic Worker extended to her the peace of Christ and everyone celebrated. The new Christian then went forth to speak out for peace in El Salvador and housing for the homeless. Her work for peace and justice now came from within the broad context of the church as symbol of human life. That community and the church in general made a bold statement of identity by embracing her.

Another image: in Washington, D.C., three blocks from the US Capitol, the inner-city parish of St. Aloysius offers spiritual support to its members, as well as shelter and food to the homeless and other poor people of its neighborhood. Community members speak out for justice and peace on Capitol Hill and around town. In the community, a strong spirit of joy and faith rocks the Sunday liturgy each week when the packed congregation of suffering and struggling people praise God and break bread together. In this setting, I led a woman and a man through the Rite of Christian Initiation. They both had been attracted to the prophetic word and living faith that they had witnessed among the community. The example of human community provided by that church changed their lives. After several months, both were baptized, to the joy of everyone.

Such examples speak well of the life of the Christian community, and its faithful commitment to the call of the Gospel. But, unfortunately, such examples are rare. In most parishes and churches around the United States, ennui rules the day. Instead of offering hope and life, most church communities seem bored and lifeless. Infant baptism, far from charging the adult sponsors to a greater fidelity—and to the witness of nonviolence—continues to be a cultural rite bordering on the superstitious.

Indeed, our inability to live up to our humanity has taken on worldwide proportions. Today, baptized, worshiping Christians wage war; refuse to be reconciled with their enemies; and worship the false gods of consumerism, money, sexism, racism, and nuclearism. Most refuse to enter into the question of what it means to be a human being. Many do not know that such a question exists, and could not conceive of it. Today, we have baptized Christians—and many Roman Catholics in particular—worshiping on Sunday mornings in their local churches, and then working on Trident submarines, or at the Pentagon, or on death rows on Monday mornings, as if their faith were separate from their normal lives. I was appalled to discover, while living in New York City, that the director of the Riverside Research Institute—a center for Star-Wars and laser-beam warfare preparations—goes to Communion at a downtown Catholic church every morning on his way to work. In correspondence with a Christian peace community that I belonged to, he wrote defending his work, and pointed to his membership in the local parish as a sign that what he was doing (preparing for the destruction of the planet) was right. He believed that the two could go hand in hand—nuclearism and Christian discipleship. Likewise, while living in El Salvador and visiting the Philippines, I learned the shocking truth that Catholics populate the death squads which terrorize the countryside. One could cite many other such scandals.

Has baptism lost its meaning? Indeed, is Christianity void of meaning for North Americans and others who long to be like North Americans? Compared with the fire of the early community described in Scripture and elsewhere, today's Christian community stands far from the sign of human love and community it was once called to be. Christians in North America are seduced by the lures and traps of the culture; they have become cultural Christians, Christians in name only. They will destroy the planet and each other in the name of Christ. In considering that nightmare, they betray the Gospel.

The struggle for justice and peace in the third world, the martyrdom of third-world Christians, and a new reading of Scripture through the eyes of nonviolent resistance shed new light on what it means to be baptized Christians.

First, baptism means that we must seriously align ourselves with Jesus Christ, the politics of the Gospel, and its narrow way of life. Following Christ will mean siding with the poor and the oppressed and speaking out for justice and peace. Following Christ will mean refusing to worship the false gods and idols of the US culture—money, materialism, the media, the presidency, patriarchy, drugs, war, and the nuclear weapon. The baptized person declares to the modern world that she or he rejects these idols of death and now follows the God of life as revealed in the Gospels.

Second, baptism signifies a specific commitment to resist actively the forces of death and violence which pervade our culture. For a baptized person, discipleship to Christ in the context of the United States will mean a constant celebration of life and the new life found in Christ's Spirit and Word, and thus a specific confrontation with death. If we are for life (or "pro life" in the true, consistent, ethical sense of that phrase), we must be against the systems of death that cause such widespread suffering. We must speak out and act against the structures of injustice—the lifestyle of the United States—which cause 40 million people to die of starvation and relievable disease each year; which cause 50,000 people to die of starvation each day; which cause over two-thirds of the world's population to live in abject poverty. The baptized person must speak out against the forty-five wars currently being fought in the world, and the stockpile of

60,000 nuclear weapons which still threaten the planet and the human race, despite the rhetoric of politicians. The newly baptized person pledges herself or himself to the narrow way of peacemaking, non-violence, and truth-telling that marked Jesus' own life.

Third, baptism will become the Christian community's way of declaring for Christ and renouncing war, oppression, and all the methods of violence which kill the body of Christ today. Through the baptism of its new members, the Christian community declares once again what it is: a community of nonviolent, peacemaking people who reveal to the world what it means to be human in a time of great inhumanity. By baptizing new adult members through the R.C.I.A. committed to this way of life, the community declares that it goes against the grain of society, against the mad addictions to violence and death which plague our world. Sponsors and parents of infants baptized today also take a bold stand with the radical Gospel, and pledge to raise the child in the alternative, nonviolent lifestyle that makes sense in light of the Gospel.

Finally, baptism remains the sign of salvation that it was to the first followers of Jesus. Through baptism, the community declares that people are saved here and now and forever through the experiential, existential way of life which is discipleship in Christ. This new life is founded first and foremost in a life of active nonviolence, as well as community living, prayer, resistance to oppression and death, and the constructive practice of seeking justice in solidarity with the poor. Through baptism, the community declares that those who have adopted and continue to follow the ways of violence, oppression, and death are losing their souls—here and now. It declares likewise that those who follow the ways of peace and active nonviolence manifested in the Gospel story of Jesus are saving their lives—here and now, and forever.

In order to grasp the political implications of baptism, and its paradigmatic quality of public allegiance to Christ as the revelation of what it means to be a human being, we must constantly return to the Scriptures to reread the first accounts of baptism after the crucifixion and resurrection of Jesus, and the implied consequences for the newly baptized. The stories are set in a time of terrible oppression, not only from Roman imperial authorities, but by the religious and local ruling authorities in Jerusalem.[3] Jesus had been publicly executed as a revolutionary (although he was a decidedly nonviolent revolutionary), a victim of torture and crucifixion, the capital punishment of his day. His friends hid out in fear of suffering the same fate. But after Jesus' resurrection and the empowering spirit that came upon the early community, the disciples and friends of Jesus went into the streets proclaiming the same message of liberation, salvation, and peacemaking which Jesus had proclaimed. They risked the same serious consequences that Jesus had risked. Facing brutal capital punishment, they took up where Jesus left off. It is in this context that the sacrament of baptism as a paradigm for human fulfillment must be understood. These new Christians followed Jesus the Christ who was then and is now the fullest image of what it means to be human. Jesus was the paradigm of the human; together, these early Christians continued to manifest that paradigm.

The author of the Acts of the Apostles traces the apostles' practice of baptizing people to the first day that they began preaching, on the feast of Pentecost. (Acts 2:37-41) The New Testament contains accounts of baptisms in a variety of settings, but in each case those who were baptized were adults who expressed their faith in Jesus beforehand.[4] The newly baptized accordingly held all things in common with the disciples, and began preaching about this new life. Beginning with Stephen, many suffered the same fate as Jesus—a bloody, public martyrdom.

St. Paul spoke of baptism in terms of a sharing in the death and resurrection of Christ, the dying and rising that Paul himself had experienced just before he was baptized. All those who were baptized had already undergone death and resurrection, and had come to embrace the new life and peace offered by the risen Christ. They were living new lives; indeed, Christ was now living in them. They were now living fully human lives, as members of the human community. They recognized the humanity of others, and reached out to others as human beings. In doing so, they shed light—in a dark time—on the meaning of our common humanity.

The times we live in are just as dark as those oppressive days in the Roman Empire. For the poor of Latin America, the Philippines or Africa, they are even darker. In these dark days, the meaning of baptism—as the entrance into human community, its assertion about the very meaning of being human, and its declaration on behalf of the God of life and justice—is just as weighty and imperative. The lives of modern disciples such as Dorothy Day, Martin Luther King, Jr., Franz Jaegerstaetter, and Oscar Romero show us well the consequential politics of baptism, the costly discipleship of Christianity, and indeed, the very definition of human life. Nonviolence, peacemaking, justice-seeking, truth-telling, compassionate love, service and hospitality toward the poor, resistance to death, community—these are signs of a human life fully lived. Today, our baptismal vows need to be reconsidered and renewed in this new light if we are to take our faith seriously. Christ eagerly awaits our pledge to start anew.

---

1 Joseph Martos. *Doors to the Sacred* (New York: Image Books,1982), p. 11.

[2] James Empereur, S.J. classnotes. unpublished (Jesuit School of Theology, Berkeley, California, September 1989).

[3] For further reading, see *Whereon To Stand: The Acts of the Apostles and Ourselves,* by Daniel Berrigan (Fortkamp Publishing Company, 1991).

[4] Martos, *ibid.*, p. 165.

31.
Christian Feminism:
A Paradigm for Peace

When some of the US Catholic bishops gathered for a weeklong retreat one summer at a Jesuit university in California, several hundred Catholic women showed up to pray and vigil. I was glad to join those women in prayer, for their struggle is at the heart of the Gospel, at the center of justice and peacemaking. They turned to the Gospel of Luke and read the story of the woman and the unjust judge. It was the woman's persistence which caused the judge to grant her request. Likewise, Jesus said, God would grant the requests of all those who cry out day and night for basic human rights. The women prayed that one day, all ministries in the church would be open to women. With such persistent prayer and steadfast determination, the ordination of women and the acceptance of the feminist vision will one day be a reality in the church.

As the vigil closed, the crowd processed forward to bless themselves with water. The women asked us to remember our baptism, the bond which unites us all as sisters and brothers, co-workers of the Christ.

Baptism missions us to ministry. The baptized person is invited by the community to serve others, to proclaim the good news of peace, to make justice a reality, and to transform our violent world into a realm of nonviolent love. It is only by their baptism that priests can claim ordination to public ministry in the church. If baptism is indeed a call to ministry, and women are not allowed to minister as men are, according to male church leaders, then, logic dictates, women should not be baptized. But, patriarchy is more insidious. Instead, women are baptized—and encouraged by men to contribute to the church by doing all the thankless tasks of organizing which few men will do. Women are allowed to be the slaves of men—not their equals, not their sisters in Christ. Women are the untouchables of the Catholic Church, a lower caste. The disease of patriarchy plagues the body of Christ. Such sexism invades every nook and cranny of the church. Today, however, cracks are forming in the foundation of church patriarchy. Women are chipping away at those cracks. One day soon, the whole structure will fall.

Sexism within the church is illogical, unjust, unfair, and evil. It should be filed away in the same drawer with the flat-earth theory and the just-war theory. Every ministerial role in the church should be open to women, including that of priest, bishop and pope.

According to the Gospels, women were the *only* followers who remained faithful to Jesus throughout his lifetime—up to and beyond his crucifixion. Given their culture, the evangelists go to great lengths to prove this point. The male disciples never grasped the mind of Christ, while the female disciples were already anticipating his death and burial. The women stood by Jesus at the cross. They did not betray him, deny him or flee like Peter and the other men. The women went to the tomb on the first day of the week. They did not remain in hiding for fear of being arrested like Peter and the other men. The women were the first to see the risen Jesus. Mary Magdalene was sent to tell the men about the resurrection. "Go tell my brothers," the risen Jesus said to her, "that I will meet them in

Galilee." Jesus deliberately decided not to appear to them first himself; he wanted the women to tell the men that he had risen. Even in his resurrection, Jesus challenged sexism. As many female theologians have noted, men today, like Peter and the other male disciples, still refuse to hear the good news that Christ is risen, that patriarchy is over. Men cannot bear the fact that women announced the good news of resurrection.

Over the years, I have found it very difficult to speak about justice and peace in the world when such a glaring injustice thrives in my own church. It has long boggled my mind how Roman church officials can justify the exclusion of women from public ministries in the church. These men claim, "It has always been this way. That is reason enough why it should always remain this way." They are misguided. Women were disciples of Jesus, as the evangelists take pains to point out, although they, too, as men, suffered from the cultural blindness of sexism. Their writings betray their sexism. If we read between the lines, we get the message: "You wouldn't believe the trouble we had with this guy! He even associated with women, accepted them as his equals, and missioned them to proclaim the gospel."

Jesus was a feminist. Indeed, recent studies by women delve deeply into the feminist implications of New Testament writings, most notably Rosemary Radford Ruether's *Sexism and God-Talk* and Elizabeth Schussler Fiorenza's *In Memory of Her*. According to Paul's letters, one woman, Priscilla, was the head of a church community. The New Testament confirms that women were deacons. The original community of disciples understood Jesus' feminism. Women were treated as equals. They were leaders. Unfortunately, over time, men took control and patriarchy was cemented into church structure.

Many women today automatically dismiss the witness of Jesus as the Christ because they cannot identify with a male savior. Their point needs to be heard and discussed. Such reservations are the fruit of two thousand years of patriarchy. I would submit as well, however, that few men identify with Jesus as the Christ. Few men follow his hard sayings and teachings. Most men want a god who is like the worst in them: violent, oppressive, domineering, and unjust. Men want the messiah of old, a warrior-king who would take charge, set things right, suppressing all minorities, obliterating all enemies. Few men admire the compassion and nonviolence of Jesus. Dorothy Day raised these questions for decades: How many of us honestly take Jesus the Christ seriously? Who in North America truly embraces the nonviolent resistance and voluntary poverty of the Gospel? How many men are willing to risk their lives in a nonviolent struggle for suffering humanity, as the nonviolent Christ did?

Christian feminism envisions God's reign of love and justice here on earth as it is in heaven. The term "feminism" is commonly misunderstood by men. Like South Africa's white, ruling class which is reluctant to end apartheid and share leadership with blacks for fear that blacks will take revenge, men are reluctant to end patriarchy and share leadership with women, because men fear that women will then take control and dominate them. Men fear that women will treat them as men have treated women down through the ages. But true feminism does not mean a matriarchy of violent retaliation. Christian feminism is the practice of equality between women and men, as Christ envisions. It bespeaks the sisterhood and brotherhood which God has already bestowed on all human beings. Feminism invites us into the Gospel truth that we are already one, already reconciled by God. Feminism insists that we are all one human family. It calls upon men to accept this insight as a living reality and repent from their erroneous ways. It challenges women to be persistent in the struggle, to insist on equality between humans, to non-cooperate with patriarchy in all its forms, and to forgive men.

Feminism and nonviolence are two sides of the same coin. For me, they are two ways of expressing the vision which we are struggling to live, the vision which is at the heart of our faith. Active nonviolence and feminism are ways to bring about God's reign here and now, ways that can heal our violent, sexist world. If we want peace and justice, we must begin with the oppression right in front of us. A paradigm of peace and liberation must confront the oppression of women by men. The peace movement must be feminist at its roots and in its mission or it will have nothing to offer. Indeed, Christian feminism is a paradigm of peace.

Patriarchy is man's original sin. Men have dominated women for thousands of years—and still do. Violence against women rages on everywhere. Many women around the world have been so oppressed, they feel incapable of fighting back. They are afraid to speak up. They have been brutalized. Social structures predominantly controlled by men, as if by some unwritten rule, bar women from leadership positions. The few women who achieve top positions—like Margaret Thatcher and Cory Aquino—resort to machismo to stay in power. As one woman observed bitterly, Thatcher and Aquino sold their souls to become "honorary men." Meanwhile, women make up the majority of the poor of the world. Most of the 50,000 human beings who die of starvation every day are women and children. Poverty is a women's issue; it is the result of patriarchy and sexism.

We men need to repent of our sexism and change our ways of thinking and acting. One reason why so few men embrace feminism is that they are afraid. Most men are afraid of the changes which would come with the abolishment of patriarchy. Men feel threatened because they know they will lose their privileged positions and their power over women. These fears mask a basic insecurity about their own identity. Men will be liberated only when women are finally liberated. We men need to embrace mutuality, equality, and service, so that all people—women and men—are empowered in the powerless spirit of nonviolence. Men should start listening to women, take them seriously, and show compassion.

Christian feminism is a nonviolent revolution, not only in world consciousness and structure, but within the church. All systems which support the evil of patriarchy need to be transformed, beginning with the church. Perhaps, the feminist revolution needs to begin first and foremost within the church. Too many of us are still trying to protect the church, to make sure it survives, as if it were the "reign of God on earth." But the church is not the reign of God; the pope is not God. We men are upholding a rich, powerful, oppressive institution in the name of God, instead of co-creating with our sisters a nonviolent community whose purpose is to serve and defend the poor, as God asks us to do. If we return to the fundamental teachings of Jesus, we will find the seeds of this mission. From the feminist perspective—the nonviolent, Christian perspective—the institutional church operates like an empire, in contrast to the nonviolent community first called together by Jesus the Christ. The feminist revolution, perhaps, needs to begin first and foremost within the church. Christian feminism clarifies the insight that the institutional church as it exists today must die and be born again—as a servant of mutuality, open to women and men, willing to lay down its life for suffering humanity.

Women have fled the church by the thousands—perhaps the millions—in recent years, because of the sexism that runs rampant within the church. Yet for myself and others, this worldwide communion is home. We stay within it and find ways to subvert it, to transform it, so that the vision of equality and mutuality, the paradigm for the human community, which Jesus died to give birth to, might become a reality. Patriarchy, hierarchy, clericalism, sexist language, and all other forms of sexism need to be confronted head on and changed now, if the church is to have anything to offer to the world, indeed, if the church is to have a future. As it stands, the church violates the Gospel and betrays the Christ, who seeks to reconcile all people into the one human family where there is "neither Jew nor Gentile, slave nor free, male nor female." It is time that women be ordained to the priesthood, that all ministries in the church be open to women, that men relinquish their control of the church and recognize the servant-leadership roles which women are called to take so that we all truly become a vision and foretaste of the reign of God on earth.

I am aware that as a man in the church, I should not say to women, "This is what you need to do to change the church." If I sound like a typical, patronizing man, telling women what to do, exerting my dominance, I apologize and will try to change. Women have to take the lead themselves, and some are. Some women are beginning a movement of nonviolent resistance to sexism within the church. This movement for justice at home needs to grow and blossom over the next years. Women will have to refuse to give money to the Sunday collection until women are ordained. Ordinations will have to be boycotted, demonstrated, and peacefully disrupted to make the point. Letters will have to be written by the millions to the Vatican. Women who work part time or full time for the church will have to go on strike and stay at home for a week to pray and fast in protest of patriarchy and in hope and in anticipation for the creation of the beloved community. Women must create this future themselves. They will have to make a scene, to cause trouble. Men in the church are not going to give up their dominance unless they are asked, indeed, nonviolently shamed into looking at their oppressive structures. As long as women obey the command not to rock the boat, change will never occur. It is time to rock the boat, the ship of church and state. Some women may have to mutiny and jump ship to call attention to the crisis. Men need to be nonviolently encouraged to recognize their sexism so they will freely be able to relinquish their dominating control. Anger and rage are essential in the face of this injustice, but love must be the underlying force for change. Our nonviolent insistence on justice must reveal the beloved community in the process of demanding it, as Christ struggled to do. Then, we will all be transformed into the beloved community which Christ envisions.

The feminist transformation is the Gospel struggle for life in all its fullness. This dangerous, subversive peacemaking activity can transform our violent and male-dominated world. This transformation will require our very lives if it is to happen at all. It is uncomfortable work for it awakens a consciousness of justice in people who would prefer to remain unconscious and who may kick and scream to prevent their own awakening. Sooner or later, men will realize that it is dawn, time to wake up and time to greet the new day. Feminism struggles for the liberation of all, oppressed and oppressors, and as such requires a truly nonviolent, loving spirit. It is costly, thankless, and necessary work which will one day bear fruit in the demise of patriarchy and the creation of an entirely new kind of world. It is a struggle worth dying for.

I learned feminism first from my mother. She has struggled throughout her life against sexism in the world of medicine, academia, and the church and has suffered in that struggle. As the head nurse in the emergency room at St. Vincent's Hospital in New York City during the 1950s, she soon realized that she would have to fight against the (male) doctors who saw themselves as superior to everyone else. Pursuing her doctorate in social psychology as a nurse at a Catholic university during the 1960s and 1970s, she struggled against the commonly held stereotypes of women. The patriarchal church environment did not help. Later, as a professor at Georgetown University, Johns Hopkins University, the National Institutes of Health, and George Mason University, she ran head on against the male dominated world of academia. Throughout those years, she raged against the sexism within the Catholic Church. From my earliest memories, I recall her anger at male domination within the church, and her demand that women be ordained to the priesthood. In such a household, I could not help but be sensitized to the oppression of women by men in our society.

My education as a feminist proceeded during my college years at Duke University, where my women classmates and Newman Center friends raised the questions of patriarchy. Over the years, as I have pursued the issues of justice and peace in various peacemaking communities, I have been challenged and reminded by the women I have met that feminism means peace-with-justice for all. From women in El Salvador, Guatemala, Nicaragua, and the Philippines, in our inner cities, in the various jails that I have been in (because of nonviolent, direct action for justice), and in the various shelters where I have volunteered, I have seen everywhere the pain inflicted by men on women.

Because I was raised in a sexist, patriarchal culture, I, too, am guilty of this original sin. My own struggle as a man in a sexist church and world requires a constant vigilance and resistance to sexism.

I write as a young Jesuit who will one day be ordained a priest. I continue on this path so that I can be of service to others, preach good news to the poor, and publicly reconcile all in the Word of God, the Body and Blood of Christ. I dream of being human to others, a servant of all, especially the poor and oppressed, and discern the priesthood as a way in which I can fulfill this mission of service to suffering humanity. My ministry of reconciliation and peacemaking must struggle for the ordination of women and the collapse of patriarchy if it is to be authentic. My own ordination will be a bittersweet moment if women are still prevented from sharing in that graced ministry. Several noble friends have left my religious community because their conscience bothered them. They felt that they should not be ordained as long as women are denied access to that ministry. My conscience bothers me as well. I wonder if I betray the Gospel by stepping forth to be ordained at this point in history when patriarchy still thrives. I wonder if I forfeit my integrity by siding so explicitly with patriarchy. But when I look around, I see so few feminist churchmen speaking out publicly against patriarchy and sexism in the church. After careful consideration and prayer, I have resolved to stay the course, and speak out boldly until that day when women are ordained priests of the beloved community. I want to work for that day when all ministries are open to women. I pledge my support to those women who are dedicated to creating a new church, a community with no trace of patriarchy, hierarchy, or clericalism, a community that always sides with the oppressed and marginalized. I pledge to listen, to take women seriously, to be compassionate, and to struggle against sexism and patriarchy as best I can. I pledge to accept the transformation of sexism and patriarchy into mutuality, equality, liberation, and justice for women, for the poor, for people of color, and for all the suffering masses.

My hope is that we may one day live in a world where women and men share life together in equality, mutuality, justice and peace. On that peaceful day, God will truly reign on earth as She does in heaven.

32.
Depending on God:
Voluntary Poverty and the Way to Peace

The words of Jesus are direct and to the point. "No one can be my disciple unless he or she gives up all her or his possessions." (Luke 14:33) Few of us have the courage to take Jesus at his word on this point. We might praise God, go to church on Sundays, and give to the collection, but give up all our possessions?

How quick we are to ignore his words. Why do we pretend Jesus never said them? Why do we not experiment with his message? Why do we refuse to give up all our possessions? Why do they challenge us so? Jesus' words confront the very premise of our culture and all the cultures of the world: that the purpose of life is to make money, to acquire possessions, and to enjoy our riches here and now. Jesus invites just the opposite: give away all your money, give away all your possessions, and enjoy your poverty, your humanity, your life, here and now.

The wisdom of voluntary poverty is a hard truth to grasp. It is a vital ingredient, a necessary prerequisite to the life of Christian discipleship. The saints of Christian history have lived this wisdom. From Francis and Clare to Dorothy Day and Peter Maurin, Christians have embraced poverty as a way of life. But they are few in number. Most of us, like the rich man of the Gospel, when asked to sell our possessions, give away the money to the poor, and follow Jesus, walk away sad.

In our own day and age, Dorothy Day stands out as the most striking example of poverty embraced in true discipleship. For her, poverty was the backbone of her faith. She wrote:

> Poverty is a strange and elusive thing. I have tried to write about it, its joys and its sorrows, for twenty years now; I could probably write about it for another twenty years without conveying what I feel about it as well as I would like. I condemn poverty and I advocate it; poverty is simple and complex at once; it is a social phenomenon and a personal matter. It is a paradox.[1]

"Poverty and destitution, like hospitality, are so esteemed by God," Day wrote, "that poverty is something to be sought after, worked for, the pearl of great price."[2]

> We need always to be thinking and writing about poverty, for if we are not among its victims, its reality fades from us. We must talk about poverty, because people insulated by their own comfort lose sight of it.... But maybe no one can be told about poverty; maybe they will have to experience it. Or maybe it is a grace which they must pray for. We usually get what we pray for, and maybe we are afraid to pray for it. And yet I am convinced that it is the grace we most need in this age of crisis, this time when expenditures reach into the billions to defend "our American way of life." Maybe this defense itself will bring down upon us the poverty we are afraid to pray for.[3]

The poverty which Jesus practiced was absolute. He lived a precarious life. He had no insurance; he placed all his security in God alone. Dorothy Day tried to do the same, and she urged Catholic Worker communities and religious orders to do likewise. For her, poverty was precariousness, that state of total insecurity and instability which the poorest of the poor know. She learned to rely on others, on her community, on the poor, and ultimately, on God. She had no social security card, no money in her pocket, no privacy, no insurance, no healthcare program, nothing: just total dependence on God, on others. Her situation was one of powerlessness and helplessness. In this state, she felt at peace, under the direct protection of God, blessed. In her weekly newspaper column, she shared a letter from a monk about precarious living.

Precarity is an essential element in true voluntary poverty, a saintly priest from Martinique has written us. "True poverty is rare," he writes. "Nowadays religious communities are good, I am sure, but they are mistaken about poverty. They accept, admit, poverty on principle, but everything must be good and strong, buildings must be fireproof. Precarity is everywhere rejected, and precarity is an essential element of poverty. This has been forgotten. Here in our monastery we want precarity in everything except the church. These last days our refectory was near collapsing. We have put several supplementary beams in place and thus it will last maybe two or three years more. Someday it will fall on our heads and that will be funny. Precarity enables us better to help the poor. When a community is always building, enlarging, and embellishing, there is nothing left over for the poor. We have no right to do so as long as there are slums and bread-lines somewhere."

Over and over again in the history of the church the saints have emphasized poverty. Every religious community, be-gun in poverty and incredible hardship, but with a joyful acceptance of hardship by the rank-and-file priests, brothers, monks or nuns who gave their youth and energy to good works, soon began to "thrive." Property was extended until holdings and buildings accumulated; and although there was still individual poverty in the community, there was corporate wealth. It is hard to remain poor.[4]

Day learned the lesson of voluntary poverty from Peter Maurin. "Peter was the poor man of his day," she wrote. "He was another St. Francis."

He was used to poverty as a peasant is used to rough living, poor food, hard bed or no bed at all, dirt, fatigue, and hard and unrespected work. He was a man with a mission, a vi-sion, an apostolate, but he had put off from himself honors, prestige, recognition. He was truly humble of heart, and loving.... He was impersonal in his love in that he loved all, saw all others around him as God saw them. In other words, he saw Christ in them.... Peter had [often] been insulted and misunderstood in his life. He had been taken for a plumber and left to sit in the basement when he had been invited for dinner and an evening of conversation. He had been thrown out of a Knights of Columbus meeting. One pastor who in-vited him to speak demanded his money back which he had sent Peter for carfare to his upstate parish because, he said, we had sent him a Bowery bum, and not the speaker he expected. "This then is perfect joy," Peter could say, quoting the words of St. Francis.[5]

Hard as it is to admit, such voluntary poverty is the calling of the Gospel, the ideal which Jesus called saints and sinners alike to follow. He expected his followers to be poor. "Give away your possessions to the poor," he says. "Give your money away. Don't spend your life trying to make money. There is more to life than dollars, bank accounts and homes in the suburbs. Joy is found not in acquiring possessions but in renouncing possessions and serving others. Store up for yourself real treasure in heaven, the spiritual treasure of blessings received here and now, the prayers of the poor who cannot repay you in any other way." He called the rich to become poor, both materially and spiritually, while he sought to relieve the poor of their unjust suffering and help them accept the spiritual dependence which they had learned in the struggle. Today, third-world churches call us in the United States to make a "preferential option" for the poor. This gnome is not just a catchy phrase: for them, it is a spiritual matter, a matter of life and death. If more people in the United States embrace poverty, share the experience of the masses in the third world, perhaps human misery will one day be eliminated.

Simple lifestyle is discipleship to Jesus who was poor and who lives now in the poor. As St. Paul wrote, Jesus was rich and powerful but became the poorest of the poor. He was born a refugee, homeless, illegitimate, marginalized, in a stable, on the outskirts of a brutal empire. He associated with the poorest people, the oppressed and marginalized all his life, and he died young, on a criminal's cross, in pain and agony, his reputation ruined. He knew the ultimate poverty, the ultimate violence of death by torturous, state-sanctioned murder. Jesus was not a yuppie; he practiced downward mobility. For us, discipleship is no less than downward mobility.

For Christians, simple lifestyle and voluntary poverty mean dedicating ourselves to meeting Christ in the distressing disguise of the poor, of the enemy, of the marginalized peoples of the world. Voluntary poverty leads us to an encounter with God. As an act of faith, it enlivens our faith and sets us on fire. It is perhaps the least likely, least popular, hardest and surest way to God, for it molds us into true dependence, the obedience which frees.

We cannot befriend the poor if we "go down" to the poor, and then go back home to our riches, our three meals a day, our TV sets, clothes and bank accounts. We need to become one with the poor, then we will befriend the poor. There, we will discover the befriended Christ who said, "What you did to the least of these poor ones, you did to me. For I was hungry and you gave me food; I was thirsty and you gave me drink; a stranger and you welcomed me; naked and you clothed me; ill and you cared for me; in prison and you visited me." (Matthew 25:35)

"Voluntary poverty is the answer," Day concluded. "Through voluntary poverty we will have the means to help our brothers and sisters. We cannot even see our brothers and sisters in need without first stripping ourselves. It is the only way we have of showing our love."[6]

It is not that we want to romanticize the poor. The poor are not perfect. But, as Archbishop Romero said, "the poor are disposed to conversion." By becoming poor, we become disposed to conversion. We open ourselves to the work of the Holy Spirit in us. We meet the God who dwells with them in their struggle, and hear God's loving invitation to join that struggle.

If we share everything with the poor, in the end, we will have shared our very lives. This self-sacrifice is the greatest love that anyone can show. It will include the willingness to suffer and die for justice for the poor. In El Salvador, to live with the poor, to walk with the poor, and to stand with the poor as Christ did, is, as Archbishop Romero explained, to share the fate of the poor. Every splenetic epithet will be used against us. We will be called communists, subversives, and radicals. We will be arrested, tortured, and killed. But, like Jesus, we will rise to eternal life, and continue the subversive work of justice and peace in the hearts of generations to come.

The Gospel call to live a simple lifestyle means standing in solidarity with the poor, becoming one with the poor, building community with the poor, advocating for the poor, and fighting the poverty suffered involuntarily by the poor. Christ's way of life urges us to measure every action, decision and word that we undertake from now on based on whether or not it will help the poor. Gandhi gave this advice: "Recall the face of the poorest and most helpless person you have seen and ask yourself if the next step you contemplate is going to be of any use to that person."

This way of life can take hundreds of different forms. Some of us may move to the Sudan to serve the hungry. Some of us may join a house of hospitality in the inner city to live with, shelter, and organize the homeless. Some of us may return to the land, take up farming and form alternative communities with the poor. Some of us may end up in prison for our nonviolent resistance to the policies of greed and war. As we discern the movement of the Spirit, the key factor is to stay close to the poor.

A young Jesuit priest learned this lesson from Dorothy Day in the early 1970s. He had begun to lose his faith. Indeed, he said he no longer believed in God. After years of study in doctoral programs, he had lost his spiritual base. He could no longer relate to Jesus. He despaired of ever understanding the Gospel. He turned to Dorothy Day for help. "What can I do?" he asked, nearly in tears. "God is nowhere to be found and I see no reason why I should continue this facade of Christianity." Dorothy looked on him with love and gave a simple, direct answer. "Stay with the poor. Get involved in the lives of suffering people. Befriend them. Help them in their struggle. There, you will find God. There, you will see how small your problems are compared to those who are poor. There, you will find a meaningful life beyond anything you ever imagined." He took her advice, moved to the South Bronx, and began a program organizing the poor in their struggle for justice. Years later, he moved to El Salvador, where he lives today. He has become a true disciple of Jesus. "Invest in the poor," Dorothy Day advised. "There you can expect to find a return." [7]

The preferential option for the poor has led me on a journey of downward mobility, a journey which I still walk. I moved from the first world life of Potomac, Maryland, to inner city Washington, D.C., where I worked with Central American refugees, the homeless and the urban poor. I have tried to stand with the poor of Central America, the Philippines, and the Middle East. I have visited death rows and been jailed numerous times for speaking out against injustice and war. And yet, the poverty I seek is, as Dorothy Day said, "a strange and elusive thing."

In my religious community, we profess a vow of poverty. Most members live a very simple lifestyle and share possessions in common. Yet as a whole, the Society of Jesus in the United States holds millions of dollars in assets. What does this wealth have to do with the Gospel poverty of Jesus? It may be needed to run large universities, but it runs counter to Jesus' request that we be poor. The Jesuits have become a success. This big business is far from the wishes of Ignatius of Loyola, our founder, who wanted us to be poor just as St. Francis was poor, as Jesus was poor. The time has come for the Jesuits to fail. They should hand over their assets to the poor and start again down the road to discipleship. I hope to see this conversion happen in my own lifetime, and I hope to be a part of it. It is not an impossible dream, for it has happened elsewhere, and it can happen here. In 1969, the Jesuits of El Salvador decided to make just this decision. They dedicated their institutions to the promotion of justice for the poor, and tried to become closer to the poor themselves. Within a few years, the results were clear: their homes were bombed, they all received death threats, and seven members of the community were killed by the government. They became disciples of Jesus and suffered the cross. They proved themselves faithful to the mandate of the Gospel, and paved a way to discipleship for the Jesuits of North America. I want to follow that journey of Gospel poverty.

Voluntary poverty goes hand in hand with a nonviolent commitment to justice and peace. As a poor person, Jesus practiced nonviolent resistance, the weapon of the poor. If we practice only charity towards the poor, the poor will never rise above their misery. There are so many suffering people on earth that we can go on forever healing their wounds, and governments will let us do this work. But we will never change the system that wounds the poor and creates generations of hungry people. While charity, service, and hospitality are essential to the Christian life, we must also advocate and speak up for the poor, and demand justice, an end to the systemic oppression which causes hunger, homelessness, disease, and misery. We do not want the poor to suffer in misery for the rest of their lives. Involuntary poverty is not a virtue. The poor deserve dignity, respect and every basic human right that makes for a full life. The poor and those who accompany them should resist the forces of oppression. We should be missionaries of charity, yes; but we must also be missionaries of justice.

Simple lifestyle is a life commitment, a life journey into ongoing, daily conversion to the Gospel. Nothing less than a lifetime commitment will be necessary if this loving transformation which Christ proclaimed is to become a reality of justice for the suffering masses. We will not, however, remain committed to the work of justice and peace for long if we are wealthy. We will cling to our possessions. These material goods and concerns will receive our utmost attention, not our suffering sisters and brothers. We will be distracted, attached, unfree. To demand justice for the poor means learning to say no to a culture which dangles creature comforts before our eyes. This Gospel life is an entirely new way of living. Simple lifestyle is, thus, an act of nonviolence itself because it is the painful process of rejecting the system of consumerism and greed which brings so much violence and poverty upon the poor of the world. It is a method of nonviolent resistance and self-defense against the onslaught of the culture. It is not only countercultural, but acultural.

Involuntary poverty is violence. It kills. Choosing to become one with the poor will mean dying to ourselves and what the culture upholds. It incarnates the Gospel call to conversion, accepts suffering for the sake of justice, and lets go of the idols that block us from God and the poor—our money, possessions, plans, and career ambitions. Voluntary poverty, on the other hand, is revolutionary nonviolence. It promotes life and the birth of an entirely new world, a world where all the earth's resources are shared equally. Today, the

United States constitutes only six percent of the world's population yet consumes some fifty-five to sixty percent of the world's resources. Such consumerism is unjust. It is radically evil. Becoming poor makes the public, political statement that hoarding the world's resources is unacceptable. Voluntary poverty shows a way out of our sinfulness.

A simple lifestyle is a serious commitment to world peace. Francis of Assisi understood this insight. "If we want to own things, we must also have weapons," he observed. "From this come all the quarrels and battles that make love impossible. And this is why we refuse to own anything." When we hoard possessions on such a large scale, it is only logical that armies and military weapons should be needed to protect our goods. If church people in the United States adopted a simple lifestyle, there would be no reason for massive military forces. Our possessions and money will be given in measure to the poor of the third world (and in our own country), so that all share an equal amount. The primary reason for war and nuclear hostilities will be eliminated.

At the heart of all our problems, all our violence and injustice, is greed. Greed is a sin. Simple lifestyle is a way to confront this sin. In the parable of the rich man who hoarded all his grain, Jesus asked, "What good will all these possessions be for you tonight when you die?" (Luke 12:13-21) This parable speaks to us in the United States. Unfortunately, our mood is not even Epicurean. We do not say, "Eat, drink and be merry for tomorrow we die." We do not think we are going to die; we think we can go on like this forever, living off the goods that we have stolen from the hungry masses and stored in our barns.

When we acquire possessions, money, and property, they become the focus of our lives. We worship them. We want more. We find ways to protect them. Property becomes a right all its own, more important than human rights. It does not occur to us in such a mindset that we cannot claim a plot of land as our own. It does not occur to us to think that God owns all property, and that we are merely God's stewards. Because of our greed, we fight to protect our possessions. We kill the people of Nicaragua who want to try a different method of economics and democracy. We will kill millions of people around the world or threaten to kill them so that no one will question whether all this food, money and resources really belong to the people of the United States, or so that no one will try to upset our enjoyment. If we have riches, if we have everything we need, we have no need for God. Violence and death are the natural consequences.

Francis provides a way out: "If you want peace, give away your possessions. Refuse to own anything." If we are greedy as individuals and nations, we will be unable to see in the face of another person, in the face of another human being, the face of God. Instead, we will see a potential robber, someone who wants our money; or we will see a thing, an enemy; or finally, we will not see anyone at all, because of the walls we have set up between us. We will be filled with fear. If we have no possessions, no property, no money, we can walk down the street and talk to anyone without the fear of being robbed. We will have neither silver nor gold and thus nothing to protect. We have only our souls, for we have become rich in the sight of God. We can then begin to see in the face of the other, the face of a human being, the face of God, Christ. If we try this as a nation, we will not be so eager to wage war or global destruction.

We will no longer see others as enemies, but as friends, as human beings. Love will be possible.

When we voluntarily embrace poverty and renounce our possessions, then everything is given back to us. God gives us the earth and the fullness thereof. We see life with new eyes and learn to appreciate the simpler beauties of life. Then, God says, "Defend it!" Defend the earth, the sky, the plants, the animals, and all living creatures through loving nonviolence.

Voluntary poverty helps us to become truly human, to get to the roots of our humanity. Society says we are human according to the number of possessions we own. But, according to the Gospel, exactly the opposite is true. We are human to the extent that we embrace our poverty before God and each other. It is the most radical witness we can give: to give away our wealth and possessions in order to join the poor in the nonviolent struggle for justice. In doing so, we side with the saints and martyrs of history. We side with Christ who gave up the riches of heaven to become the poorest human being. Simple lifestyle will help us to evangelize not through words but through the way we live our lives. Our integrity and Gospel authenticity will evangelize the world and show others that we do believe in God, that we rely solely on God, and that we are serious about justice, peace, and nonviolent love. With our very lives, we can become good news for the poor, a sign of hope.

Voluntary poverty is a walk into the unknown future, into the reign of God. If we take that walk, the Holy Spirit will grant us enough light for each step on the journey.

In the final analysis, becoming poor prepares us for our death, for eternal life. None of us will be alive one hundred years from now. We may live to be sixty, seventy, eighty, or ninety years old, or we may die tomorrow. Voluntary poverty says, "Get ready now. Learn to let go. Give away your possessions and prepare for the ultimate letting go of your final possession—your body. Then, your soul will be ready to enter the reign of God."

To become poor is to inherit the reign of God, for the poor are blessed. The reign of God is theirs. But the good news is intended for all of us. We all inherit the reign of God as we embrace our poverty. In the acceptance of our humanity, God bestows abundant blessings upon us. Let us rejoice then, become poor, and join the struggle.

---

[1] Robert Ellsberg, Ed. *By Little and By Little: The Selected Writings of Dorothy Day* (New York: Alfred A. Knopf, 1983) p. 109.

[2] *Ibid.*, p. 114.

[3] *Ibid.*, pp. 106-107.

[4] *Ibid.*, p. 108.

[5] *Ibid.*, pp. 123, 124, 126, and 127.

[6] *Ibid.*, p. 109.

[7] "Dorothy Day: Exalting Those of Low Degree," *Sojourners*, December 1976, p. 12.

33

Thou Shalt Not Disable:
Disability, War and Peacemaking

One day, several years ago, while vacationing at the beach, one of the assistants of a L'Arche community (the network of communities for physically disabled and non-disabled peoples) asked some of the physically disabled children to draw pictures in the sand. "Can you draw a house?" she asked one child. The child drew a beautiful house in the sand. "Can you draw a cat?" she asked another disabled child, and the child outlined the figure of a cat in the sand. Finally, to a third disabled child, she requested, "Draw me a picture of joy." The child looked at her, looked all the way down the end of the beach, then turned and looked down the other way. "There's not enough room for joy," the child said.

Such is the wisdom of children with disabilities.

Throughout my life, I have worked with and befriended people with mental and physical disabilities. I have also worked with refugees, the sick and dying, prisoners, the homeless and the hungry. From these poor and marginalized peoples, I have learned what it means to be human, what it means to seek justice, what it means to love God and humanity. From mentally and physically disabled children, I have learned the value of life and the need for constant celebration and joy. Such children are for me a touchstone, a living reminder of what it means to be a human being. From these and all people who are the declared enemies of the United States government—the people of the Philippines, El Salvador, Guatemala and Nicaragua, the mentally-disabled, the homeless, the poor, those on death row, those with disabilities—I have heard the urgent call to create a nonviolent society, to stop the torment of violence and injustice that runs rampant through our lives and our world. The message I hear is simple: the violence, the injustice, the lack of compassion must stop. It is not right to disable people.

In his novel, *The Clowns of God*, Morris West makes dramatic the simple truth that people with disabilities offer a special gift to society. Jean Vanier and L'Arche communities have lived the truth of this reality for years. Those who suffer physical and mental disabilities are a great blessing to us all. They teach us how to love, how to be compassionate. They offer us a way to peace. They call us to the basic truths of life, to notice our common humanity, our poverty, our common need before God. People with physical and mental disabilities are peacemakers, children of God. They witness to the peace of God, manifesting God's love for humanity in their own sanguine love and mirth.

The true fiber of every society can be found in the way it treats its so-called "weakest" members. In our society, in our world, those called "weakest" get stepped on, ignored, abused, pushed outside, and sometimes killed. People with disabilities, the homeless, children, those dying of AIDS, the elderly, those in prison, the unborn, minorities, women, people from foreign lands—all are looked down upon in our society. All suffer and are rejected. All are marginalized. The culture judges them to be less than human. According to the standards set by the media and the white, male elitists who run the country, they do not count. Instead, the culture glamorizes only its sexist, racist, and militaristic idols.

But as people of faith, we are beginning to learn a deep spiritual truth. All human beings are equal in God's sight. All are God's children. All are brothers and sisters of each other. We are all one. In particular, people with disabilities are fully human; they are our very sisters and brothers. They have basic human rights that need to be defended. People with disabilities have the right to their dignity and humanity, just like every other human being in the world, and society should protect that human dignity.

Those who work with people with disabilities are engaged in a holy work, for they seek in a spirit of love to defend those who are defenseless. This work, like the work of sheltering and feeding the homeless, the work of organizing anti-nuclear and anti-death-penalty demonstrations, is a work of justice and nonviolence. It is all part of the lifework of peacemaking. Working with and for people with disabilities is intimately connected with all work for liberation and peace. Standing up for people who are disabled is part of the broader work of social justice.

Perhaps the best way to meditate on this truth is to look at its converse. Not only does our culture reject and marginalize people with disabilities, it actively disables other people. Our society, addicted to violence and death as it is, is intent on disabling those people it does not like. All those who are declared the enemies of the US government become victims of its military violence. Once they are declared to be "the enemy," to be less than human, then the government actively seeks to disable them. Enemies are disabled by war.

Injustice and war disable people. Millions of people in our country and in our world spend all their time and talents and energy deliberately, actively disabling other people. Most government leaders in our world spend their time on this work. Our own country is number one in the business of disabling people. In fact, the disabling of people is big business. Disabling other people is very profitable.

The greatest disability that war inflicts on people is death. Death is the ultimate disability. In our world, millions of good people are working in places like the Pentagon, the White House, the Concord Naval Weapons Station and Livermore Laboratories to bring death to people. In such places, people build bombs, ship the bombs, organize bombing raids, and give orders for the bombings. All this leads to a lack of funds for social programs for the needy here at home and to the massacre of peoples in faraway places like El Salvador, the Philippines, Guatemala and elsewhere. Because these addictions continue unchecked, the forces of evil in this world charge forward intent on disabling the poor and all humanity. The nuclear bomb threatens to disable the planet and the entire human race. In this addiction to violence and the infliction of pain and death on others, we remain perilously close to nuclear war and the total disability of the planet. By looking the other way in light of the 50,000 children and women who die each day from starvation, by supporting the existence of 60,000 nuclear weapons and the continued testing of new weapons, we participate in this disabling work of death. With the daily destruction of the environment and the dangerous computer-controlled, nuclear-weapons systems, we are only moments away from catastrophe. This predilection for violence shows our contempt for human life. It is not surprising, then, that in such a society those with physical and mental disabilities fall through the cracks. Yet they are the ones who can heal us and teach us to love life once more.

Why are the disabled forgotten? Why are people with disabilities and all others who suffer not the centerpiece of society? Why doesn't our society spend all its energy working to serve and heal those in need? Why do we spend billions of dollars for stealth bombers and Trident submarines and Star-Wars, but only pennies to meet the needs of the disabled, the homeless, those with AIDS? Why do we even have to be advocates for people with disabilities? The answer, unfortunately, is simple: because killing people is more important than helping people live. The US wars in Central America are more important to our government leaders than helping the disabled. Continuing the nuclear-arms race is higher on the agenda than serving people with disabilities, or the homeless, or those with AIDS, or anyone in need. Official rhetoric to the contrary notwithstanding, our society is still dead set on its course with death.

The Gospel parable which speaks most dramatically to our recalcitrance and hardheartedness is the story of Jesus' healing of the Gerasene demoniac and the subsequent reaction of the townspeople. (Mark 5:1-20) According to the story, Jesus encountered a man "with an unclean spirit" who lived among the tombs and cried out day and night. Before healing him, Jesus asked, "What is your name?" The unclean spirit in the man said, "My name is Legion; for we are many." Jesus ordered the unclean spirit to leave the man, and it went into a herd of 2000 swine. As soon as the evil spirit entered the swine, they rushed off the cliff and drowned in the sea. When the townspeople saw the healed man and realized that their profitable herd of swine were gone, they asked Jesus to leave the area.

It is significant that the word chosen to describe the evil spirit is "Legion." In Jesus' time, a "legion" was a large unit of Roman soldiers. In this subtle way, the parable explains how Jesus attempted to liberate people from the violence of Roman occupation. The people, however, did not want to be liberated. They profited from the status quo, even though the imperial forces wreaked havoc and injustice in the lives of many. Those soldiers allowed them to reap enormous profit from the sale of those swine. The price for healing just one person in need was too high: it cost an entire herd of swine, the major source of income. The villagers did not want to pay such a price. They lived high on the hog, as it were. Jesus came along and tried to set them right, but they were less than grateful. His way of doing things was rejected.

We North Americans have the same attitude as those villagers. We would rather not be healed from our addiction to violence because it will mean an entire change of lifestyle. We would have to transform our military economy. We would rather not heal the needy person. The cost is too high, and those in high places know it. If we are going to heal the thousands of mentally-ill homeless women and men who walk our nation's streets, if we are going to provide adequate care for the disabled, if we are going to comfort and heal those dying from AIDS, we will have to spend millions of dollars on housing and healthcare. We will have to refocus the money and energies spent on war toward programs that serve those in need. Yet we prefer spending those funds on war, on intervention in Panama and El Salvador, in the Persian Gulf, on the death penalty, and on preparations for nuclear destruction.

Meeting the needs of the poor and those with disabilities will mean a transformation of our society. One city which has grappled with this transformation is Berkeley, California. Berkeley is home for many people who have severe disabilities. It is not uncommon to see scores of people with severe physical disabilities moving around the city streets in motorized wheelchairs. They have settled in Berkeley because the city has worked to make all public facilities accessible to them. The city has made them welcome by focusing on their needs, respecting their dignity and rights, and treating them like human beings.

If we want to help and advocate for the disabled and the poor, we have to work to end war and the causes of war. Those who serve the physically disabled should speak out against the disabling policies of our government.

Oddly enough, however, once we begin to speak out against war and the deliberate disabling of the poor, we will discover that our message is rejected. We will find ourselves disabled by our government. We will be placed under arrest, handcuffed, brought before a judge, and eventually put behind bars.

Our regular witness for peace at the Concord Naval Weapons Station, the Pentagon, and elsewhere is not well received. The authorities handcuff us, chain us together, and then put us behind bars, effectively disabling us. And yet, because our cause is right and just, and our method peaceful and loving, our action touches the lives of the Marines and police officers who arrest us, as well as those in the military and in the surrounding community, and the suffering people of the world. People begin to reconsider the deadly business of death. The victims of US policy find hope that transformation in our society might occur. When we are disabled and put behind bars, we find ourselves spiritually enabled to be the instruments for the societal transformation from violent destruction to nonviolent co-existence. We are enabled by the spirit of love to touch the lives of our sisters and brothers at Concord and within the US military.

In his effort to stop the war in Central America and the forced disability of the Central American people by our weapons shipments, Brian Willson was run over by a train. He lost both legs and was disabled. Just prior to this event, Brian had traveled extensively in Nicaragua and met with hundreds of children who had lost their legs because of land mines. These children were deliberately and knowingly disabled by the US-backed Contras. Brian responded to the violence done to his body in a spirit of nonviolent love and forgiveness. He continued to call for an end to the industry of war. His nonviolent spirit touched the hearts of people across the nation.

In war, one group of people deliberately disables another group of people. Brian Willson has shown us how to stop people from disabling others by taking a stand in a loving spirit which can enable others to see the wrongness of our military arsenal. This work is difficult and costly, but it is a holy work and the duty of all those who have been spiritually enabled by God and conscience to speak the truth in love about the USA's preferential option for war.

The story of Ron Kovic, portrayed in the movie "Born on the Fourth of July," bridges the extremes of these truths. Kovic waged war against the poor. With other US soldiers, he inflicted the cruel disability of war on the people of Vietnam. In the process, he was shot and physically disabled. In his subsequent search, he learned the truth that war is wrong, that killing people is inhuman. From his wheelchair, Kovic lifted himself out of his spiritual disability and became a spokesperson for peace. His story, like the story of Brian Willson and other disabled veterans for peace, shows the possibility of a transformation in our culture, from warmaking to peacemaking.

These issues of injustice and war are spiritual matters. They are matters of life and death. For us not to get involved, to sit back silently while our country supports the murder of people—including the Jesuits—in El Salvador and elsewhere, is to be complicit in the crime. It is to be complicit in this evil work of disabling millions of people. Because our country is so hostile to the needy and the physically disabled, so violent to the poor of the third world, so misguided in its mad addiction to death in the nuclear arms race, we can conclude that as a people, we are morally and spiritually disabled. Those who prepare war and wage violence against the poor and maintain

Trident submarines and support the death penalty are spiritually and morally disabled. Those who consistently respond to human need through violence, fear, contempt and hostility are spiritually and morally disabled. Dr. King suggested that such have lost their souls. "A nation that continues year after year to spend more money on military defense than on programs for social uplift," he declared in 1967 shortly before he was assassinated, "is approaching spiritual death." The mad spiral of violence is much worse now than when he made that statement.

The good news is that there is a way out. Through active nonviolence, by speaking up publicly for peace and justice, we can help end the wars. We can create a disarmed world. We can end world hunger. We can transform our nation and our world. We can make life more comfortable for those who are physically and mentally disabled and accept the gift of love and compassion which they offer us.

Unlike war, the spirit of nonviolent love enables people to grow, to be spiritually healthy. The spirit of love, compassion, and nonviolence enables people to live in peace, to know their dignity, to have enough food, clothing, and healthcare. Such a spirit calls us to be human with one another.

We are called to speak the truth, and to do so humbly and without judgment on others, in a spirit of nonviolent love and respect; to be on the side of life and to help make life fuller for others. This is what it means to be a human being, what we have learned from our sisters and brothers who are disabled. We are called to dedicate our lives to the creation of peace and social justice, to serve the physically and mentally disabled, and to stop the wars which terrorize and disable the human family. For this vision of life, peace, and justice, we must risk our lives. As people of good will, we are called to make justice and peace a reality in the world, to speak the truth, to nonviolently resist war and injustice and the idols of death which we worship, and to stand with the poor and for peace. Ours is a preferential option for the poor and a preferential option for peace.

In the tradition of Martin Luther King, Jr. and Jesus, our task is to practice nonviolent love, to love our enemies, to become peacemakers. Our task is to be advocates for the poor, to stop the unjust, forced debilitation which our nation inflicts on so many.

It is a beautiful and noble task, a holy work. May we do it with joy and know the joy which our disabled sisters and brothers offer us in love.

34.
The Long Haul Keeps Looking Longer: Spirituality and the Journey of Peace

It had been a busy day. As usual, I had been running around, doing my errands, talking on the phone, studying, visiting with people, planning an upcoming peace conference, going to meetings, preparing to face trial with other churchfolks on charges of disturbing the peace in opposition to war, cleaning the community house in anticipation of a friend who was due to visit, a million thoughts in my mind, a hundred things to do. Such is the life of a peace activist—too much activity, too little peace.

I was home alone that afternoon in our community house in Oakland, California, sweeping the house, when I decided to throw the dust in the dustbin outside. As I stepped onto the front porch of our house, I heard the door shut behind me, and I knew I was in trouble. I had no keys with me and there were none hidden for just such an emergency. All the doors were locked and there was no way back inside. My community members were not due back for two hours.

I was locked out of the house! I visited with the neighbors for a while, then returned to sit on the front porch. So much for those well laid plans!

For some reason, I did not get angry or become frustrated. I didn't find myself swearing. Actually, I started laughing to myself. "You'll do anything to get me to spend some time with You, won't You?" I asked, looking up to the sky, waiting for God to answer. "Okay, You win. I get the message. Let's spend some time together praying."

For the next two hours, I sat on the porch of our community house, in a peaceful stillness, praying for peace, praying for justice, praying for my friends, family, community members, for all the suffering peoples of the world, from the homeless poor to the campesinos of El Salvador to the sugar-cane workers of the Philippines to the peoples of the Middle East, for the whole human race.

As I sat on the porch, it occurred to me that this episode was a parable for my life. I am always reluctant to take time to pray, thinking that everything else I do is more important, and yet I know that prayer is essential, especially if I want to be a peacemaker, a person who does justice.

As the sun began to go down and the weather turned colder, I prayed that God might let me into God's house, and send someone with a key that I might live there forever. The episode became a metaphor for my personal journey. Like every sojourner, I am locked out of the house of God, trying to get in, praying that God will let me into God's house, the house of peace, the house of justice, the house of love. Eventually, someone arrives with a key and lets me in, where I can sit down to a heavenly banquet.

It might be a parable for all of us.

Those moments of prayer on the front steps of our house helped me to understand the importance of prayer and spirituality if I want to be serious about peacemaking and doing justice. I need to take time every day to stop what I'm doing and put myself before God in prayer. In that moment, everything is refocused and I am centered in the peace that I so long for in the world. Out of that prayer, I find the grace to see reality in a new light. Indeed, I discover that all my activity for justice and peace is not my doing at all, but God's work. In such moments, I realize that God is in charge and that I am merely God's instrument. Then, I can surrender myself totally to God and ask God to lead me according to God's will, that I may indeed be an instrument of God's peace in our warring world.

A spirituality for the life of peacemaking and doing justice entails a life of prayer and contemplation, a steady diet of reading the Scriptures, community worship and other prayer services, and also sitting quietly, in solitude, in God's peace. Peacemaking is a lifetime commitment. If I am going to be in it for the long haul—and the long haul keeps looking longer these days—I will need to drink daily from the well of prayer. This prayer helps me to focus on the truth of our peacemaking mission. Whether I am successful or not (and I cannot expect to improve on the crucified Jesus, a failure as far as the world is concerned), I can rest in peace knowing that our calling to be peacemakers is true, that God will use us to make peace.

Such a spirituality puts into practice the Way of nonviolence which Jesus and Gandhi called us to live. By keeping a contemplative rhythm to our days, we can be nonviolent with ourselves and resist the mad rat-race of the world, including the endless activity that so easily traps us. In this spirit, we can walk in peace, and give thanks to God for our lives and for God's love, even as we continue to confront systemic evil in our world and seek to transform injustice into justice.

In light of the injustices and wars that terrorize our world, and the imperial systems that institutionalize violence; in light of the 50,000 children who die each day from starvation—we know we need to turn to God to find how to respond in faith. As we go public then in acts of nonviolent love to make peace and do justice, and receive a lukewarm reception, even a hostile response, we will discover anew the need to rely wholeheartedly on God.

As we try to live out God's peace in our lives, and turn to God in quiet prayer, we can hear an inner voice, the voice of God, whisper: "Come to me and draw from the springs of peace. Seek peace and you will find peace. Be merciful and you will find mercy. Where there is no love, put love and you will find love."

Those contemplative moments, when we dwell in the peace that God offers us, can sustain us through the long days of peacemaking, and the long haul of living. In this light, we are able to see the world around us with new eyes, to look for God in all those we meet, and to see God in every human face. In this spirit, we can find God in the poor and in our enemies. We can encounter God in the nonviolent struggle for justice, in our daily life, in the world itself. In this spirit, we discover that God is alive, present, real, aware of us, loving us, calling us forever to dwell in peace and nonviolent love.

Spirituality develops as we let go of power and control, of the imperial ego that takes over our lives and prevents us from dwelling in God's peace. It emerges naturally as we take risks for peace— publicly, peacefully, lovingly—risks like opposing war, demanding housing for the poor, and speaking out against the death penalty. Be vulnerable before God and take the risk of peacemaking, the mystics tell us, and then God can use us as instruments of God's peace—in ways we never dreamed possible. In that vulnerability, God can tame the savagery of the human spirit, as Aeschylus wrote, the violence and anger that linger within us all. In that prayerful mindset, we will be free to walk into the world and make peace. Gandhi put it this way: "Prayer from the heart can achieve what nothing else can in the world." Not only can heartfelt prayer center us in God's peace, it will send forth a ripple of peace from us out into the world.

Perhaps the best way to develop such a spirituality, calling us back to the basics of our humanity and God's divinity, is to live and work among the poor and the marginalized. In the poor, we meet God calling us to be with God, to do justice, to transform the institutionalized violence of our world, and to be compassionate. The poor can teach us a spirituality of peacemaking.

In the midst of my activities for justice for the poor and peace among peoples, I always discover a need to go deeper into the well of prayer in order to keep a spirit of peace about me. The struggle, I have learned, is to stay centered in the nonviolent love of God at all times, and thus to be fully present to people and aware of God's presence at all times—even as I speak the truth of peace, walk with the poor, march for peace, and sit in against war.

During such times, I found myself turning to favorite books from those who have gone ahead of us, marked with the sign of faith. One book that I keep returning to is *A Vow of Conversation*, the journal which Thomas Merton kept as he was beginning his hermitage experience. What a symbol for me during the hectic days of peacemaking and working with the poor! There he is: at the height of the Vietnam war, alone, praying, in solitude, in his hermitage in the Kentucky woods. Deliberately silent. Cultivating the Spirit of Peace. Saving it for the rest of us, for future generations. In prayerful moments, I feel the gift of his solitude, keeping me calm, guiding me with a vision that holds my heart and soul intact, at peace, contemplative, at one with the God of peace. On many an evening, his words transformed my restless spirit into silence and a deep peace.

From his hermitage, he wrote,

Only here do I feel that my life is fully human. And only
what is authentically human is fit to be offered to God....
What more do I seek than this silence, this simplicity, this
"living together with wisdom?" For me, there is nothing
else, and to think that I have had the grace to taste a little of
what all men and women really seek without realizing it! All
the more obligation to have compassion and love, and to
pray for them.... I can imagine no other joy on earth than to
have such a place to be at peace in. To live in silence, to
think and write, to listen to the wind and to all the voices of
the wood, to struggle with a new anguish, which is, nevertheless, blessed and secure, to live in the shadow of a big
cedar cross, to prepare for my death and my exodus to the
heavenly country, to love my brothers and all people, to pray
for the whole world and offer peace and good sense among
people. So it is my place in the scheme of things and that is
sufficient. Amen.

What an alternative lifestyle, a counter-cultural sign to the nation at
war. His witness challenged all Christian activists, for it called us to
go back to the roots of our faith. Merton's peacemaking was existential. It meant breathing the fresh air, watching the birds, looking at
the sky. Merton walked ahead of us, revealing to us God's call to become a community of peacemakers. He showed us a vision of the
whole human being—at peace, nonviolent, contemplative, at one
with God, nature and all humanity. For Merton, peacemaking and
spirituality were the same thing.

His insights into silence, contemplation, and the peace which is
already given to us by God, sustain me in a spirit of grace as I try to
witness to peace in a world that seems—in these recent days, by all

appearances—to have lost all sense of grace, all sense of love, all sense of sanity.

Whenever we feel off track from these basic contemplative rhythms, we must retreat from our activities, cut back our workload, sit outside, listen to the birds, look at the trees, and dwell in God's peace all over again. The good spirit of God wants us first and always to be at peace if we are going to seek peace, speak peace and promote peace with justice in God's name. All the way to peace is peace filled, the ancients said. "While you are proclaiming peace with your lips, be careful to have it even more fully in your heart," St. Francis wrote long ago.

St. Ignatius Loyola, the founder of the Jesuits, urged his companions to take fifteen minutes at the end of every day for a prayerful review with God of that day, and in this way, ensure that one's heart is centered in God's peace as we fulfill our mission of doing justice. His *examen*, as he called it, can help us today as we seek to become a nonviolent people, centered in peace, responsible, committed to justice for the poor, willing to risk our very lives for our fellow human beings.

Begin by asking for light and understanding to see the day from God's perspective; then review the events of the day without judgment, and notice where I felt or saw the presence of God. Give thanks for those moments, and then reflect on those times when I failed to be at peace, when I was not nonviolent or loving, when I did things which I shouldn't have done and didn't do things which I should have done, for God's sake. Repent of those sins, ask for God's forgiveness, and pray for strength to be a better peacemaker for the next day. Ask God what God has to say to you about this day and that tomorrow. Conclude with a prayer of thanksgiving and resolve to be a better peacemaker the next day—more faithful, more nonviolent, more daring, more loving, more hopeful. This *examen*, Ignatius believed, with God's grace, would help us to become a people of peace.

Such is a spirituality for everyday peacemaking. Be rooted in a nonviolent love for all; be gentle with everyone, beginning with yourself; practice humility and kindness; accompany the poor and let go of possessions; join a community of peacemakers as they study the Scriptures and seek the way of peace; speak the truth and act on it; say No to war and Yes to the Way of nonviolence, and accept the consequences—and most of all, be centered in God who calls us to be peacemakers, to be God's very sons and daughters. In this way, we will truly be blessed. Indeed, we will find ourselves dwelling in the house of God, the house of nonviolence.

My community members eventually returned home and I entered our house, but in the meantime, I rediscovered a simple truth: the key to the house of God, the house of peace is in our hands. We can enter anytime.

35.
The Making of a Peace Church:
Pax Christi, a Catholic Peace Movement

We are peaceful or not; peacemakers or not. There is no middle ground. The choice is always before us. We are called to be so immersed in the tide of peace that every thought, word and deed is a blessing of life, for ourselves, others and all creation. This task of unity is our lifelong mission—interiorly, spiritually, publicly, communally, internationally, politically, socially.

Etty Hillesum, a twenty-nine-year-old woman who died at Auschwitz in 1943 and who left behind a spiritual diary of tremendous depth, put it this way: "Unless the smallest detail of your daily life is in harmony with the high ideals you profess, then those ideals have no meaning."

These words cut to the heart of the matter. Life is to be lived at the highest level at every moment. One dare not speak of peace and fashion oneself a peacemaker without first exploring the depths of war in one's own heart. It is an ancient truth, honored by every positive religion, yet dishonored by our constant inability to put it into practice. To look at the roots of nuclear war in our own hearts is painful and costly. To disarm those violent roots will bear fruit for generations to come. To live in a spirit of nonviolence will mean the reign of God on earth.

Though we may wish to be peaceful, we can't help ourselves: we respond with violence. Few of us in the United States can imagine living a life of active nonviolence. Not only do we adamantly believe in violent self-defense and the old "eye for an eye" theory, we are so addicted to violence that we let our lives continue "normally" in the face of war, hunger, homelessness, the death penalty, abortion, sexism, racism, and torture. To make matters worse, like the addict who completely loses control and drinks himself to death, we have threatened to destroy the entire human race and our planet. We are drunk on violence.

Such thoughts lead me to think that one of the functions of the peace movement—the church—is to offer a way out of our addiction to violence through basic, support communities of nonviolence. We need a group of "Violence Addicts Anonymous," like the "Alcoholics Anonymous" groups, where we can gather to say, "Hi. My name is John and I'm addicted to violence." Perhaps through these peace communities, we can transform ourselves, one another, our nation, and our world. I think this is what Jesus was trying to do with his life.

One of the most exciting developments these days in the Catholic Church is the emergence of Pax Christi as a voice for peace and justice. Pax Christi may provide a way for us to be healed from our addiction to violence, as individuals and as a society. In Pax Christi groups around the country, people have a chance to become sober. Not only are they facing their own personal violence and converting to Gospel nonviolence, but people are beginning to look seriously at the world's violence and injustices and to work together to heal the human community.

In a few short years, Pax Christi has blossomed into an image of what the church could be: a peacemaking community. With over 12,000 members including over 100 bishops, sponsored by over 300 communities and provinces of religious orders from coast to coast, made up of over 250 local grass-roots groups meeting in parishes, neighborhoods, high schools, colleges and seminaries in every state, Pax Christi is fast becoming a leaven in the church and in society. Perhaps, it can help us learn what it means to be a Catholic Christian in the United States in the 1990s headed towards the 2000s.

Pax Christi USA has its roots in Pax Christi International, the international Catholic peace movement, founded immediately after World War II by two people, Mrs. Dortel-Claudot, a French lay woman, and Bishop Pierre-Marie Theas of Lourdes. Their fledgling peace group grew from a desire to reconcile French and German Catholics during and immediately after the war. Bishop Theas began working for the reconciliation of France and Germany while he was imprisoned in a German war camp. In the early months of 1945, several French Catholics, imprisoned by the Germans, began a "crusade of prayer" for the German people. Bishop Theas, newly freed from prison, blessed the crusade. This prayer vigil was the beginning of Pax Christi. At the war's end, French and German Catholics made a peace pilgrimage to Lourdes.

The goal of the Pax Christi founders was to work "with all people for peace for all humankind, always witnessing to the peace of Christ." Soon after the war, Pax Christi groups were established in France and Germany. In 1948, Pope Pius XII gave Pax Christi his blessing and the movement spread throughout Europe and to Australia. In 1952, Monsignor Montini, who became Pope Paul VI in

1963, gave his blessing to Pax Christi as an international Catholic peace movement.

Cardinal Feltin of Paris, Pax Christi International's first president, summarized Pax Christi's program for peace as three steps: prayer, study, and action. The movement focused its early efforts on disarmament, peace education, contacts with the Eastern Bloc, the arms race, and the arms trade. As church historian Ronald Musto notes in his book, *The Catholic Peace Tradition*, the growth of Pax Christi "reflected the church's gradual abandonment of the just-war theory after World War II."

During the 1950s, Pax Christi sponsored well-publicized international marches in which people from all over Europe were brought together to live in peace, pray, and discuss peace problems as they made their way from village to village. They carried a "cross of reconciliation" back and forth between France and Germany, sowing seeds of reconciliation between these divided nations.

Today, Pax Christi International has branches in over thirty nations, including Canada, the United States, Australia, the Philippines, and Haiti. In 1988, Sr. Mary Evelyn Jegen, SND, international vice president of Pax Christi, traveled throughout Asia, boosting Pax Christi in Pakistan, India, Hong Kong, and New Zealand. With the worldwide embrace of Catholic peacemaking in Pax Christi, a new chapter is beginning in the history of Catholicism. Pax Christi is becoming a worldwide, base-community movement where people become sober and nonviolent, alive in the Gospel of peace and justice. With the help of Pax Christi, the church is moving away from a general acceptance of the just-war theory into the embrace of Gospel nonviolence in action. Perhaps with the growth of Pax Christi, we are on the verge of loving one another, loving our enemies, and refusing to kill—*as a people, on a societal level.*

Pax Christi International continues to promote disarmament, human rights and the rights of conscientious objectors and political prisoners. It has tried to be a link between East and West, especially between the churches, as well as a voice against torture, racism, capital punishment, and war. It has always used both education and research, study conferences and grass-roots activities, prayer and Eucharist as the means of teaching and making peace among peoples. It has made significant contributions worldwide to the spirituality of peacemaking and since 1979 has held status at the United Nations.

In the United States, Pax Christi USA has undertaken similar peacemaking efforts. Although Pax Christi was founded in the early 1970s, its roots go back to 1957, when Gordon Zahn, the noted pacifist, sociologist, and biographer of Austrian martyr Franz Jaegerstaetter, attended a European meeting of Pax Christi International and tried to start a chapter on his return home. In the 1960s, the Catholic peace group PAX, coordinated by Eileen Egan and Gordon Zahn, grew to include Thomas Merton, the Berrigans, and Dorothy Day as leading members. In the late 1960s and early 1970s, PAX affiliated with Pax Christi International, and Bishop Carroll Dozier of Memphis and Bishop Thomas Gumbleton of Detroit agreed to act as moderators of a new Pax Christi USA. In May 1975, in New York, Eileen Egan, Dorothy Day, Gordon Zahn and others met at Manhattan College to pray for and form the new Pax Christi USA. A larger national meeting was held in Dayton, Ohio, later that year. By 1979, a national office was set up. Based on its foundation as a movement of Catholics committed to forming communities of prayer, study, and action, Pax Christi USA set goals to promote Gospel nonviolence, peacemaking, disarmament, works of justice, and disarming the heart.

In the early 1980s, the national office moved from Chicago to Erie, Pennsylvania, where it received great help and sponsorship from the nearby Benedictine community, under the leadership of Sr. Joan Chittister, OSB. Sr. Mary Lou Kownacki, OSB, succeeded Sr. Mary Evelyn Jegen, SND, as the national coordinator. A quarterly magazine was launched, and Pax Christi USA gradually emerged as a leading voice for peace.

Throughout the 1980s, Pax Christi has vigorously promoted the US bishops' peace pastoral and published a wide array of materials on nonviolence and peacemaking. Indeed, they have taken the bishops at their word in the call to be peacemakers. This reflective work has led Pax Christi to challenge the bishops to move beyond their acceptance of deterrence into the Gospel message of Jesus: "Love your enemies. Do not kill."

In 1985, Pax Christi offered its members a vow of nonviolence as a way to confront our addiction to violence and to commit ourselves formally to Jesus' way of nonviolence. Thousands of people around the country and the world have privately and publicly professed the vow since then. As a channel of grace supporting and strengthening our commitment to nonviolence, the vow encourages and reminds us to remain faithful to the Way of nonviolence:

> Recognizing the violence in my own heart, yet trusting in the goodness and mercy of God, I vow to practice the nonviolence of Jesus who taught us in the Sermon on the Mount: "Blessed are the peacemakers, for they shall be called the sons and daughters of God.... You have learned how it was said, 'You must love your neighbor and hate your enemy,'

but I say to you, Love your enemies, and pray for those who persecute you. In this way you will be daughters and sons of your Creator in heaven."

Before God the Creator and the Sanctifying Spirit, I vow to carry out in my life the love and example of Jesus by striving for peace within myself and seeking to be a peacemaker in my daily life; by accepting suffering (in the struggle for justice) rather than inflicting it; by refusing to retaliate in the face of provocation and violence; by persevering in nonviolence of tongue and heart; by living conscientiously and simply so that I do not deprive others of the means to live; and by actively resisting evil and working nonviolently to abolish war and the causes of war from my own heart and from the face of the earth.

God, I trust in your sustaining love and believe that just as you gave me the grace and desire to offer this, so you will also bestow abundant grace to fulfill it.

The vow of nonviolence, in particular, offers people a challenging new beginning into the way of life which is Gospel nonviolence. As a covenant of nonviolence, the vow professes our acceptance of God's transforming, disarming love at work in our hearts, mobilizing us in turn to transform and disarm others, and the world.

In the 1990s, under the leadership of Bishop President Walter Sullivan and national coordinator Anne McCarthy, OSB, Pax Christi USA has five priorities:

1) *Disarmament.* Pax Christi works for nuclear and general disarmament, and the reordering of national budgets from military spending into programs that benefit human needs.

2) *Alternatives to Violence.* The Gospel calls us to become people of nonviolence, and so, Pax Christi promotes nonviolence in our personal lives, in our church, in the nation and in the international community. It offers concrete steps to help members become nonviolent people.

3) *Education.* Pax Christi promotes the study of peace and justice for people of all ages, as recent popes and bishops have urged. Pax Christi publications on peacemaking are designed for use in parishes, schools, homes, and communities.

4) *Primacy of Conscience.* Pax Christi upholds the right to conscientious objection to war, selective conscientious objection, nonviolent civil disobedience, and the designation of taxes for nonmilitary purposes through the Peace Tax Fund.

5) *Just World Order.* Pax Christi advocates universal human rights through economic and political justice and an end to all forms of institutionalized violence. It strongly endorses the work of the United Nations as a means to promote a more just world order, and works to end apartheid in South Africa, poverty in Haiti, US intervention in El Salvador and the Philippines, and religious war in the Middle East.

On the fourth anniversary of the US bishops' peace pastoral, May 5, 1987, Pax Christi sponsored a national gathering at the Nevada Nuclear Test site. Hundreds of Pax Christi members traveled from around the country to pray and keep vigil in the desert. Many decided to cross the line onto the grounds of the test site, including two bishops. This marked the first time Catholic bishops committed civil disobedience because of our nation's continued support for nuclear weapons. During the forty-fifth anniversary year of the bombing of Hiroshima and Nagasaki, Pax Christi members around the country gathered at the twelve largest nuclear-weapons bases and military centers to call for an end to the arms race. They walked onto the bases carrying bread and roses, as signs of love and hope for a future of peace.

Every year, Pax Christi offers national assemblies and regional workshops; issues reports on third-world matters; releases statements on national and international events; promotes the consistent life ethic linking pro-life, justice, and disarmament issues; and seeks to witness in simple ways to the Gospel message of peace and nonviolent love. The cumulative effort of this growing movement for peace will be the transformation of the Catholic Church into an active peacemaking community rooted in the Gospel of Jesus.

Considering the world's addiction to violence and death, Pax Christi makes a significant contribution in its call for a nonviolent alternative. For that reason, I believe every Catholic in the United States should consider becoming a member of the Pax Christi movement. Each local Pax Christi group acts as a support group for people who wish to explore nonviolence as a way of life and active peacemaking as a joyful duty. Indeed, such groups help us accept God's transforming grace in our lives, so that as a people we can move from our addiction to violence into the freedom of nonviolence. As a support group, a la Alcoholics Anonymous, Pax Christi members could confess their addiction to violence, and through communal prayer, study, and action seek to live in the Spirit of the nonviolent Christ.

The development of Pax Christi shows that the Spirit of God, the Spirit of peace, is alive and moving among us. This movement of the Spirit of peace may transform our lives and our church, not to mention the world.

An astounding feature of human life is its connectedness. Everything affects everything else. We are all one. Our souls, our relationships with one another, our attitude toward the world, our way of life, our inner peace, our struggles, our thoughts spoken and unspoken to others—all are connected. We are all one, together, sharing the same experience on this planet. We are all given the gift of life and the freedom to do with our lives as we choose. One day, we shall all be held accountable for how we lived our lives, and how we upheld our unity.

In reality, life is a journey towards spiritual integration, a journey into that unity of life. When fully sought after and lived to the fullest, life is a deepening of nonviolence and love, a journey of the spirit that has political and social ramifications of justice and peace for all. Life is this integrity of spirit. The road to its daily deepening is called nonviolence. When every human being pursues that journey with a heart full of unconditional love, then all of creation bends toward the full integration of spirit to which it was created. The God who created us all will reign completely then on earth as God reigns in heaven. Justice will prevail for all. There will be no more tears shed, no more blood spilt, no more hungry bellies, no more lives snuffed out. As Julian of Norwich foresaw, all will be well and every manner of thing will be well.

We are whole, but it takes us a lifetime to realize it. We are all one, but it takes us a lifetime to ponder that mystery of justice and love. We are already at peace, but it is so difficult for us to accept the unity already given to us. The culture of violence tells us that we are divided, that we have nothing in common with each other, that we are each other's enemies, that we are at war with one another. We have to believe every minute of the day that we are one with all humanity, one with all creation, one with God.

Every minute of life is an invitation to enter into the struggle of unitive love. To enter that nonviolent struggle, to believe that we are one in love, to lay down our lives for suffering humanity, that is to live. Pax Christi seeks to help Catholic Christians live this underlying unity of peace which Christ has given us.

May we all dwell in that peace of Christ.[1]

---

[1]For more information, contact Pax Christi USA, 348 East Tenth St., Erie, PA 16503 (814/453-4955).

Part Seven:
The Christ of Nonviolence

We Christians do not bear arms against any country; we do not make war anymore. We have become children of peace, and Jesus is our leader.

Origen

The only people on earth who do not see Christ and his teachings as nonviolent are Christians.... Jesus lived and died in vain if he did not teach us to regulate the whole of life by the eternal law of love.

Mohandas Gandhi

If Jesus taught us anything, he taught us how to die, not how to kill.

John McKenzie

36.
Jesus' Narrow Path of Nonviolence

The first thing to be disrupted by a commitment to nonviolence, as Jim Douglass points out, is not the system, the government, or the world, but our own lives.

I think he's right, and perhaps that's why we don't want to plumb the depths of Gospel nonviolence. It disrupts everything, beginning with our own lives, plans and ambitions. Nonviolence is truly a personal challenge, a struggle, a way of life, something much more than a tactic, or an occasional experience. It is a transforming spirit of love and truth which begins in our hearts and reaches out to touch the world.

As our nation practices war in the Middle East, El Salvador, the Philippines, and elsewhere, perhaps the time has finally come for us as a people to look more closely at this spirit of active nonviolence.

For myself, I know such a prospect is daunting. I'm no expert on nonviolence; like everyone, I'm an expert on violence and injustice. I'm addicted to violence, a victim of the American culture, a violent person trying to follow the nonviolent Christ in a world of violence. On top of this, I'm a recovering white male.

What might it mean that God is nonviolent, that Jesus practiced and lived nonviolence, and that we are called to be followers, co-workers of the nonviolent Jesus? What would Jesus say to us today? How would he mission us to practice nonviolence? What does it mean for us to be nonviolent? What does it mean to be a human being? How do we respond to this calling? Such questions require our attention these days.

I am convinced that Jesus lived, taught and practiced a Way of nonviolence. His whole life, his actions, his death and resurrection are nonviolence personified. His great lesson for us is to practice active nonviolent love, to love one another, to love our enemies, to go public with love for all people.

Jesus is our model of nonviolence, a peacemaker who challenges the world's addictions to violence, its love of death. He brings life to the world by turning over the tables of the culture and insisting on justice for the poor, on reconciliation with all people. He calls us to do the same.

Jesus invites us to experiment anew with the nonviolent alternative. "Love, love without ceasing," he says. "Love even those declared to be the hated enemies of your empire. Do not be afraid. Become nonviolent. Do not practice violence anymore. Do not hurt one another. Forgive everyone. Seek the truth, speak the truth, and accept the consequences. Always seek justice for the poor and peace with everyone. Stop hoarding the earth's resources. Help transform the world into my reign of nonviolent love. Take up the nonviolent cross and follow me."

He says to those who would follow him—to us: "If any one would come after me, let them deny themselves, take up their cross of nonviolent resistance to evil and follow me. Follow me on the narrow path of nonviolent love. I cannot guarantee you success or great results. In fact, all I can guarantee you is persecution, conflict, abuse, hassles, frustrations, inconvenience, pain, suffering, public harassment, death and eternal life, and a community of sisters and brothers to share the struggle."

Such is the invitation of Jesus.

What is our response? We cringe in horror! "You must be kidding, Jesus!" we exclaim in unison. "It's all well and good for you, but we live in the real world. It's easy for you to say those things."

On second thought, we realize it was not easy for Jesus to be nonviolent, loving and truthful. He was killed by the ruling authorities as a revolutionary and yet he still manifested a nonviolent spirit. This witness scares us even more.

Why do we cringe at his invitation?

I recently saw a television commercial for a bank that summed up our plight. "Americans," it concluded, "are not satisfied with survival. We want success."

The problem for us Christians living in the United States is that we have been trained for success, but Jesus does not promise us success. All Jesus promises is survival—albeit a survival for the long haul, eternal life.

What's our reaction? Deep in our guts, we all ask: "Jesus, isn't there another way to eternal life, to salvation, to follow you, to see God, to be human?" And deep in our hearts, we know that the Jesus of the Gospels answers, "No. There is only one way: My life, the narrow path of nonviolence."

The disciples also cringed at his invitation. They had three years with Jesus—over 1000 days of retreats on nonviolence—and yet they never quite grasped the meaning of nonviolence until after Jesus had been executed. Perhaps some of the women disciples understood him, since they stayed with him to the cross and beyond, to the resurrection, though they too ran in horror at the prospect of a martyr calling them to go forth with the message of revolutionary nonviolence.

We read that everywhere those followers went with Jesus, they kept asking about the limits of nonviolence. They kept proposing one last exception where, maybe, Jesus would let them off the hook, let them be a little bit violent, let them relax a bit from the commitment.

But Jesus would not give in.

We can imagine the many conversations:

"Jesus, I'll follow your way of nonviolence, but first let me say goodbye to my family and friends and take care of my business."

"Now is the time," Jesus explains. "Repent and believe the good news and come and follow me now. The need is too urgent. No one who sets a hand to the plow and looks back is fit for the reign of God. I need people who are totally committed to me, to the Way of nonviolence, now and forever, people who won't turn back when the going gets tough. I don't want people to say, 'Yes, I'll be nonviolent,' and then not practice it. I prefer those who say no or wrestle with it, but then go and live it, act it, be nonviolent."

"Jesus, those guys in that neighboring nation are invading our territory; they're challenging our nation's manifest destiny. Don't you think we should do the holy and righteous thing like the prophet Elijah and call down lightning from heaven and wipe them out and protect our interests and be the policemen of the world?"

"No way," Jesus replies. "Love your enemies. Love one another."

"Jesus, I fast, I pray, I organize for peace, I go to demonstrations for peace. I professed a vow of nonviolence; I'm not violent like others. What more could you want? In fact, I'm one of the greatest disciples you've got, aren't I?"

"If you would be perfect and compassionate, sell everything you have, give the money to the poor, and come and follow me. There is no greater love than to lay down your life for your friends, for the poor, for me. Whoever is like the least among you, like a child, the servant of all, the poorest, the most loving, the freest, the one who risks her life for love of suffering humanity—is the greatest in the reign of God."

"Jesus, what about that guy who insulted me? He took off his glove, and struck me with the back of his right hand on my cheek. That was the most insulting thing a person could do! I have to defend my honor."

"Turn the other cheek. Refuse to be humiliated, but refuse to hate and do not respond with violence. Look him in the eye until he sees that you are a human being with dignity."

"Jesus, how often do I have to forgive? Seven times? That's a lot, isn't it?"

"Seventy times seven times. An infinite number of times. Forgive everyone, even those who kill your loved ones. I would even forgive people if they were killing me."

"Jesus, increase our faith. We want to have a great faith, so we can follow your way of nonviolence."

"If you had faith this small, the size of a mustard seed, you could say to this mountain, get up and move and it would."

"Jesus, we're gonna need resources for the nonviolent revolution, for the reign of God, for the journey."

"I say to you: Sell your belongings and give alms. Seek God's reign of nonviolence alone, and everything else will be provided for you. You can't serve two masters: God or money. So trust in God, work for justice, and your needs will be met."

"But Jesus, you know we have to pay our taxes; what do you expect, we could get into trouble?!"

"Give to Caesar what is Caesar's, and to God what is God's. Of course, once you give to God what is God's, there's nothing left for

Caesar. So don't pay taxes, don't join the military, don't go to war, don't fight, don't support the Pentagon. Be peacemakers, not warmakers. Give everything to God and God's movement for nonviolent change."

"Jesus, we need some kind of game plan, some new political system that will enforce justice. Maybe you could become king or president or take over the world and solve the problems?"

"No," Jesus responds. "No one should take over the world; no one should have that much power. I have no new system. I have only the truth and the good news that the reign of God is at hand and I'm going to Jerusalem, and there, I'm going to confront the powers and the principalities. I'm going to speak the truth and use nonviolence to try to wake up people, but this will be a failure, as far as worldly politics and effectiveness are concerned. It will be a disaster. They will arrest me, torture me, and murder me. Nevertheless, I will still love and forgive them and call them to conversion, and in that resurrecting spirit, they will have a change of heart, which is what needs to happen first. And I want you to follow me on this non-systemic, non-ideological, non-powerful, non-political, nonviolent path."

"Okay, Jesus, just show us what to do, how to live, the way to go, so we can change the world."

"I am the way—my life of unconditional love, committed nonviolence, limitless forgiveness, and steadfast truthfulness—this life is the way. This is what I want from you."

"Yeah, Jesus," Philip interrupts, "but we want God to come down, intervene, and do something to shake folks up. Just show us God."

"This is God! God is in this way of life, in my life of active nonviolence. God is going to Jerusalem with me. God is nonviolent. How long have you known me, anyway?"

"Okay, Jesus," Peter declares. "I'm prepared to live just like you, to go to prison and die for you. I'll be your best follower, the best peace activist, the most nonviolent person you know."

"You'll deny even knowing me at the first sign of trouble."

Later, when the soldiers came to get Jesus, Peter speaks up, "Don't worry, Jesus; I've got this sword here and I'll protect you, you and your crazy nonviolence; I'll chop this guy's ear off and..."

"What are you doing with that sword?" Jesus asks in dismay. "Put away the sword and practice nonviolent love. Those who live by the sword will die by the sword. Those who use violence will suffer from violence. Those who hate will be overcome by hatred. Instead, be nonviolent and loving, come what may. It is the only way to live."

Jesus had a difficult time teaching his friends about the wisdom of nonviolence. The disciples never really learned the message of Jesus until after he was brutally tortured and crucified, until he was raised from the dead and still preaching and practicing nonviolent love. Then, they understood that the way of nonviolence is indeed God's way. They learned the message by heart and passed it on so that others could learn. Today, 2000 years later, we are still struggling to learn and live Jesus' way of nonviolence.

In some ways, we have it easier than the disciples. We know about the resurrection. We have the Holy Spirit to guide us along the narrow path of nonviolence. All we have to do is go and live the way of the nonviolent cross and risk crucifixion; we know what is ultimately to come: the resurrection of the beloved community. But, in some ways, we have it harder: we are facing powers and principalities that could destroy the entire planet and the whole human family. The witness we are called to profess publicly could mean life or death for many.

The life of nonviolence is a kind of high wire act. We're up in the air, walking across a tightrope, balancing a bar, sitting on a bike, with everyone watching us. We could easily fall. If we stop, we will fall, so we have to keep going forward to the other side. It will take our entire lives to get there. All along the way, we can hear the crowd's reaction, "Oh, look at him! He's trying to be nonviolent. How ridiculous! How daring!"

Jesus called his way "the narrow path." Few make it, he said. "Enter through the narrow gate," he said, "For wide is the gate and broad is the road that leads to destruction, and many enter through it. But small is the gate and narrow the road that leads to life, and only a few find it." (Mt. 7:13-14) That sounds very discouraging; many walk the road to destruction, as the record of war testifies. Narrow roads are found in mountains or hills and are usually dangerous. How can we walk the narrow road to life? On further reflection, however, perhaps this image is encouraging. A few do find the road and walk it; a few do live the life of nonviolence. We can do it. A life of steadfast nonviolence is possible. We can walk the road to life.

Nonviolence is a never-ending well of grace and peace, love and truth from which we are called to drink ever more deeply. We can always go further into nonviolence; no one ever becomes perfectly nonviolent; but one day, when we finally let go and are truly empty of all power, ego and violence, we will be swept up into the reign of nonviolence, into the love of God.

The struggle, the journey, the life lived, the effort to be faithful—this is what the disciples were called to try. What they learned, they passed on to us. Yes, we can be nonviolent; we can help transform the world's violence into love. But we must try to be faithful to the calling with all our hearts and souls. This is what God, what Jesus, asks of us: to become nonviolent, peaceful, peacemaking, justice-seeking, truth-tellers; to enter into a daily conversion of heart, a nonviolent transformation.

Gandhi said, "The possibilities for every person to develop nonviolence are infinite. The more you develop it in your own being, the more infectious it becomes till it overwhelms your surroundings and by and by might oversweep the world. I have not the shadow of a doubt that any man or woman can achieve what I have, if he or she would only make the same effort and cultivate the same hope and faith.

"When the practice of Jesus' nonviolence becomes universal, God will reign on earth as God reigns in heaven."

Such a dream is possible. For Jesus, it is essential. His word to us? "Come, make the dream real. Embrace nonviolence as a way of life."

37.
Imaging God:
Despite the Fall, Grace

In an effort to challenge my convictions, a theologian once diagnosed me as a classic "apocalyptic fundamentalist." I found the cumbersome phrase insightful rather than antagonistic. I have always desired to cling to the fundamentals of the Word of God, a Word which quickly gets to the heart of the matter. Such a desire can mean nothing less than staring reality in the face and insisting on love, truth, and justice. I think every Christian is an apocalyptic fundamentalist, in the sense that every one who claims discipleship to Jesus should practice the urgent message of the Gospel—love one another, love your enemies. Such extreme love, if put into practice, can be nothing less than apocalyptic.

To this end, I have found few theologians who inform my search. Most seem to me to be out of touch with reality. From Augustine and Aquinas to Bultmann and Rahner, most speak of Christ as if he were in the clouds instead of present today in the nonviolent struggle for justice. Because they do not see Christ in this struggle, they ignore the reality of death as it plagues the world. They support the governments and empires which rule the world, because they do not see the political implications of the nonviolent Gospel. I do not want to be anserine or naive, but I can not take these writers seriously because they have not renounced violence with their very lives. They support war, calling it just and necessary, even as they wax rhapsodic about the love of God. I have difficulty reading Rahner's rigorous tracts, for example, knowing that he did so little to resist the Nazi rule which roared all around him. I do find stimulation, however, in the challenge of Bonhoeffer, Day, Solle, King, and the theologians of the third world who sweat out their liberating fundamental truths with their own blood. I find a spiritual home in their struggles for liberation, justice, feminism, and nonviolence, and in their theological reflections. Life makes most sense to me in their messy theology.

Theologians so often miss the point of the Gospel. Instead, they cling to an argot which does little to serve the poor or the truth. An episode may explain the point. I once attended a lecture by one of the leading Roman Catholic nuclear ethicists. This priest had earned several degrees, written many books, and won many honors. He had worked diligently on the US Catholic bishops' peace Ppastoral, and his handiwork can be found throughout the document. He vigorously defends nuclear deterrence and "just" war. A large crowd came to hear his address. As he prattled on about the blessings of the bomb, I became increasingly annoyed. His words did not ring true; they had the sound of a cracked bell. He never once mentioned the witness of Jesus, and how that might impact on the topic for us as Christians. Indeed, he betrayed the spirit of the Gospel in the name of a nuclear theology. Someone asked him, "Why don't you side explicitly with Jesus, and advocate love for one's enemies and nonviolence?" His response sent a chill down my spine. "I am a Roman Catholic," he replied, "not a biblical Christian." I made a fast exit through a side door.

Though I am a Roman Catholic, my allegiance is to the Christ, the biblical Word of God which speaks to our condition here and now and calls us to justice. If that makes me an apocalyptic fundamentalist, so be it. I desire to be a nonviolent resister to evil, a follower of Jesus the peacemaker, a keeper of the Word. As the Hebrew Scriptures urge, doing justice *is* my religion. Resisting evil is my faith in action. I do not advocate Pelagianism (the belief that salvation can be earned through one's good works). I speak of an authentic life, a life beyond words. The Christian life witnesses to God's reconciliation already won for humanity. It addresses the political realities of poverty and injustice which terrorize the world.

My own active life has helped me to see that the theological images of God, sin, grace, and salvation must be rooted in nonviolence, justice, agape, peace, truth, and compassion. They must be firmly grounded, in other words, in the peacemaking Christ of the Gospel.

For me, God is indeed a personal being. God is truth. God is peace. God is unconditional love. God is infinite forgiveness. God is the spirit of nonviolence, love, and truth. God is much more than I can ever imagine: neither male nor female, yet an overwhelming presence of truth and nonviolent love. This image of God goes beyond the tradition handed down to us, a tradition which portrays God as a Michelangelo figure condemning us all to eternal damnation. Yet, it fits within that tradition as well. Unfortunately, the structures which defend the tradition are also busy defending the status quo, the systems which oppress and kill the poor. God rises above the status quo. If Love is God, and Truth is God, and Peace is God—then the Person of God is revolutionary, as far as the world is concerned. To get to know God, I have to establish a relationship with the Person of Peace, the Person of Love, the Person of Truth.

God is God for me precisely because God is nonviolent, still steadfast in the desire for justice and peace. Anyone can be violent. But nonviolence is of the divine. Those who pursue active nonviolence for humanity—the peacemakers—are indeed sons and daughters of the divine because God is nonviolent, peacemaking, reconciling, just, merciful. Jesus reveals the divine to me because he was nonviolent, compassionate, truthful, and active in resisting evil. He was a resister, a liberator, a feminist, a revolutionary—non-aligned, non-ideological, and nonviolent to the core. As Daniel Berrigan says, Jesus was God in trouble for being human.

The concept of the Trinity is so mysterious and murky that we usually dismiss it from our thoughts. For me, its inherent simplicity catches my breath. Our faith teaches us that God is creator, redeemer and spirit. God is a *community* of love and truth. In particular, the Spirit between the Creator and the Christ is the feminist spirit of peace moving among us, urging us towards love, justice, peace, and mercy. This Spirit reveals to us the *basaleia*, the reign of God, as we share in God's active nonviolence and resistance to death.

The Holy Spirit is that presence of nonviolence among us when we resist evil and live life in love and truth as sisters and brothers, as one human family. This Spirit is God's presence in us—when we are weak, human, nonviolent, in crucifixion or resurrection. William Stringfellow put it this way:

Biblically, the Holy Spirit names the faithfulness of God to God's own creation. Biblically, the Holy Spirit means the militant presence of the Word of God inhering in the life of the whole of creation. Biblically, the Holy Spirit is the Word of God at work both historically and existentially, acting incessantly and pervasively to renew the integrity of life in this world.[1]

The presence of this Spirit conveys a personal relationship with God. The spiritual journey is a path into deeper awareness of this ever-present, personal, loving God. Like every human being, I have experienced vaguely conscious moments of this presence. I become aware of God when I lose myself among the poor of the third world, among the homeless, the marginalized, and the dying; and when I end up in trouble for speaking truth to power, and in jail. Once, when I was arrested for demonstrating at a nuclear-weapons facility, I was pushed into the back seat of an empty police car where I sat handcuffed and alone for a long while. In that moment, I felt a Presence, what I would call the Spirit of God, come upon my spirit. There is no way to describe such a presence, and yet one tries anyway. It was perfect peace, unconditional love, the truth in a place of terrible injustice and untruth. These moments of consolation are, for me, signs of God's abiding, loving presence.

William Stringfellow has helped me a great deal to understand the world in biblical and political terms; that is, the world as it is. He is unafraid to say that everything in the world is under the reign of death. Everything, everyone is victim of the fall. Stringfellow wrote that "the fall is not, as the biblical literalists have supposed, an event in time. The fall is the era of time as such; the fall is the time of time, as it were.... Time is the realm of death. Death is a reality only in time; indeed, death is the essential reality of time."[2]

Death is the ultimate factor that must be confronted in human life. Death takes so many forms and we do everything we can to avoid it, even to the point of denying its existence while we plan the destruction of the planet. The struggle of the Christian life is to face up to death and to witness to Christ's transcendence of death. We worship the idols of death, and pay for that worship with a world of violence, injustice, and despair. "The fall is about the militancy of death's presence within all relationships, in the reality of our present existence, and in the history of this world."[3] It describes "an estate of subjection to the power of death which both people and things in this history suffer."[4] He continued:

> The fall refers to the profound disorientation affecting all relationships in the totality of creation, concerning identity, place, connection, purpose, vocation. The subject of the fall is not only the personal realm, in the sense of you or me, but the whole of creation and each and every item of created life. The fall means the reign of chaos throughout creation now, so that even that which is ordained by the ruling powers as "order" is, in truth, chaotic. The fall means a remarkable confusion which all beings—principalities as well as persons—suffer as to who they are and why they exist. The fall means the consignment of all created life, and of the realm of time, to the power of death.[5]

We live in a situation of massive *social sin.* Sin is systemic; we are born into it and give in to it. This homage to death invades every area of life. The systems which kill are the powers and principalities of Scripture. Our quiet acceptance of these systems is our original sin. We are not necessarily ogres; we are sinners, each and every human being. This addiction to death invades each human heart. Each one of us is capable of the most abominable, hideous crime. Every human being is capable of pushing the button which would start a nuclear war. Every human being is capable of killing someone. Every human being is capable of driving the nails into Christ. Every human being at one point or another wants to kill God.

The glorious news from God is that we are forgiven. God loves us unconditionally and invites us not to sin anymore, but to be transformed from this addiction to violence and death into the freedom of nonviolent love. "The theme of the Gospel from the first moment of the fall is God in search of humanity," Stringfellow declared. "The emphasis is upon the initiative God takes toward people in the world."[6] God seeks us out, like lost sheep, and showers us with forgiving love. In this love, we can turn to others and offer the same forgiving love, and thus make peace. Life is discovered and redeemed in the process of overcoming our original sin and systemic evil. It is a gift that requires our acceptance.

"If everything is providential," Stringfellow writes, "then providence refers to God's capacity and God's willingness to redeem all of life. It means that no circumstances ever arise which are beyond God's care or reach." He continues:

> It means that the power and reality of death at work concretely in the world is never so ascendant or successful that resurrection—the transcendence of death and the restoration of life—is either irrelevant or precluded. If everything is providential, then the issue in living is the patience and ingenuity of God's grace, and people need never live bereft of hope.[7]

Grace is the instrument of God's movement for justice and salvation. It is God's instrument of revolution which causes us to opt for the poor, speak the truth, and love our enemies. It is a gift we must pray for and accept with open hearts when it is given, and God gives us many graces at every moment of the day. Indeed, as St. Therese of Lisieux said, "All is grace."

God acts through grace against sin—in us—making right the world, as St. Paul says. Grace is the Holy Spirit, God's presence in us, transforming the world. Grace is the nonviolence of God, the Spirit of God in action that works through movements for justice, for the poor, for peace, which turn unjust structures into nonviolent structures that serve all people. This transforming grace operates on all levels, from the individual human heart to the broadest international level. If we change our hearts, that grace can move us to change the structures of evil around us. If we change the structures of evil around us into the service of nonviolence and justice for the poor, grace will move us to provide the physical needs of the poor.

In the liberation, feminist, justice, and nonviolence movements, grace is the process of nonviolent love which transforms the structures of sin, and us as well. God's Spirit present and active is the social grace of transformation. The personal struggle is learning to let go and open my soul to God so that God's Spirit can transform me and my life. It is a process of surrender to God, a process over which I have no control. All I can do is set the stage by following the life outlined by the Christ, a life of active nonviolent love that seeks justice and resists evil. In this life, I can cooperate with grace and God's work can be done.

A life of nonviolence is a life of grace, a way of living without any control over another, over oneself, or over God. A graced life is a life of freedom. In grace, we are out of control, so to speak. We are disciplined in nonviolence and dedicated to the service of justice for the poor. Such grace is a lifelong process of recovery from our original sin, a process of daily conversion and transformation until we become like God, fully human beings.

People resist nonviolence and love because they want to have control over everything and everyone. This control is violence; it leads to unjust wealth, war, hunger, poverty, and death. It means living in denial. This addiction to sin in its various deadly forms is a way of controlling reality. Stringfellow observed: "God's grace overcomes all human barriers, forgives all alienations, heals all brokenness, absolves all distinctions, pacifies all strife, purifies all iniquity, sanctifies the vulgar, redeems from sin, and defeats the last enemy, which is death."[8] God's grace is good news in a bad time.

The term "salvation" is equally mysterious to most of us. What does it mean to be saved? When are we saved? Scripture sheds light on this truth, if we are willing to dig deep and look for it. Unfortunately, most of us deny that we are in need of salvation.

For myself, salvation is here and now. It is choosing to be chosen by God, living as if the truth were true, as if the reign of God is here and now, as it is. When nonviolence is practiced everywhere on earth by everyone, then God will reign on earth as God reigns in heaven and we will experience perfect salvation. Converting and opting for the poor, for justice and peace—these are signs of our salvation.

Salvation requires dying now before we die. It means living in the resurrection now. The physical death we undergo at the end of our lives is the final act of something that began long ago. Our physical death is the last letting go, the last of a thousand spiritual deaths that we undergo every day when we choose to love unconditionally and seek justice without regard to the personal consequences. Conversion is a painful process, but not a one-time event. Every day we are invited to be converted anew. As we convert to God's will, we step closer to the experience of a salvation which is already guaranteed in the life and death of Christ. The poor have involuntarily suffered the pain of conversion and they experience salvation, the reign of God in their midst, as they struggle for justice. If we want to look for salvation, we have to look to the way they live and enter their struggle.

Christ invites us to this salvation here and now. He paved the way, once and for always, through his crucifixion and resurrection, by turning over the tables on the reign of death. The way of the cross, the way of nonviolent resistance to evil, is the way of salvation. Stringfellow wrote:

> People hate the cross because it means a salvation not of their own choosing or making, but rather of God's grace and mercy. People hate the cross because it means a salvation which is unearned, undeserved, unmerited. People would much prefer God to punish them than to forgive them because that would mean that God is dependent upon people and needed their obedience to be their God. Then God would be in fact no different from an idol of race, nation, family or whatever.[9]

We can choose to reject the offer of salvation, and continue with the bloody business of greed and war. But God's mercy, nonviolent love, reconciliation and forgiveness are infinite, and one day we will come to our senses. In this regard, the afterlife is not a question of primary concern. Fifty thousand people die of hunger every day; over one billion people are homeless or refugees. Three-quarters of humanity lives in misery. This suffering should not happen. It is our duty to end this needless pain. Salvation must address this unjust suffering or it is no true salvation. The life of Jesus shows that salvation involves the nonviolent struggle for justice; indeed, the struggle is our salvation. Salvation is choosing to act, speak, and live on behalf of suffering humanity. In that solidarity— the cross of Christ—we are saved.

God calls us, transforms us, and uses us to transform the world into God's reign of justice and peace, so that there will come a day when there is no more violence, no more war, no more death. For the rest of my life, I can expect God to keep calling me, forgiving me, challenging me to stand with the poor, and for justice and peace, no matter what the cost or situation. Being a sinner, I will continue to resist that call; but with God's grace, I will also be able to answer it.

As God draws me into the practice of nonviolent love, justice, and peacemaking, I can expect to suffer the consequences which Jesus knew. I can expect the cross, but I can also expect the redemption and salvation which is resurrection.

God wants this paschal mystery to happen in my life, for if everyone embraces that journey, God's transformation of humankind will be fulfilled. In this journey, I can expect God to suffer with me. God will be with me because God in Jesus has already gone ahead, suffered the consequences and shown us how to live and die. I can expect crucifixion and resurrection if I believe in God and put that belief into action through a life lived for justice. God is active in the lives of the poor and the oppressed, and there I will find God. God is actively nonviolent and active wherever people nonviolently resist the powers of death on earth, and there also, I will find God. God is present with us now in our hearts, in our silence, in our sacrificial love. Salvation is the great "Amen" and "Alleluia" sung in response to God's great gift.

Nonviolence is the great test of our faith. It is the great leveler, the revealer which bears all hearts.

The ultimate question of theology is one so simple that we easily miss its piercing light. In looking for God, we look to humanity. The question is: *What does it mean to be a human being?* God wrestled with this question and got into serious trouble. We can do no less.

"The only vocation to which a Christian is called," Stringfellow observed, "is to be a mature human being."[10] To be human means to work for justice for the poor and for peace and to do so always in a spirit of nonviolence, love, compassion, mercy, forgiveness, and steadfast resistance to the forces of death. To be human means to be willing to suffer for others as I nonviolently struggle for justice, for the poor, for peace, and for all humanity.

Stringfellow goes further. Being human ultimately means enjoying life, living in the resurrection. It means loving everyone and doing what is right. "The vocation of people," Stringfellow noted, "is to enjoy their emancipation from the power of death wrought by God's vitality in this world. The crown of life is the freedom to live now, for all the strife and ambiguity and travail, in the imminent transcendence of death, and all of death's threats and temptations [are overcome]. That is the gift of God to people in Christ's resurrection. People of this vocation count all trials as joys, for, though every trial be an assault of the power of death, in every trial is God's defeat of death verified and manifested."[11]

In the end, I do not mind being called an apocalyptic fundamentalist, because it implies a willingness to stare reality—including the everpresent evil of death—in the eye. This piercing look sees through death and beyond, to the light, life, and love which God bestows upon us in the spirit of resurrection. It is the mark of a Christian, the sign of a human being. May we one day together see the light.

---

[1]William Stringfellow. *The Politics of Spirituality* (Philadelphia: The Westminster Press, 1984), p. 18.

[2]William Stringfellow. *A Second Birthday* (New York: Doubleday and Co., 1970), pp. 122-123.

[3]William Stringfellow. *Imposters of God: Inquiries into Favorite Idols* (Dayton, Ohio: Witness Books, 1969), p. 31.

[4]*Ibid.*, p. 106.

[5]*The Politics of Spirituality, op. cit.*, p. 38.

[6]William Stringfellow. *Count it all Joy* (Grand Rapids, Michigan: Eerdmans Publishing Co., 1967), p. 29.

[7]*A Second Birthday, op. cit.*, p. 121.

[8]*Count it all Joy, op. cit.*, p. 35.

[9]William Stringfellow. *Free in Obedience* (New York: Seabury Press, 1964), p. 33.

[10]*A Second Birthday, op. cit.*, pp. 67-68.

[11]*Count it all Joy, op. cit.*, p. 92.

38.
Jesus and the Minjung:
A Call to Solidarity

Two of the most influential Christians in the United States this century, Dorothy Day and Martin Luther King, Jr., dedicated their faith lives to an active solidarity with the poor and oppressed. For Dorothy Day, that meant founding the Catholic Worker movement and its houses of hospitality which reach out to the homeless and hungry who crowd our city streets. For Martin Luther King, Jr., it meant speaking out for equality and integration and against racism and segregation. He marched in the streets with oppressed blacks of all walks of life, joining them in a movement for positive social change. As the years went on, he broadened that movement to include oppressed peoples throughout the world, including the victims of US war in Vietnam. Such solidarity cost him his life.

The poor and oppressed peoples of the world have been rising up and demanding justice and peace throughout this century. The most dramatic influence of these movements for social change on the church can be felt in Latin America, where liberation theology has articulated the cry of the poor in their demand for justice and peace. But while the call for liberation and justice has arisen from Central and South America, it can also be heard in Africa and Asia, and most recently, in Korea.

Korea's liberation theology, known as minjung theology, has made significant contributions to our understanding of the Christian responsibility of solidarity with the poor and oppressed. Korean theologians articulate a new reading of the Gospels which has emerged from the struggling people of Korea, just as the liberation theologians have given voice to the movement of liberation and justice among the masses of poor people throughout Latin America. The Korean struggle has produced a vision of Jesus in solidarity with the oppressed masses, the marginalized, and the outcast. The Korean term for the oppressed is "minjung." Their new minjung theology may help Christians in North America hear more clearly the call to solidarity with the poor—and to nonviolent resistance of the forces which oppress the poor—which the Gospels address.

Korean liberation theologians such as Ahn Byung Mu have begun to shed new light on the political significance of the Gospels by investigating the social character of the people who followed Jesus. In an attempt to examine their economic, political, and cultural make up, as well as the social structure and place of the people around Jesus, Ahn begins by examining the evangelists' use of the Greek word for people, *ochlos*.[1] The more common Greek word, *laos*, would be expected, since it is used frequently to refer to the people (specifically, the people of Israel as the people of God). The word *laos* occurs over 2,000 times in the Septuagint alone. But altogether, *ochlos* appears 174 times in the New Testament, including eighty-four times in Luke, while *laos* occurs only 141 times.

Mark's Gospel, the earliest, deliberately avoids the word *laos* and cites instead the word *ochlos*, which appears thirty-six times in Mark. *Laos* appears only twice, in a quotation from Scripture and in the words of the chief priests and lawyers (14:2). Mark did not want to refer to the crowds of people around Jesus as those within the national and religious framework defined by the Pharisees. The word *laos* would imply that context. Mark's use of the term *ochlos* for people is distinctive in the New Testament and probably influenced the other writers, notably Luke. Specifically, Mark used the word *ochlos* to describe the rabbinic expression *'am ha'aretz,* the "people of the land," who were the lower class, the uneducated, the poor, those ignorant of the Law. They were looked down upon, oppressed, despised, and marginalized by the culture. Rabbis taught that Jews should neither share meals nor travel together with the *'am ha'aretz*; yet Mark portrays Jesus doing even more than that with the *ochlos*.[2] As Ahn notes, Mark uses the rural outskirts of Galilee to set the background for his reference to the people with whom Jesus associated. The victims of oppression at that time comprised the *ochlos*.

Mark emphasized that the people around Jesus were marginalized and abandoned by society. Ahn writes that Mark's term is defined in a relational way, that the poor are *ochlos* in relation to the rich, ruling class; that the tax collectors are *ochlos* in relation to the Jewish nationalist establishment. Further, the *ochlos* are not organized into a political bloc. They exist as a crowd, without a common destiny, united only in their common alienation and powerlessness. Jesus specifically sets no conditions on the *ochlos*; he sides with them and accepts them. He never rebukes the so-called "sinners"; he only rebukes those who criticize and attack the *ochlos*, including the disciples. He does not force them to proclaim him their ruler; he stands in solidarity with them. He becomes one of them. He offers them new hope by declaring the coming of God's reign.

"Jesus stands with the minjung and promises them the future of God," Ahn writes. "God's will is to side with the minjung completely and unconditionally. This notion was not comprehensible within the framework of established ethics, cult and laws. God's will is revealed in the event of Jesus being with them in which he loves the minjung."[3]

Ochlos specifically referred to sinners and tax collectors, according to Ahn. The category of marginalized Galileans would have included prostitutes, the sick, the hungry, widows, women in general, fishermen, farmers, children, and Zealots. It was thought that such people had violated the law and were therefore to be shunned. Some, because of their occupation, did not keep the legal standard of "cleanliness." Others were considered criminals because they had somehow incurred the wrath of God, and hence were made sick or widowed. Knowing full well the legal ramifications of solidarity, Ahn notes, "Jesus unconditionally embraced the alienated and despised class of his community."[4]

Jesus made what we now call a preferential option for the poor. "Jesus never showed what may be called universal love," Ahn explains. "He loved people with partiality. He always stood on the side of the oppressed, the aggrieved, and the weak."[5] Markan scholar Ched Myers, author of the acclaimed work, *Binding the Strong Man: A Political Reading of Mark's Story of Jesus,* writes, "The portrait now emerging is of a Jesus who is continually surrounded by the poor, who attends their importune cries for healing and wholeness, and who acts not just to bind up their wounds but to attack the structures that perpetuate their oppression."[6]

Jesus does not relate to the minjung as subject to object, Korean theologians suggest. He is one with them. This solidarity becomes clear early on. In Mark 3:34, Jesus declares that the people, the *ochlos*, are his mother, his brothers and sisters. His union with the poor and the oppressed surpasses the ties of blood relations.

This insight into Jesus' solidarity with the oppressed has renewed our understanding of Christian discipleship, Korean theologians suggest. Jesus was an advocate for the poor. He was totally open to their needs. So should it be with those who follow him, they assert.

"The leper, the sinner, the woman, the child are all to be received unconditionally as subjects of the kingdom," Myers writes. "Jesus teaches his disciples to live among them and look at life from their perspective. This receptivity is not based upon any inherent goodness on the part of the poor, but as a sign of Yahweh's unconditional acceptance of them as minjung."[7]

Jesus came to call the minjung into God's reign of peace. Korean theologians insist that we should do the same, for the plight of the minjung is at least as horrific in our times as in Jesus' day. Theologian King Yong-bok explains:

> Kingdoms, dynasties, and states rise and fall; but the minjung remain as a concrete reality in history, experiencing the comings and goings of political powers.... Power has its basis in the minjung. But power as it expresses itself in political powers does not belong to the minjung. These powers seek to maintain themselves; and they rule the minjung.... Women belong to the minjung when they are politically dominated by men. An ethnic group is a minjung group when it is politically dominated by another group. A race is minjung when it is dominated by another powerful ruling race. When intellectuals are suppressed by the military power elite, they belong to minjung. Of course, the same applies to the workers and farmers.[8]

The duty of every Christian is to stand in solidarity with these min-jung.

The Gospel of Mark sets a striking contrast between the way Jesus dealt with the oppressor class and the way he dealt with the oppressed. Toward the end of Mark's Gospel, Jesus encounters two stereotypical characters—the rich man (Mk. 10:17-31) and the blind beggar, who is given a name, Bartimaeus (Mk. 10:46-52) With these two divergent caricatures, Mark portrays Jesus' different approach to the rich, ruling elite and to the minjung.

The story of the rich man begins with the rich man's challenging question to Jesus and builds to Jesus' dramatic response. It takes several stages:

First, the man runs up to Jesus freely, without being stopped by the disciples, kneels down in front of Jesus, and offers a flattering compliment to Jesus, presumably expecting one in return. He poses a question, "Good teacher, what must I do to enter eternal life?" The focus of the question centered on the power of this man to act to save himself. The man tries to engage Jesus in a scholarly discussion about eternal life (as opposed to life here and now in the world).

Second, Jesus challenges the man immediately, asking, "Why do you call me good?" Then, Jesus says, "You know the command-ments," and proceeds to list several of the commandments. How-ever, Mark includes one item which is not listed in the original com-mandments, "You shall not defraud."9 Jesus is testing the rich man.

Third, the man claims to know all these commandments, and thus did not pick up Jesus' insertion of a false commandment! The reader notices Jesus' test, but Jesus makes no comment. Rather, he looks at him with love and says, in effect, "Well then, go and sell what you have and give to the poor; you will then have treasure in heaven.

After that, come and follow me." Jesus challenges him to give away everything and come and follow him.

In the end, the man goes away sad, unable to do what Jesus says, unable to follow Jesus because, we are finally told, he has many possessions. He is rich. Jesus then declares how hard it is for the rich to enter the reign of God. The disciples marvel at his words, but do not understand them. We are told that "they were completely overwhelmed at this."

The story of the blind beggar Bartimaeus is set up in an exactly opposite fashion. We read:

First, Jesus is leaving Jericho. He is about to enter Jerusalem and confront the Temple system. He knows he risks crucifixion. A blind beggar sitting by the side of the road calls out, "Jesus, Son of David, have mercy on me!" His plea recognizes Jesus as the Anointed One, and requests that Jesus take action for him, a poor blind beggar. We are told his name, "Bartimaeus," which could mean in Hebrew, "son of the unclean." This poor person acknowledges Jesus as savior, messiah, and healer. His focus is on Jesus, whereas the rich man's focus was himself.

Second, the disciples "scold" the beggar for calling out to Jesus and disturbing Jesus, but the beggar calls out even louder. The disciples do not want Jesus to be bothered by a poor, "worthless" beggar. They do not understand Jesus' solidarity with the minjung. In contrast, the rich man was allowed to walk right up to Jesus. They showed deference to the upper class.

Third, we are told that when Jesus heard the plea, he "stopped." It is significant that Jesus took action, stopped his plans, and let the blind man come to him. He did not do this for the rich man. Jesus called the beggar to come to him. Jesus shows deference to the poor.

Fourth, the disciples then encourage the beggar to come to Jesus saying, "You have nothing to fear from him. Get up. He is calling you." The disciples change their attitude because of Jesus' decision.

Fifth, the beggar drops everything to go to Jesus. Mk. 10:50 is the crux of the story. We read, "He threw aside his cloak, jumped up and came to Jesus." If he was a poor, blind beggar, then his cloak would have been the only possession he owned in the world. It probably would have lain on the ground for people passing by to throw coins on it. The cloak symbolized not only all his possessions, but his entire means of livelihood (which would have been meager at best).[10] When he was called, this beggar gave up everything he owned in an instant to follow Jesus.

Sixth, when Jesus sees this devotion and realizes what the beggar has done, he places himself completely at the service of the beggar. "What do you want me to do for you?" Jesus asks. It is the question Jesus always asks the poor. It is the attitude of God to those in need. It is an expression of solidarity and compassion. The rich man gets no such question. Such is Jesus' politics of compassion.

Seventh, the blind man declares, "Rabbi, I want to see." His request concerns his suffering here and now, not his disposition in the afterlife. From Mark's standpoint, this request for "vision" bespeaks a deep understanding of discipleship. Jesus responds, "Be on your way; your faith has healed you." Jesus does not tell the man to follow him and Jesus does not claim to have healed the man. He states rather that the poor beggar's own faith in throwing away his coat and trusting in Jesus is what has healed him. With that, Bartimaeus receives his sight immediately. It is Bartimaeus' initiative of faith which is responsible for the healing, for the vision. Jesus merely affirms the steadfast spirit of the poor person who believes.

In conclusion, Mark records, Bartimaeus started to follow Jesus "up the road." Since they were in Jericho, that road would have led to Jerusalem, where Jesus would confront the Temple system and face the consequences of crucifixion. The blind beggar realized this and without hesitating followed Jesus. He was not even invited to follow Jesus, yet he followed Jesus without hesitation. The rich man goes away sad, unable to follow Jesus; the poor man has the exactly opposite experience. The poor man follows Jesus to the cross. Jesus' solidarity with the poor evokes their solidarity with him.

The contrasts between these two episodes make a strong statement about the nature of discipleship and Jesus' relationship with and attitude toward the minjung. The story of the rich man has been misinterpreted and watered down for centuries. He is not a young man or a ruler as popularly perceived, and only after he turns away from the call to discipleship, are we told the punchline—that he is a large landowner.[11] Initially, he approaches Jesus with a request like the leper in 1:40. But we quickly learn that Mark's account of the rich man is a judgment upon the wealthy class, as the passages immediately following make clear (See Mk. 10: 23-31.) Jesus declares boldly, "The first will be last and the last will be first." (Mk. 10:31) These passages proclaim in no uncertain terms that one could not be wealthy and be a disciple at the same time.

The Bartimaeus story speaks from another point of view. The setting is the final turn before Jerusalem. All the Passover pilgrims travel this path, and would encounter blind beggars like Bartimaeus, looking for a handout. As Myers notes, the encounter is "a paradigmatic story of discipleship.... The poor join in the final assault on the dominant ideological order, and the rich have walked downcast away."[12] Myers sums up the passage:

Mark draws a devastating contrast between this beggar's initiative and the aspirations of the disciples. Upon their approach, Jesus had asked James and John, "What do you want me to do for you?" (10:36) To the beggar's petition, Jesus responds with exactly the same words. But how different the requests! The disciples wished for status and privilege; the beggar simply for his "vision." The one Jesus cannot grant, the other he can. It is Bartimaeus who is told to "take courage" (*tharsei*), as the disciples were told earlier, during their dangerous crossing of the sea (6:50). And it is the beggar who follows. The narrative discourse of hope is now clear in this last discipleship/healing episode. Only if the disciples/reader struggle against the internal demons that render us deaf and mute, only if we renounce our thirst for power—in a word, only if we recognize our blindness and seek true vision—then can the discipleship adventure carry on.[13]

Bartimaeus represents the minjung. Jesus is open and disposed to Bartimaeus and the minjung, to all those who are poor and social outcasts.

Jesus does not try to organize or motivate the minjung into a specific program for change, according to Ahn:

Jesus does not give the impression that he intends to organize the *ochlos* into a force. He does not provide a program for their movement, nor does he make them an object of his movement. He does not forcibly demand anything from them. He does not ask to be their ruler or head. He "passively" stands with them. A relationship between Jesus and the minjung takes place and then is broken. They follow him without condition. They welcome him. They also betray him. In a word, Jesus informed the minjung of the "advent of God's kingdom."[14]

As the Bartimaeus story reveals, Jesus was open and receptive to the minjung. He associated with them, to the shock and scandal of the elites in society. While I agree that Jesus walked freely among the minjung through Galilee without a specific "program," I think that through his calls to discipleship, Jesus was inviting the minjung to a specific, new, daring way of life. His "Way" was not a program, but it was a specific "way." From my reading of Mark, and the other Gospels, I believe that "way" was a steadfast commitment to nonviolence as a way of life and resistance to the powers of injustice and oppression that enslave the minjung. That meant for Jesus eventually going to the Temple and turning the tables on the culture's symbol of injustice, oppression, and imperialism. Through nonviolent resistance, Jesus was revealing God's reign to the minjung. Such news would have been eagerly received by the minjung. Jesus recruited his disciples through this call, and was open to the minjung, if they wanted to join him in the nonviolent struggle. It is because of this invitation and the possibility that the minjung might follow Jesus in nonviolent resistance—a nonviolent revolution for justice—that Jesus was arrested, tortured, and legally executed on the cross.

As Jesus walked this road of nonviolent resistance, he associated with the marginalized and voiceless, and was ostracized and criticized for this solidarity. Such solidarity in today's world breeds the same hostility and ostracism, as well as the same seeds of challenge and conversion. Such solidarity with the minjung was exemplified in the lives of the Jesuit priests and their co-workers assassinated on November 16, 1989, in San Salvador. They were killed because they sided with the poor and called for justice through a steady movement of nonviolent resistance and truth-telling.

In South Africa, the minjung are the black people, suffering under the systemic, racist oppression of apartheid. They are the masses who sing, dance, and call out "Amandla." In South Africa, blacks have suffered and been killed by the thousands under the apartheid system. To associate with them, to stand as one with them, is to follow the example of Jesus who was one with the minjung.

In the United States, the minjung suffer and cry out for God. If the historical Jesus of the minjung were alive today, he would stand with the minjung of the United States: the homeless, the hungry, people with AIDS, gays and lesbians, the elderly, prostitutes, refugees, the sick, prisoners, women, children, the mentally and physically disabled, all who are marginalized. These minjung wander aimlessly, like sheep without a shepherd, as Jesus characterized the minjung or *ochlos* of his day (Mk. 6:34). Ahn's description of Korea's minjung applies equally to the minjung of the United States:

> The minjung have the potential of liberation. We do not consider the minjung either morally or ethically "sinless," and we are not glossing over anything. We acknowledge the ordinary depravity of the minjung; ethically and morally the simple people can often be even worse than others. Yet, we have had the amazing experience again and again that among the minjung something akin to self-transcendence can occur. By this we mean especially the minjung's readiness to expend their efforts, their non-laziness and their willingness

for sacrifice. To us this is a phenomenon. We cannot analyze such occurrences according to the subject-object schema.[15]

The minjung throughout history have been open to the truth of God and the life of nonviolent love and justice for which we are created. From the creation of the world, through the times of Jesus, to the movements of the poor, oppressed, and marginalized of the world today, the minjung have been open to the good news of God, God's reign of justice and peace.

Occasionally, a prophet of peace in the tradition of Jesus comes forth from the minjung in the United States to call for justice and peace. Martin Luther King, Jr., and Dorothy Day are two such figures in the minjung movement of the United States. There are others. But the minjung continue to suffer in silence, to be pushed outside society, and in this way, to live and die in oppression. The good news of liberation and nonviolent resistance needs to be proclaimed more than ever today if the marginalized are to find hope and live.

The implications of the minjung movement for the world today challenge our culture, and all who submit to its madness, to repent and convert to the way of peace and love revealed in Jesus, the mirror of the minjung. For Christians in the United States, this will mean the slow process of entering the world of the homeless, the sick, the dying; the world of gays and lesbians, feminists and antinuclear activists; the world of the Salvadoran refugees who live here "illegally"; the world of all those who do not "fit" the image of the "all-American". Such solidarity with the minjung—at home and abroad—sows a seed of nonviolent revolution which could transform this culture and its addiction to violence into a new creation of nonviolence, equality, community, and justice. Everything will be called into question, and everything will be redeemed, as it already has been by the minjung movement of God.

---

[1]Byung Mu Ahn. "Jesus and the Minjung in the Gospel of Mark." in King Yong-Bok, (ed.) *Minjung Theology* (Singapore: The Commission on Theological Concerns, 1981), p. 136.

[2]Ched Myers. *Binding the Strong Man* (Maryknoll: Orbis Books, 1988), p. 156.

[3]Ahn, *op. cit.*, p. 150.

[4]*Ibid.*, p. 143.

[5]*Ibid.*, p. 145.

[6]Myers, *op. cit.*, p. 156.

[7]*Ibid.*, p. 440.

[8]*Ibid.*, pp. 439-440.

[9]*Ibid.*, p. 272.

[10]*Ibid.*, p. 281.

[11]*Ibid.*, p. 272.

[12]*Ibid.*, p. 281.

[13]*Ibid.*, p. 282.

[14]Ahn, *op. cit.*, p. 150.

[15]Byung Mu Ahn. "A Reply to the Theological Commission of the Protestant Association for World Mission," in Jung Young Lee, (ed.) *An Emerging Theology in World Perspective* (Mystic, Connecticut: 23rd Publishers, 1988), p. 205.

39.
A Letter to the Churches in Washington, D.C.

I, John, an apostle of Jesus the Christ and witness for the Gospel of peace and justice, to all God's beloved who are called to be saints in the churches in Washington, D.C., in God our Father and Mother and Jesus the Christ, our redeemer and our peace, Grace to you and peace from Jesus the Christ and God the Creator.

I continue to thank and bless our God for the unity in Christ, the union of hearts and minds in the faith which you show to one another and the world, and for the love of peace and life you show towards all. I give thanks to God always for you and the grace that has been bestowed upon you and which you manifest so clearly to one and all through the power of Jesus the Christ, and his cross, his way of love which you all remain so steadfastly faithful to, no matter what trial or temptation or smooth talk confronts you. God be praised for God has called you and strengthened you—though you be poor and powerless in the eyes of the world, in the eyes of the rich and powerful—to stand up and proclaim yourself a follower of the Way who is Jesus our peace and life. You know well that we have all been saved by the power of God in Jesus the Christ; that is, that we are already one, all redeemed, all equal, all brothers and sisters now in the new peace with justice bestowed on us through this abundant grace which is life in the Gospel. You have not renounced the Gospel I preached to you, which you received not from me but from the saints and martyrs through the ages, and thus directly from Jesus the Christ.

I write to strengthen you in your struggle against all the forces of division and hostility, all the powers and principalities of this world, which you know well, that beset you with every trial and tribulation, blocking the vision of the Gospel—the peace which God has given to us in Christ Jesus—from becoming real in our hearts and lives and world. For truly, we are already one; we are all equal. We are all brothers and sisters in Jesus Christ, and in the light of this grace and peace, we see every human being as our very own sister and brother, a child of God, called to be in the peace of God and at peace with one another in the love and justice of God. You recall the words of the apostle Paul, in his letter to the churches in Galatia, near the time of Jesus, that "in Christ Jesus, you are all daughters and sons of God, through faith. For as many of you as were baptized into Christ have put on Christ." (Gal. 3:26-28) He continued to state, in effect, that there is neither Jew nor Gentile; there is neither slave nor free; there is neither black nor white; there is neither rich nor poor; there is neither male nor female; there is neither Catholic nor Protestant; there is neither cleric nor lay person; there is neither gay nor straight; there is neither young nor old: "for you are all one in Christ Jesus." In your own city, you heard the words preached to you years ago by the apostle of peace and justice, the prophet and martyr for the Gospel, our brother Martin Luther King, Jr., who spoke of his dream of the new creation in peace:

> I have a dream that my four children will one day live in a nation where they will not be judged by the color of their skin but by the content of their character.... that one day little black boys and black girls will be able to join hands with

little white boys and white girls as sisters and brothers;... that one day every valley shall be exalted, every hill and mountain shall be made low, the rough places shall be made plain, and the crooked places shall be made straight and the glory of the Lord will be revealed and all flesh shall see it together.... When we allow freedom to ring from every village and hamlet, from every state and city, we will be able to speed up that day when all of God's children—blacks and whites, Jews and Gentiles, Protestants and Catholics—will be able to join hands and to sing in the words of the old Negro spiritual, "Free at last, free at last; thank God Almighty, we are free at last."

I remind you of these words and this Gospel vision of peace given to us first by Jesus because, as you well know, you live in division, separated along lines which Christ has already broken down, yet which you still uphold—and not only you, but the nation as well. I do not like the reports I hear from Washington, D.C., how the racial division has flared up even more, how your communities have failed to unite everyone beyond mere differences in the color of human skin.

You may not realize it but your city is really two cities with a Berlin wall between them: one city, the land of the powerful, the rich, dominated by white men; the other city, one block away, another world of terrible poverty, abandoned houses, murder, violence, addiction, hunger, homelessness, illiteracy, poor health care—and all divided according to the color of skin. This is not the Gospel! This is contrary to the Gospel of our Lord Jesus Christ, who reconciled us all by the blood of the cross. How can you continue to flock to your churches on Sundays and yet live the rest of the week in two camps, failing to practice the Gospel of reconciliation which you know in your baptized hearts to be true and just. You cannot continue to live like this, for this division makes a mockery of your faith and your witness. I know that some of you have turned over your lives to enter into Christ's reconciliation between our black and white sisters and brothers. The rest of you should learn from them, how we are all one, how racism is the spirit of the evil one who seeks to divide the Body of Christ on earth, here and now. I have heard reports from some of you regarding the schism that you have begun, how some of our black, Afro-American sisters and brothers have left the churches to begin their own community, where they will look after their own people and worship in their own Afro-American liturgy. I understand this well, for too long have our Afro-American sisters and brothers suffered under a white reign within our own communities: this, too, is contrary to the Gospel that was preached to you. I commend their boldness in confronting the issue of racism and exposing the racism within your communities for all the world to see, and I am deeply pained by the blindness that is revealed. Please, I beg you then, as a servant of Jesus and brother to you all, to rededicate yourselves to the task of breaking the racial barriers that separate you, uniting with each other, and being the one body that you are, that Jesus prayed that you would be. Let all others elsewhere who hear this word commit themselves as well to the racial justice which the Gospel insists upon for us all.

Similarly, I hear reports of your divisions along economic lines, how they have not only increased, but caused more violence than ever; how the have-nots have no place among the haves, as Paul would say; how some 15,000 homeless walk your streets while many of you have two and three homes; how the powerful among you do not stoop to help the powerless in their struggle just to survive—much less join them in that struggle of life, as our Lord Jesus Christ did. We have all heard, for example, how the US Catholic Bishops' Conference opened their new spacious offices near Capitol Hill, a building complex which cost some $23 million. In light of the sufferings of the poor who stand among you and walk your streets, this construction is a scandal to all the faithful, a stumbling block to all who should rightly find a home among us. I have heard how a small number of sisters and brothers vigiled outside the building at its grand opening, calling for the use of the building as a shelter for the poor in the evenings. I commend their request to you, and recall the exhortation the early Jerusalem community gave to Paul, that you should at all times "remember the poor," which he said was "the very thing I was eager to do." (Gal. 2:10)

These matters are at the heart of our faith. Not that we are justified by works alone, for surely God has saved us all through faith in Jesus Christ. And yet, we do make a lie out of that faith if we do not then proceed to live according to the Gospel of Jesus, and the Gospel is clearer than most of us are willing to admit. Do you not recall the teachings of Jesus? "Sell your possessions, and give alms; provide yourselves with purses that do not grow old, with a treasure in the heavens that does not fail, where no thief approaches and no moth destroys. For where you treasure is, there will your heart be also." (Lk. 12:33-34) Or elsewhere, when Jesus said to the rich man, "Sell all that you have and distribute to the poor, and you will have treasure in heaven; and come, follow me." (Lk.18:22) With the parables of the man who helped the Good Samaritan (Lk. 10:29-37), and the poor man Lazarus who went to heaven while the rich man did not, (Lk. 16:19-31) the Gospels exhort us to side with the poor, as God in Christ did. Our lives in Christ need to be at the service of all, especially the poor among us, so that they may have decent food, clothing, shelter, education, and medicine to live now fully in God's reign as Christ wants them to.

I have heard, too, how refugees from Central America, especially El Salvador, who flock to the city, continue to be turned away and arrested by the police and shipped back to El Salvador, where they face certain imprisonment and execution. The Salvadoran and Central American people who flee for their lives are our brothers and sisters, Christ come to us in disguise. Do not reject them, for in rejecting them, you reject Christ. Show your love and faith by welcoming them into your churches, homes, and lives. Your reward will be great, not only in the life to come, but here and now, as you will discover the risen Lord in them, in their faith and joy, which is the most profound I have ever experienced in all my travels.

By neglecting the poverty which the poor in your own midst suffer, you aid and abet the violence which runs rampant in your city, the capital of the nation, and the nation itself. For the poor who turn to drugs and guns, who kill themselves and each other on your city streets, do so because they do not have the opportunities that the rest of us have. First of all, they suffer in terrible housing, if they have any; their futures look bleak. They do not have the hope of faith that means the pursuit of God's kingdom "on earth as it is in heaven"; rather, they turn to the easy money that can be made selling drugs, even if that means killing others. Life is cheap because violence is cheap. Your nonviolence must make life precious again.

You cannot keep worshiping in your churches without addressing the suffering and despair which is all around you, in blacks and whites. Some of you need to stop and become sober yourselves, through programs for alcoholics and drug addicts anonymous, and from there, seek to rescue the lives of your sisters and brothers who still suffer these addictions.

Finally, you need to address the city's addiction as a whole to violence and death. Those of you who hold government positions cannot expect the people on the streets to stop their violence while you wage war against the poor of Central America, the Philippines, and elsewhere. You cannot expect people to put down their guns while you are set to the pull the trigger of the nuclear weapon which you hold aimed at the heart of the entire planet. You who claim to be followers of Christ, who continue to wage war and threaten to use nuclear weapons on anyone anywhere—whether you work at the White House, the Pentagon, the Capitol, the Department of Energy, the Central Intelligence Agency, or the Naval Surface Warfare Center—you are mistaken and are not following the Way of the Gospel, the way of peace. Have you forgotten the words of Jesus, as he was taken to his death? "Put down your sword. Those who live by the sword shall die by the sword." (Mt. 26:52) If you continue to use violence, and make violence your way of life, you will die by violence and bring violence to others. Christ, on the other hand, offers the way of peace as a new way of life. If you live by the peace of Christ, you shall live forever, and bring life to others, even those who suffer the violence of war and poverty, in your own city and around the world.

Christ has saved us through love, and his death on the cross was a manifestation of his love. He loved us, and thus resisted our addictions to violence and death. We killed him legally for his loving resistance, his civil disobedience and divine obedience; but now in the light of the resurrection and in his Spirit which he has given us all, we know the way of love for ourselves and are called to live it and manifest it with our whole lives, even unto death in the pursuit of justice for all.

We can no longer support the systems of death from the centers of power in Washington, D.C., unless those who work there renounce violence and manifest love. We need to transform those systems into programs of service through true nonviolence. But it is by their very nature that they are violent and deadly. Thus, we are in a spiritual war with these powers and our weapon is the truth shown in a spirit of love which is becoming contagious, bringing about the kingdom of God in our midst, something which is already here if we have eyes to see it.

In this light, remember the words of our Savior, who said: "You know that those who are supposed to rule over the Gentiles lord it over them, and their great men exercise authority over them. But it shall not be so among you; but whoever would be great among you must be your servant, and whoever would be first among you must be slave of all. For the [Human One] also came not to be served but to serve, and to give his life as a ransom for many." (Mark 10:42-45) To this end, not only can you no longer partake of the structures of violence, represented by the Pentagon, but you cannot support the clericalism and patriarchy that plague our churches as a whole, for Christ did not come to set up and affirm old standing systems of oppression, but to tear down all the walls of division that have ever existed. If we are to be the faithful disciples that we are called to be, we cannot let any form of domination enter into our lives. I am very grateful for the work of the Women's Ordination Conference in Washington, D.C., which has dedicated itself to removing every trace of domination and patriarchy within the Catholic Church.

We are called to be servants of all. In our society today, the way to do that is to associate with the lowly, the outcasts, the marginalized, the homeless, the hungry, the poor, as Jesus did in his day. I beg you to do this with your lives, as you have learned from the Gospel.

These are points I do not make lightly. You know I have labored to live the Gospel for many years, and have suffered through nearly three dozen arrests and jailings around the country for demonstrating against our addiction to violence and death. You know well my life among the poor, on the streets of D.C., with the homeless, the hungry, and the Central American refugees; as well as in Central America, in a Salvadoran refugee camp, a daily witness of the US bombings there. I have been a prisoner for the Lord, and suspect that I shall be again, so that the Gospel of peace and justice may be furthered and proclaimed anew throughout the country, just as our brother Martin Luther King, Jr., and our sister Dorothy Day labored to bring forth the vision of Christ anew in reality for the poor, for the oppressed, and also for oppressors.

Be transformed in the peacemaking vision of the Gospel of Jesus! That is my prayer and hope for all of you. I have been transformed in Christ and continue to swim the deep waters of peacemaking which keep transforming my life. This is a great grace, given to us in the Gospel of Jesus Christ. Would that this grace would spread into the consciousness of the world, as it has already into every heart.

My greetings of peace and joy to all the brothers and sisters who continue to witness to the peace of Christ, especially to all at the Dorothy Day Catholic Worker Community, to the Olive Branch Catholic Worker Community, to the Sojourners Community, to all at St. Aloysius' Church, especially George Anderson, to the K Street Jesuit Community, and to the sisters at the Sursum Corda Community. I write this in my own hand, from Oakland, California, where I have come for a short while to listen and learn and minister, having been led here by the Spirit of God. I shall return shortly.

May the God of peace come and grant you every blessing to your life witness; and may your spirit and soul and heart be kept strong in the vision of peace and justice which resists every form of violence and evil. Keep me in your prayers and hearts, as I surely do keep you in my prayers and heart. I am with you all in the Spirit.

The grace of our Lord Jesus Christ be with your spirit, sisters and brothers. May we all dwell in Christ's peace and justice, now and forever. Amen.

Epilogue:
Seeds of Nonviolence in the Day of Violence,
A Diary Kept During the Persian Gulf War

The just-war theory should be filed in the same drawer that contains the flat-earth theory.

Bishop Carroll Dozier

Darkness covers the whole of humanity.

John Paul II
Holy Week, 1991,
after the Persian Gulf War

Wednesday morning, January 16, 1991

At midnight, the US "deadline" for war with Iraq, the United Nations' permission for the US to wage war, passed. Now, we sit, holding our breath, hoping and praying for a miracle of peace, that war will not break out.

This is a very dark moment in the history of the world. Unfortunately, and in many ways, it was to be expected. With 60,000 nuclear weapons in the world, with the world deeply divided by greedy, consumeristic, militaristic societies, even empires, this moment, as we hang on the brink of war, is the natural consequence of such worldwide violence.

I have been out speaking at churches in the San Francisco Bay Area, calling people to pray for peace, trying to spark a spirit of nonviolent love for all the people of the Persian Gulf, especially our "enemies," the Iraqis. Yesterday, I joined tens of thousands of people who took to the streets in the San Francisco Bay Area to protest this impending war. We shut down the Federal Building and blocked streets. Some folks even closed the Bay Bridge connecting Oakland and San Francisco. The message that we do not want war was strong and was heard around the world, but there is such a spirit of anger and violence in the crowd, that I fear the addiction to violence in the American people is about to be unleashed, even and especially in young people calling for peace. We may yet learn how deep is our violence, how deep is our division, and how deep is our need for conversion to the Spirit of nonviolence.

As our poor, broken world hangs on the precipice of war, one can imagine the God of peace looking down on us with great sadness, seeing all the masses of starving and poor people, and now the nations lining up for war. God has tried to teach us the way of peace through the Scriptures, through the life of the Christ, and the lives of the saints and peacemakers, but we have always been slow to respond. When one looks at history, and then at today's news, it is clear that we are addicted to violence and death as our way of solving problems. We prefer war to peace.

I think of Jesus these days and how meaningful his words and life are before the world, even though they are so ignored or misunderstood. Here is someone dedicated to justice and peace, someone not addicted to violence, someone who is sober, someone who is nonviolent, a true peacemaker. God must surely have been pleased with Jesus the peacemaker. So many claim to be his followers, yet these same people speak of "just wars" and the need to "annihilate Iraq." The words of Jesus still speak to us today: "Love your enemies, love one another, thou shalt not kill. Do not wage war; do not prepare for war. Be peacemakers. Let the people who have never waged war be the first to drop a bomb. Be perfectly nonviolent and loving to all people, just like God."

Jesus lived a life of peacemaking. He told the truth, practiced nonviolence and spoke up and criticized society when it went against God's ways. His message was not well received, and so he was executed, a victim of capital punishment. And yet, as we know, God vindicated God's chosen servant. God raised Jesus, who then went about calling people to live a life of peacemaking, to be sons and daughters of God.

I am convinced by my reading of the Gospels, no matter what other church leaders say, that God does not support war either by George Bush and the Americans or by Saddam Hussein and the Iraqis or for that matter, the Israelis, Saudis, Salvadorans or anyone.

For God, war itself is the enemy. War is never the solution. War is never the answer. For God, there is no victory in war; there are no victors in war. Violence only begets violence. There is no such thing as a just war. God wants us all to live together in peace, as fellow human beings, as brothers and sisters, children of our loving God.

Jesus calls us to the truth that all life is sacred; that we are all brothers and sisters; that war is immoral, wrong, and evil; that we do not have to kill; that we can oppose violence and injustice through nonviolent means; that the options for peace can never be exhausted; that we can, for example, nonviolently oppose the Iraqi government's takeover of Kuwait; that indeed, we can love our enemies.

Love your enemies, Jesus says. This Scripture is Jesus' answer to the question of war. It is Jesus' prayer for peace. Jesus prays that we will love our enemies, that we may all be one, that there will be no war. His prayer is an invitation for us to become a disarmed people, people with disarmed hearts, peacemakers.

This call to love is very important to keep in mind as we pray for peace in these days of war in the Persian Gulf. We are a people who pledge to keep the hard commands of Jesus, a people who love our enemies. When we come together in prayer for peace, we come to put that message of love into practice.

Jesus always advocates nonviolent love, that exceptional, total, sacrificial, non-retaliatory, unconditional love for all people. Thus, even if the whole world goes to war, I must still try to love my enemies. I will still oppose war. I will nonviolently resist evil and stand up to oppression and injustice, but I will never kill anyone, nor will I advocate killing or war. I shall make his words my own so that they sink into my heart and take root there for all the world. The time for killing is over. We are all reconciled. It is time for us to see every human being as our very own brother or sister. I pray that the scales may fall from our eyes, even in this crisis; that we may put away the whole concept of war, and vow never to wage war again.

It is very important, in these days ahead, that I remain rooted in this love of God, this love for all people, including our enemies. As these days unfold, as I watch the news, I must continue to pray for peace, and be rooted in love for everyone. If I find myself praying, somewhere in my heart, that our troops will win and kill the Iraqis, I am not praying in the spirit of Jesus.

Imagine, as Mark Twain did in his "War Prayer", God listening to the prayers of the world, listening to Christians in the United States praying for their side to win and Muslims in Iraq praying for their side to win. In God's eyes, we are all one, all equal, all God's children. God does not want us to kill one another. God wants us to dwell in peace and nonviolent love together.

With Jesus' command that we love our enemies, we realize that God wants us to pray for peace by praying for everyone, the Americans, the Iraqis, the Saudis, the Kuwaitis, the Israelis, and the Palestinians; to pray that there will be no war, that we may all be spared the horrors of war, and come to our senses. We are to pray for peace with love in our hearts for the Iraqis. We are to walk as peacemakers calling for peace with a love for all people rooted deep within our spirits.

If God hears us praying for each other around the world in a deep spirit of love; if God hears us praying especially for the Iraqis; then indeed the Holy Spirit of God, the Spirit of peace, will be unleashed in the world and reach out and touch even the hearts of George Bush and Saddam Hussein. Only then will war be stopped. This is our hope. Prayer rooted in love for one's enemies is a powerful weapon indeed.

If we are going to set out to love our enemies, if we are going to be followers of Jesus, if we are going to be peacemakers, indeed, if we are going to beg God for a miracle of peace, then we must first disarm our own hearts, put away all the hatred, violence, and anger inside of us, hand it over to God, and allow God to fill us with God's spirit of unconditional love. We can't ask for peace and be filled with hatred, violence, and anger. We can't ask for peace and be filled with violence and war in our own hearts and personal lives.

As part of my prayer for peace, I must try to reconcile with everyone I know. I must try to forgive those who have hurt me and seek forgiveness, loving everyone I come in contact with, and thus truly build peace around me from now on. Then, I can pray for the grace to truly love the so-called "enemies" of the United States, in this case, the people of Iraq. Then, along with others, I can send a spiritual signal to God and the people of Iraq that we are serious in our prayer for peace. We want peace; and to show that we are serious, we will reconcile our own lives, heal the divisions in our lives, forgive others and seek forgiveness, and love everyone around us, so that this great love, the love of God, will spread like a ripple of peaceful water around the world.

In this spirit, I find hope. I can be united and centered in prayer; I can trust in God and know that God has heard our prayers. In this spirit, I can continue to pray always, as St. Paul says, for peace. In this spirit, I can dedicate my life truly to the Gospel message of peacemaking, and decide once and for all, that I am going to become like Jesus, a peacemaker, a nonviolent person. In this spirit, I can encourage young people to become conscientious objectors. In this spirit, I can risk arrest in nonviolent civilly disobedient protest and go to jail. In this spirit, I can take to the streets and march for peace, as a loving, nonviolent person who, like Jesus, speaks out publicly and says NO to war, saying with others that we do not want our friends, relatives and fellow Americans killed; nor do we want the Iraqis, Kuwaitis, Saudis, or Israelis killed. In this spirit, we can all walk with Jesus as he tries to make peace in the hearts of the people of the world.

O God, give us hearts of love, disarmed hearts that love those around us, hearts of love that go beyond the borders of our nation into the hearts of all people everywhere, especially the people of Iraq and the Persian Gulf. Help us to love our enemies in practice, and give us eyes to see you in the face of our enemies. Help us to see all people as our very brothers and sisters. Help us to know, now and forever, that we are all one, your beloved children. Enlighten the minds and fill the hearts of George Bush and Saddam Hussein with the power of your creative love. Guide their actions so that all civilians and soldiers in the gulf area are protected from the sufferings of war. Inspire their decisions so that this crisis in the Middle East may still be resolved peacefully. May we live in peace as brothers and sisters with each other; may the day come when we will never go to war again. O God, grant us a miracle of peace. May Your reign of nonviolence come soon, O God. Amen.

Wednesday evening, January, 16, 1991

At 3:50 p.m., the news came from a friend that the United States has begun a massive bombing raid of Iraq. Surely, many people have been killed already. Who knows how long, how awful this insanity will continue, now that it has been unleashed.

I went to a scheduled meeting of religious organizers to plan a response to the action, where I found everyone, like myself, deeply saddened, in shock, feeling betrayed by their country. We planned prayer services in the churches, and all agreed to meet tomorrow morning for the nonviolent demonstration at the Federal Building in San Francisco to protest the US war. We also began to organize a religious funeral procession for this Friday, which will start at the Catholic Cathedral and proceed down one of the main thoroughfares to the Army headquarters, the Presidio, near the Golden Gate Bridge, where waves of people will come forward to kneel down and risk arrest for an end to the war.

After this meeting, I traveled to the San Jose Mission Church in Fremont, where some fifty people had gathered to start a new chapter of Pax Christi USA, the national Catholic peace movement. We shared our sorrow and pain on this dark night of war, as well as our hopes that this mustard seed community could blossom and bear the fruit of peace for people in the Bay Area.

As I go to bed and prepare for a long day tomorrow, reports come in over the radio of further air raids and bombings in Iraq, and rioting by demonstrators at this late hour in San Francisco. The Bay Bridge has been closed again by the demonstrators and the police are beating people with clubs to get them off the bridge.

It is a day of sorrow, and I have the sad feeling that it is just the beginning.

I come before Jesus on the cross tonight in my prayer and I look at him with eyes of love as he dies once again. In this image, I see Jesus dying under the US bombs in the people of Iraq. May God forgive us. May the fighting stop. May we repent of the killings.

Thursday evening, January 17, 1991

A long, awful, beautiful day. The news tonight is dreadful: Iraq has bombed Israel. There were rumors that Iraq had even dropped chemical weapons on Tel Aviv and Haifa. At the very least, these bombs destroyed several buildings and injured many people. But certainly the war has expanded. We are on the verge of World War III, although nobody is saying it. Today brings to light the old truth: violence only begets violence. An eye for an eye only ends up making the whole world blind.

I left my community house at 5:00 a.m. to join the demonstrations at the Federal Building in downtown San Francisco. More than 8000 people came out onto the streets to march and sit in at the doorways. Most were peaceful and nonviolent, but there was tension in the air. Last night, demonstrators marched again onto the Bay Bridge, and this time, turned violent. They torched one police car which exploded in a ball of fire. Such violence not only discredits the growing anti-war movement, but threatens the lives of the demonstrators and police officers. Someone easily could have been killed.

To counteract this violent anger, some 300 religious activists gathered in a large circle, holding hands, at the corner of the Federal Building this morning. We prayed, we sang, we knelt, we preached, we cried. Then, we walked hand in hand to the next street corner. It continued like this all morning as we encircled the Federal Building, singing and praying in front of the thousands of angry, bitter, anti-war demonstrators. The effect of our prayers and songs was immediate. The crowds became noticeably silent, then joined in our songs, then gave us a round of applause before we moved on. A powerful experience of nonviolence and prayer aimed at an unruly, potentially violent crowd. Our action may have helped calm the mob; the police (and the press) thanked us afterwards.

Finally, at 11:00 a.m., we came to one side of the building where violence was about to break out between one group of demonstrators and the police. We approached the crowd and the police line as they faced each other in the middle of the street. Just as we came forward in song, the police threatened to tear gas, Mace and beat people. One contingent had already been Maced a few blocks over. All of a sudden, the hundreds of demonstrators crowded just ahead of us turned around, and in a wild moment of panic, started to run toward and through us. Our group of three hundred religious folks immediately knelt down and started singing. Our gesture calmed the crowd and people stopped running. I went up and spoke with the sergeant in charge, and told him we were trying to keep the crowd peaceful and nonviolent, and that he need not use violence on us because we were determined to keep everyone calm.

And so, we knelt and eventually sat down in the street. A line of police officers appeared behind us and we were boxed in. With helicopters flying over us, and scores of TV cameras and reporters surrounding us, we continued to sing, kneel, and offer words of peace against the war. At noon, the arrests began. I was arrested by an officer who ran up to the sergeant in charge and asked if he could arrest me. Since I was dressed in clerical garb, I attracted some attention. The officer handcuffed me and with a smile, asked where I came from. When he heard I was a Jesuit, he broke into a grin. "I graduated from a Jesuit high school!" he exclaimed. He then proceeded to list all his Jesuit friends. "This is a great moment for me," he said, "to arrest a Jesuit." I said something feeble like, "Well, I'm glad to meet you, but you do not have to arrest me. Why don't you join us in the protest against the war?"

Before I could get his name, I was pushed into a cramped police van where I spent the afternoon talking with the other demonstrators, a beautiful hodgepodge from punk-rockers to prim grandmothers, all against the US war, all for peace through nonviolence. We were taken to the basement garage of a nearby police station, and fenced in cages for up to 200 people each.

Subsequently, we learned that the police arrested 1087 people today—the largest arrest in the history of San Francisco. And there was no mention of this day of protest on any of the major network newscasts. It is becoming abundantly clear that the media have given the full weight of their support to President Bush and the Pentagon for this war. The television news broadcasts whatever the Pentagon says, without any critical analysis. There is no mention that people are taking to the streets by the thousands across the nation. There is no reporting on the number of Iraqis killed. No one questions the morality—the immorality—of this war.

While I was being booked by the police, I was asked if I had heard the news: Israel had been attacked by Iraq. I left the police station in shock and sadness. All the way home on the subway, I prayed that the God of peace might give us strength for the days ahead and help us to speak out to help end the war.

Tonight, I'm gathering my strength to take to the streets again tomorrow for our religious demonstration.

May God have mercy on us all and help us put an end to this war. May we renounce violence and embrace God's way of peace.

Friday evening, January 18, 1991

An exhilarating day, given the fact that the world is at war. After a long meeting of religious peace activists from around the Bay Area, several hundred church people gathered in prayer on the steps of St. Mark's Church in downtown San Francisco to grieve and mourn the loss of life, to pray for an end to the war. Then, we processed across town to the Presidio, the West Coast Army and Reserve Officers headquarters.

Our prayer was somber, but imbued with a spirit of peace and love. The opening plea expressed our deep sentiments as our nation rushes ahead to war:

> O God, we gather today to mourn the deaths of our brothers and sisters who have died in the Persian Gulf because of this war—the people of Iraq, the US soldiers who have been killed since the preparations for war began, and the people of Kuwait and elsewhere. We mourn the loss of all those who will die because of this senseless tragedy, this horrible war. We are filled with sorrow for all those who have been injured, including the people of Israel, Iraq, Kuwait, Saudi Arabia, and the United States. We are filled with sorrow at this war, at the insanity of this commitment to killing and bombing, this feast of death. We support and love all people in the Persian Gulf. We love our fellow Americans who are in Saudi Arabia. We also love the Iraqis, Kuwaitis, Israelis, Palestinians, and all the people of the region. We want the war to stop. We come here to mourn. We come here to take to the streets this afternoon in a funeral procession, to grieve

for the loss of life and the loss of the soul of our nation and the nations of the Persian Gulf as they continue to rush ahead with war, instead of pursuing your way of peace and nonviolence. O God, we want peace. We want your gift of peace. We pray for peace in our world, and we do so in a spirit of nonviolent love toward all people, including the people of Iraq, Kuwait, Saudi Arabia and Israel. Send us your Spirit of peace, that we may walk in a spirit of peace, and together, with you and one another, find hope and strength to continue to witness to our world your way of peace and nonviolent love. Be with us now as we hear your word. And hear our prayer that the fighting may stop, the killing will end, that a day will come when there will be no more mourning and more more war. Amen.

We read from the Hebrew Scriptures, the Koran, the Christian Scriptures, and in particular, Mark's account of the crucifixion of Jesus. "At noon," Mark writes, "darkness fell over the whole land until three in the afternoon." Such was the feeling of darkness today.

We sang a hymn, then began our procession across town. We were Christians, Jews, and Muslims, people of faith and people of peace. In the spirit and tradition of Dr. Martin Luther King, Jr., and the civil-rights movement, we knelt in silent prayer every fifteen minutes along the way, staying centered and calmed, prayerful and nonviolent.

Finally, we arrived at the Presidio to find a wall of young Marines holding three-foot clubs, waiting for us, just on the other side of a police barricade. We knelt again in prayer, and prayed aloud for peace, for them, for all humanity, that we might find a way to live together as one. While prayers continued, some fifty of us, still carrying crosses, moved to the back of the crowd and slipped down a side street of the residential neighborhood until we came to a low wall marking the Presidio property. Only two Marines were guarding the wall, so we calmly climbed over it and immediately knelt down again to pray the Lord's Prayer. Marines came running down hills from every direction and formed a line right in front of us, holding their clubs aloft. We started singing "We shall overcome," again, adding the verses, "We shall live in peace," "We are not afraid," "We'll walk hand in hand," and "Love will overcome." The young Marine woman who gave the order for us to disperse was visibly shaken when we did not leave but continued to kneel and sing. Eventually, they began to arrest and handcuff us, one by one. As we took turns speaking to the Marines, they calmed down and realized we were a peaceful group. By the end of the day, they were joking and laughing with us—even as we urged them to search their consciences and to refuse to support the war.

This evening brings more reports of new Iraqi raids on Israel. The Pentagon claims to have organized the largest bombing campaign since World War II, with 18,000 tons of bombs dropped on Iraq in the first hours of the war alone.

I go to bed with a prayer for peace and heartfelt gratitude for our prayerful procession through the streets. We did what we could. We sent a message to the city, the nation, and the world that people of faith oppose this war. May our voice be heard and heeded.

Saturday, January 19, 1991

This morning, I awoke to reports of the war. The fighting has intensified (if that was possible), and a general has announced that the "campaign" was only beginning. Tel Aviv has been bombed and everyone fears that Israel will retaliate.

I write this as I head out the door for another day of peacemaking in the streets. Major peace demonstrations are set to occur around the country, with the largest in Washington, D.C., New York, and San Francisco. We are trying to send a signal to the White House and the war department that this war is not fought in our names, that we do not approve of the bombings, that we still want negotiations and peace. And yet, it is abundantly clear to all of us that we are well into a major war. Our role now is to resist it—actively, nonviolently, publicly. We must break the silence which is betrayal. We must question the whole bloody business of this war. We must shatter the public perception that this war is moral or justified. It is neither. It is the abomination of desolation.

Another long but glorious day. Some 100,000 people walked through the city of San Francisco today, calling for an end to the war, calling for peace, calling for an end to the insanity. A peaceful, nonviolent, disciplined, militant, loving protest. A strong message to the war machine that many people do not want this war to continue.

And yet the war continues. The US carpet bombing has turned from attacking the Iraqi military installations, to bombing the Iraqi soldiers themselves. The cost in human life will be in the thousands, perhaps the hundreds of thousands. Iraq has attacked Israel again. The world holds its breath as we await the further consequences of this addiction to violence.

Sunday, January 20, 1991

A cover-up of worldwide proportions is playing out before our eyes on the television screens. We are being told that the largest bombing operation in the history of the world is under way. So far, some nine young men from the United States have died or been captured. But what of the Iraqis? Not a word. It is as if they do not exist. As if the bombs fall on sand. Perhaps thousands upon thousands of people have been killed in the past few days. I tremble when I think of such things.

The largest bombing raid in the history of the world! What does that mean? I cannot comprehend it. I cannot comprehend the meaning of one bomb, much less Hiroshima or Nagasaki. Now, the bombing of Iraq. I cannot comprehend how such accomplishments are proclaimed with such pride by the network newscasters, as if this bombing raid were something to rejoice in, as if this war effort were something to brag about. But, few public figures dare even raise an eyebrow of doubt.

Indeed, the president was "jubilant," almost gleeful, when he announced on television last week that the war had begun. It seemed to me that he had to keep from smiling from his excitement. What kind of people have we become? How can we get out of the predicament we have placed ourselves in? How can we as a people turn to the God of peace?

A morning meeting in San Francisco to help plan the upcoming march this Saturday, January 26. Lots of work to do. Many good people of every variety and background coming together to walk and speak out a message of peace, in hope that this war will be stopped. Later, another meeting, this time in Berkeley, with some friends from various churches, to plan a weekly response by the churches. We discussed a candlelight procession through the city of Oakland to be held next week.

Tonight, reports that Iraq has bombed Dahran and Riyadh.

O God, guide me during these days of war that I might hasten your day of peace.

Monday, January 21, 1991

Today is the official birthday holiday of Dr. Martin Luther King, Jr. And yet, as with all prophets of peace, he is ignored. No one in the government acknowledges him, mentions him by name, invokes his spirit. Indeed, the war was set to begin on his birthday, a deliberate insult to the legend of Dr. King. The news proceeds as usual: "War, war, war. It's going great."

My thoughts and prayers turn to Dr. King. I hear the voice of God in his word to me. His life gives me strength to witness and proclaim the good news of peace, the Way of nonviolence. Dr. King's life demonstrates to me how I too can be a Christian, a peacemaker, in a time of war.

I have been rereading his speeches and books during these days, to gather strength for the days ahead. "A nation that continues year after year to spend more money on military defense than on programs of social uplift is approaching spiritual death," he declared in his famous speech calling for an end to the war in Vietnam. "Let us rededicate ourselves to the long and bitter—but beautiful—struggle for a new world. This is the calling of the sons and daughters of God, and our brothers and sisters wait eagerly for our response."

What would Dr. King say today? He would be calling for the end to the war with Iraq, and preaching a message of nonviolence, unconditional love and peacemaking. He would be traveling across the nation, organizing the churches to take to the streets in a mass movement of nonviolent resistance to transform the nation from its addiction to war to the sober life of peace with justice. I want to continue his work. Not only do I want to end this insane war, I want to help speed up the day of transformation, when we all embrace the love of Christ in our hearts, when we are born again as a people, as Dr. King said, when we agree to beat swords into plowshares and study war no more.

Tuesday, January 22, 1991

Iraq continues to fire missiles into Saudi Arabia, and the Pentagon claims to have shot them all down. Saddam has broadcast interviews with three captured US pilots whose planes were shot down. Meanwhile, no word about the sufferings of the Iraqi people themselves. Both sides lie and cover up their violence. Aeschylus was right: the first casualty in war is the truth. But I recall the words of Dr. King: No lie can live forever.

Religious leaders from around the country gathered in Washington, D.C., today at the invitation of Pax Christi to pray and speak out for peace. They met at St. Aloysius' Church and then walked to the US Capitol, where some knelt in silent prayer for peace and risked arrest.

This evening, one Iraqi bomb landed in suburban Tel Aviv, killing three people and injuring ninety-six people. The Israelis have pledged to retaliate with a bombing raid of their own. The Iraqis have set three oil refineries on fire. Ecologists say these oil fields could burn smoke into the sky indefinitely, because the war will permit oil supplies to surge to the surface fire. Who knows the ecological disaster this alone will bring to us? Throughout all this, the US bombardment of Iraq continues. Reports are beginning to emerge describing the destruction of Iraq, the many civilians killed, the loss of all water supplies, and the destruction of all plumbing systems in the cities. The war department is beginning to say we're in this for "the long haul." Coretta Scott King has called for an immediate cease-fire. The Pope has asked that the fighting cease. Their pleas go unheeded.

For me, these days are an experience of powerlessness. The powerful powerlessness of the crucified Christ! On the one hand, there is nothing I can do to end the war. I cannot speak to those in power who are waging this war and convince them of its insanity. On the other hand, I can offer myself to God to be an instrument of peace. I can act for peace as the Spirit moves me, whether by fasting and prayer, organizing demonstrations, writing and speaking out publicly, and risking arrest in nonviolent direct action at military installations, or by a combination of all these. The main thing is to discern God's will and to speak the truth—publicly, boldly, without fear—to register our extreme dissent with this nation's policies, and our obedience to the God of peace.

I am powerless and I am not powerless. I am helpless and not helpless. As Dr. King says, "We have a power greater than atomic bombs and Molotov cocktails: the power of nonviolence as a corrective for peace and justice in the world." May that power of nonviolence, rooted in a deep and humble love, move us more deeply towards the end of this war and the transformation of our world.

Wednesday, January 23, 1991

The Pentagon has succeeded in covering up the war so that day-to-day life goes on as usual. We are not in World War III, they say.

Yes, this is war, but we are not going to give body counts or the numbers of Iraqis killed; we need not be concerned with that. Saddam is evil and must be destroyed, they say; some are calling for his assassination. Do what you are told; go about your business; don't worry about the war, we'll handle that. Trust us, the Pentagon officials say.

And so we slide down the slippery slope of violence, the never-ending spiral of hatred, anger, bitterness, bombings, murder, and suffering.

War fever has hit the nation, but at the same time, the numbness is shocking. Perhaps when the US body bags start coming home, there will be a change of opinion. But one gets the eerie feeling that even body bags will not wake this sleeping nation. We seem to have forgotten the lessons learned from the horrors of the Vietnam War. Perhaps the nation is not asleep. Perhaps it is dead.

Meanwhile, yesterday, in El Salvador, all the adults in a tiny village were massacred during the middle of the night. Some fifteen people, brutally tortured and killed, under the pretext of a robbery. The Archbishop has condemned the massacre and accused the military of massacring the farmers. The Bush government has released $1 million a day in military aid to the death-squad government of El Salvador, which now feels free to run a rampage of killing. They've been given the OK sign to go ahead. They got away with the murder of six Jesuit priests; certainly, they figure, they can get away with the murder of poor villagers.

If Mr. Bush is truly concerned about brutalities waged against the people of Kuwait, why is he not equally concerned about the brutalities waged against the people of El Salvador?

How long, O Lord, until justice and peace flourish?

Thursday, January 24, 1991

A long and restless night, thinking of the many things to do, the fighting in the Persian Gulf, God. At dark moments in the middle of the night, I offered a silent prayer, simply put, to be with God, to see God face to face, that my life might be pleasing to God, that I may do God's will, and only God's will all my days. When I woke, the quote from Gandhi's autobiography rang in my mind: "What I want to achieve—what I have been striving and pining to achieve all my life—is self realization, to see God face to face. I live and move and have my being in pursuit of this goal. All that I do by way of speaking and writing, and all my ventures in the political field, are directed to this same end." Amen. All that I am trying to do is to do God's will, to see God face to face, and in the process, to help others do God's will so that they too might see God face to face, and live with God in peace forever.

My days are filled with meetings. Last night, the Committee Against Another Vietnam War in the Middle East, planning the big peace march on Saturday. This morning, the Interfaith Witness for Peace in the Middle East, planning various public religious gatherings and conferences for peace. This afternoon, the Bay Area Religious Peace Action, planning next Thursday's candlelight procession from the Oakland subway station to the Oakland Army Base. Long, arduous, tedious, hopeful. Many ideas, much work, a good spirit, a simple response to the US war with Iraq, which continues ahead like a runaway train. May our effort be God's effort and thus be graced with the peace that bears good fruit.

This morning, Mr. Bush declared, "We will succeed, all the way." One Pentagon general announced that they were "very satisfied" with the first week of war. And so it goes. We try to offer a different spirit, to call for nonviolent alternatives. We are doing what we can, responding as best we can to the crisis before us. That may be all that we can say about ourselves, in the end. As Dan Berrigan has written, we did not succeed in preventing or stopping the war, but we tried.

I rode the crowded subway train to the organizing meeting in San Francisco this morning and all along the way, absorbed in prayer, I imagined myself sitting in a prayer circle, joining hands with the Christ, the God of peace, the peacemakers of history, praying for peace, dwelling in God's peace. A centering prayer that calmed my spirit and set the tone for a peaceful day, come what may.

Sunday, January 27, 1991

Some 200,000 people of every variety, from the labor groups to socialists to the church folks, minority groups, students and grandmothers, marched today through the streets of San Francisco. It began with prayers by Muslim, Christian and Jewish leaders at the Embarcadero Plaza near the Bay Bridge. Very consoling to be with so many people in opposition to this war—people who do not want the United States to be the policeman of the world, people who do not want the United States to achieve new records in carpet bombing, people who want our nation to be peaceful, if that is possible. Joan Baez concluded the day with a song and an invitation to take up the lessons of Gandhi and Dr. King.

Meanwhile, this morning's paper says Iraq has suffered more destruction in the last week than in eight years of war with Iran, a war which left over one million people dead.

Wednesday, January 30, 1991

The forty-third anniversary of the assassination of Mohandas Gandhi. The massive bombing raids continue, along with the outbreak of fighting on the Kuwaiti-Saudi border. There are no reports of the numbers of Iraqis killed, but some refugees tell of US bombs falling on civilians, cities, even buses fleeing the country.

Last night, a small group of Catholics gathered in a San Francisco home to discuss forming a Pax Christi group—an altogether different way of peacemaking than last Saturday. There were only a dozen of us. We prayed and discussed what we were looking for. Everyone wants to gather in community to search out together in a prayerful spirit how they can live in Christ's peace and become more nonviolent. We are all violent, they confessed. Indeed, one gentleman told the story of holding a sign on Saturday's march that read, "Pax Christi: We want peace, not war." When a beggar began to hassle him and his wife, he argued back loudly and almost hit the beggar over the head with the Pax Christi sign! Such is the violence within all of us, especially those of us who want to be peacemakers! And so, they committed themselves to weekly gatherings of prayer and discussion in the hope that together they might become better Christians, a people of nonviolence.

Thursday, January 31, 1991

Tonight, one hundred people of faith gathered at a subway station in Oakland for a prayer service and candlelight procession for peace through the inner city to the Oakland Army Depot, one of the military headquarters for the West Coast. Once again, we begged God for a miracle of peace, and spoke out publicly against the war in the hope that a cease-fire could be negotiated. Along the way, we knelt down at various points to keep centered in the peace we were seeking. Finally, at the main entrance to the Army Depot, we sang "We Shall Overcome," exchanged a sign of peace among ourselves, spoke with the soldiers and police officers, and left our candles along the entranceway as a sign of our desire for peace. Reporters told us it was the first peace demonstration at the depot since the Vietnam war, when thousands of people were arrested for demonstrating against the war.

Sunday, February 3, 1991

George Bush has called for a national day of prayer, and yet he continues to rain a shower of bombs on the people of Iraq. I am disgusted at this hypocrisy, and yet I too turned to God in prayer for peace today. I hope it was a prayer rooted in Jesus' love for one's enemies. I prayed for both George Bush and Saddam Hussein, for all the people of Iraq and the United States engaged in war, for everyone in the Persian Gulf, that the war would end, that peace would become a reality.

It seems to me that Mr. Bush has succeeded in numbing the country. The strict censorship that has been imposed on the media is largely unquestioned so that all special reports have stopped, and life has returned to "normal." Suddenly, people no longer speak out against the war, people have returned to their jobs with a spirit of resignation and the war is pushed out of everyone's mind. In many ways, Mr. Bush has already won the war on the home front. Meanwhile, he has led the most destructive bombing campaign in the history of the world. Iraq has suffered more damage than any time in the history of Mesopotamia. There has been one bombing raid over Iraq every minute since the US invaded Iraq.

The US soldiers who were killed in the bloody battle a few days ago along the Kuwait border, it now turns out, were killed by "friendly fire." They died from shells that came from other US soldiers. The Pentagon's attitude? "These things happen. Look at the plus side: some twenty-six Iraqi tanks were bombed during that same battle, so it was worth it."

Monday, February 4, 1991

The first local funeral, a young Marine, killed in Saudi Arabia last week. Hundreds of Catholic school children were lined up to see the hearse drive up to the church. The priest spoke of the Marine's dedication to his country. He left a young wife and two small children behind.

Oh, the insanity of war and the patriotism which blinds people! My heart breaks for these poor people, caught in a web of lies, yet they do not even know it.

Wednesday, February 6, 1991

This morning I sat down and read the book of Lamentations. How deep is the pain and grief of the poet, writing after the destruction of Jerusalem in 587 B.C. "Look at the ashes! Think of the dead! Why has this happened? Where is God?" Such are the thoughts that race through the author's mind, thoughts of grief and sadness during a time of war. The descriptions tell the story of the current crisis in Iraq: "Dead in the dust of the streets lie young and old; my maidens and young men have fallen by the sword...." (Lam. 2:21) The author confesses a deep desolation, yet even in that dark pit, musters the strength for a prayer of hope: "Even when I cry out for help, God stops my prayer.... My soul is deprived of peace, I have forgotten what happiness is; I tell myself my future is lost, all that I hoped for from the Lord.... But I will call this to mind, as my reason to have hope: The favors of the Lord are not exhausted, God's mercies are not spent; they are renewed each morning, so great is God's faithfulness. My portion is the Lord, says my soul; therefore will I hope in God. Good is the Lord to one who waits for God, to the soul that seeks God. It is good to hope in silence, for the saving help of the Lord.... Let him sit alone and in silence." (Lam. 3:8-9, 17-28)

"I have called upon your name, O Lord," the poet continues, "from the bottom of the pit. You came to my aid when I called to you; you said, 'Have no fear!' "(Lam. 3:55-57) This is my own experience. "The joy of our hearts has ceased, our dance has turned into mourning. Woe to us, for we have sinned! Over this our hearts are sick, at this our eyes grow dim...Lead us back to you, O Lord, that we may be restored: give us anew such days as we had of old." (Lam. 5:15-21)

Tonight, further reports from Iraq that many people have been killed by US bombing raids. Over 150 people are dead from the bombing of one apartment building alone. Every now and then, a glimpse of reality sneaks past the censors—images of blood on the sidewalk, a single shoe, a burning corpse. Oh, how could we do such things? Of course, I oppose Iraq's takeover of Kuwait, but how in the world does that justify killing more people? My soul identifies with the sorrow in the book of Lamentations. I am beside myself with grief and anguish. I turn to God once again for solace, guidance, and mercy. I am lost in grief. In prayer, I imagine Jesus standing on the hill overlooking the beautiful city of Jerusalem, weeping. "If only you had understood on this day the message of peace. But alas, it is hidden from your eyes." (Luke 19:42) And today, Jesus says these same words to us through his heavy tears. He stands overlooking Washington, D.C., and Baghdad, Kuwait City and Tel Aviv, London and San Francisco. If only we had understood the message of peace. Alas, alas.

Friday, February 8, 1991

How can this be happening? How is it that people could be so cruel? How is it that entire nations could be filled with so much hatred for other peoples? How is it that people could approve of bombing raids on schools and mosques? How is it that people could consider using nuclear weapons on other people, as Dan Quayle and Pentagon generals are now hinting? How is it that people call this feast of death patriotism? How is it that people think that God supports this war? How can people continue to go to churches that support the war? Why aren't people taking to the streets by the millions upon millions? Why aren't young people refusing to fight for this corrupt government? When will we ever learn? How long, O God, how long, until justice and peace are truly established on earth as they are in heaven?

Jim Douglass and other religious leaders and peace activists are going to begin a fast in front of the White House and then keep vigil in front of the US Capitol.

Ash Wednesday, February 13, 1991

On Monday, many of us in the religious peace community suddenly received notices to appear in court today. The nonviolent action at the Presidio was canceled and we geared up for our court hearing. This morning, some seventy-five of us gathered in a prayer circle in the plaza in front of San Francisco's Federal Building, where the courtrooms are located. We read from the book of Jonah and then, as we all held hands and stood in silence, someone walked by each of us and put ashes on our foreheads. "Repent from the sin of war and believe the good news of peace," he said to us.

Just as he finished, police officers appeared and began handcuffing people! We were shocked. Some broke off from the circle to avoid arrest while others bowed their hands and awaited arrest. I could not idly stand by and so I approached the police and spoke out in a loud voice, "How can you arrest us? You haven't even given us a warning!" The arresting officer looked very perturbed, even frightened to be arresting church people in the middle of public liturgy. "I was told to arrest everyone," he responded. "But you have to give us a warning first," I implored. "What you are doing is illegal," I said.

With that, he stopped putting handcuffs on my friends and walked off with the other officers to look for a bullhorn. "Let's all go up to the courtroom now," I announced. As we entered the building, we could hear the orders coming over the bullhorn, "You are all under arrest...." Luckily, those who received the plastic handcuffs, were able to take them off easily.

An illegal liturgy! We had prayed for an end to the war and for peace and had repented of our own complicity in our nation's war. We can only conclude that in a nation gripped with war fever that such behavior is subversive! The message we received? Repentance is revolutionary activity; it is treasonous.

Inside the court, we endured the usual litany of legal gibberish from well-meaning lawyers and were subsequently called forth to make our plea before a magistrate. Some forty-three of us pleaded not guilty, and will return for trial before a US District judge. Perhaps we will have the opportunity to put the war on trial. Or perhaps, once they realize that the thousands of demonstrators who have been arrested all want to go to trial, they will drop all the charges to prevent the court system from shutting down.

After the hearing, we heard the heartbreaking news: US bombers deliberately obliterated a shelter in a Baghdad suburb killing some four hundred unarmed people, primarily children and women. The newspapers and television are filled with pictures of weeping husbands, injured women, and dead children holding stuffed animals. The horror of it all. I am so ashamed of my country. Once more, grief and mourning.

Sunday, February 17, 1991

On Friday, Saddam Hussein offered to pull out of Kuwait if the US would force Israel to recognize the Palestinians. The offer was totally rejected and the bombing was stepped up! The White House and the media are preparing us for a bloody ground war and there is more talk about the possible use of nuclear weapons on Baghdad, if the war continues beyond March and April.

Last evening, a long dinner conversation with Jim Flaherty, one of my community members, on the daily struggle to live and witness for peace in a country blinded by arrogance and violence. "God is brokenhearted," he said. "All God can do is love and then love some more, yet this great love is rejected by so many people. Someday, in another life, we will have to face the realities of what we as a nation have done, and repent of our sins."

Tuesday, February 19, 1991

Since January 16, the United States has dropped the equivalent of at least one Hiroshima bomb per week on the Middle East. Friends are continuing to keep vigil and fast in Washington, D.C., for peace in the Persian Gulf. They cite the words of Jesus in the Gospel of Luke, "Unless you repent, you will all likewise perish." (Luke 13:5)

Wednesday, February 20, 1991

On Monday, we had another prayer service in downtown San Francisco followed by a funeral procession through the streets of the city to the Presidio, where some people climbed over a low wall onto the military base to kneel in a prayer for peace. We carried two coffins, one draped with a US flag, the other with Iraq's flag. At the Presidio, several people called upon the scores of Marines who greeted us to consider becoming conscientious objectors and refusing to go to Saudi Arabia to kill or be killed. Along the way, I found myself kneeling with my friends, in a silent prayer for peace, stunned by the beauty of the witness and the continued shock of this war.

The news is bleak. A ground war is imminent. The president has once again refused to accept Gorbachev's peace proposal with Iraq. Mr. Bush wants a ground war. The Iraqis admit that at least 20,000 Iraqis have been killed so far, but the number may be over 200,000 killed so far with over 100,000 more injured.

While President Bush attended a church service in Kennebunkport, Maine, on Sunday, John Schuchardt of the Plowshares Eight stood up and demanded that Mr. Bush stop the murder of Iraqi children. He was hauled out of the church, but continued to speak loudly all the way into the police van. The church service continued and the president ignored the plea. Thank God for John Schuchardt: he defended the name of God by breaking through the blasphemy.

In Amherst, a young college student who had spoken out against the war walked to the town square, poured paint thinner over himself, and set himself on fire. He was dead within minutes. May God have mercy on his troubled soul, and grant us an end to the war now.

Saturday, February 23, 1991

Saddam Hussein has agreed to a Soviet peace plan orchestrated by Mikhail Gorbachev, but George Bush will have none of it. Iraq said that it will withdraw from Kuwait the day after a cease fire begins. In response to this hope for peace, Mr. Bush announced yesterday evening that Iraq must begin an immediate withdrawal by noon today or the ground war would begin by this evening.

Iraq did not withdraw and late this evening word came that the US had begun the ground war. Our immediate shock and sorrow were overwhelming. I thought of the words of Jesus as he knelt in prayer in the garden of Gethsemani, awaiting his own arrest, torture, and execution by the ruling authorities: "My soul is sorrowful unto death." (Matthew 26:37) Who knows how many countless young men and women, especially Iraqis, will die because of this arrogance, greed, and insanity. This war did not have to happen, but our government has insisted upon it. It did not have to start in the first place, and it does not have to continue, but George Bush wants war and the Pentagon needs it to survive. Tonight the news reports that many months ago, the president and the Pentagon generals picked this time and date, 8:00 p.m. Eastern Standard Time, February 23, 1991, as the start of the ground war. Everything had been set in motion these past weeks. The schedule had been set; the war would begin on time. There could be no reason to break from their plans, according to George Bush, not even peace!

We are all shocked and saddened once again. A wave of despair and sorrow has come upon all my friends in the peace movement. I was told the news after a large Eucharistic liturgy for peace this evening, which was presided over by Bishop Antonio Fortich of the Philippines who is visiting and promoting the zones of peace in his war-torn island of Negros. When it was over, as we were leaving, a friend told me the ground war had begun. Her young son is on the front lines, and she is in tears. All I could do was offer her my prayers and support. God have mercy on us all.

Tonight, I sit in prayer imagining myself before the dying, crucified Jesus who is being crucified all over again in those who are being senselessly killed in the Persian Gulf. I look upon Jesus—brutalized, bloodied, his body broken and crushed, the laughing-stock of the military and passersby. My heart is broken as I think of those who will die tonight and in the days to come, and with a spirit of love, I offer this broken heart to the crucified God who can somehow raise us up if we would only choose the Way of nonviolent love.

God have mercy on us all.

Tuesday, February 26, 1991

This morning at 6:30, some one thousand of us gathered in front of San Francisco's Federal Building to protest the continued war and aggression of the United States in the Middle East. It was a mixed bag at best: anger, frustration, and downright hostility by the protesters toward the bewildered—and scared—police officers. But not all was lost: some one hundred people of faith formed a circle of prayer and song that defused the tension and eventually led a procession to the Chevron building, where a service of prayer and repentance was offered. At one or two critical moments, several ministers put themselves between angry protesters and the police officers with their raised billy clubs and transformed a potentially violent, even deadly situation. The religious presence brought a definite peaceful character to an otherwise unpeaceful peace demonstration. One of the bad fruits of this war is the flowering of the violence within all of us—especially those who demonstrate for peace in a spirit of anger. I do not judge or condemn them; I only hope and pray that we can all be transformed into a spirit of nonviolent love, that we can channel our anger and fury into active nonviolent love that will become contagious to the point of transforming the hearts of us all, in our city, our nation and our world. As Jesus our Savior has showed us, nonviolent resistance in a spirit of unconditional love will spark an eternal spirit of love that can live forever and spread throughout the world. Indeed, Jesus is our only hope.

Reports are now coming through that as many as fifty thousand Iraqi troops have surrendered, but one is left to wonder about how many thousands have been killed. Mr. Bush has announced that half the Iraqi army has been immobilized: that means 250,000 human beings, either captured, injured or killed. Last night, Saddam Hussein announced that he is definitely pulling out of Kuwait, but George Bush is furious at this and calls it "an outrage." Apparently, Mr. Bush is determined to kill as many Iraqis as possible; he wants the war to last long. Perhaps, he is mainly concerned about keeping the focus on Iraq instead of our failing economy, the plight of the poor at home, and the staggering domestic problems that face our rotting culture. It is "outrageous" to him that he is not the clear winner, that Saddam Hussein has not come crawling on his knees, that the US has not taken total control of the entire Middle East like some new Alexandrian or Roman empire. The *New York Times* reports that because all water in Baghdad has been cut off, thousands upon thousands of people, primarily children, will soon die from every variety of disease and epidemic, including typhoid, dehydration, and diarrhea. The children are the innocent victims of our greed. They do not have to die, but we kill them to ensure "the new world order," a new US hegemony. Meanwhile, we are having a drought here in California and people are upset because they are being requested not to water their front lawns.

This evening, reports that the US has taken over Kuwait City and that the US continues to bomb and fire upon tens of thousands of Iraqi troops as they flee from Kuwait.

O God, have mercy on us all. Forgive us these sins of war. I repent of this sin of war. I repent for the people of the United States. I repent for the people of Iraq, Kuwait, Israel, and the Middle East. I repent for the human race. O God, forgive us; we know not what we do. In your mercy, in your compassionate love, may the fighting and the killing stop. May we as a people have a change of heart and begin once again the long struggle of disarming our hearts, our nation and our world.

Wednesday, February 27, 1991

Last night, the president declared on national television that Kuwait has been "liberated" and that a cease fire has been declared. This morning, thank God, the fighting and the bombings have stopped. And here in the Bay Area, for the first time in months, a day of rain, an answer to prayers, a blessing for us all. Mr. Bush says

that the "Vietnam War syndrome" is over, that Americans are proud
again of their military and how the bombing campaigns defeated "the
enemy."

One morning newspaper headline declares "Victory!" but it does
not feel like victory to me. Where is the victory in this war? Where is
the glory in this slaughter? Reports are leaking out that thousands and
thousands of Iraqi soldiers were killed in the last two or three days as
they fled Kuwait in their tanks on their way back to Iraq. How can
we repair the damage of this massacre? What good has come from
the killing? Have we really solved anything by murdering over a
hundred thousand people in Kuwait and Iraq? Haven't we only sown
new seeds of violence and division, and ensured a future of violence
and bitterness for decades to come?

This is a day of gratitude; yes, I thank God that the bombing has
ceased. But it is still a day of grief and mourning. I am stunned and
shocked at the devastation which this country has wrought upon the
peoples of the Middle East; I am equally appalled at the euphoria and
blind patriotism that continue to sweep the nation. I think of Camus
and wonder: "I long for the day when I will be able to love my country as well as justice."

One could spend a lifetime pondering the many claims made by
the US, for example, that Kuwait has been "liberated." Biblically
speaking, true liberation, the liberation that not only transforms unjust structures and situations but goes to the spiritual roots of our
problems, only comes through active nonviolence. Instead, we have
enslaved Kuwait to a future of violence, just as we have sown seeds
of violence throughout the Middle East and for future generations of
North Americans.

New world order? What the US has unleashed looks to me like
more of the same old, stale world order—an order of imperial vio-

lence, warfare, lies, aggression, military intervention, betrayal, affliction of the poor at home and abroad, domination, racism and sexism, bombing campaigns, and more. The only thing new about this new world at war is the technology that enables the killing to take place faster and more decisively. We are better at killing than any nation in the history of the world. Indeed. But is this something to take pride in? Is mass murder a cause for rejoicing? Is the killing of anyone a cause for celebration?

This is a time of repentance and prayer, a time for regrouping in the faith-based peace movement, a time to form new base communities of nonviolent resistance. We have a long road ahead, a long nonviolent struggle—to fight the war on war, through prayer, fasting, community building, and active nonviolence. These are apocalyptic times we live in here in the United States. We are setting out on a new journey, a journey of nonviolent resistance from within the empire. We have to start all over again, proclaiming the good news of Christ's way of nonviolence, peacemaking, justice for the poor, community, and steadfast resistance to evil, rooted in unconditional love. Perhaps those of us in the faith-based peace movement are about to learn what the people of Latin America learned in the early decades of this century: that the struggle would last a lifetime, and that the only way to persevere in this nonviolent struggle for justice and peace is through the formation of active base communities and a spirituality of hope and forgiveness that does not allow us to be eaten up by anger and bitterness. As we have grown in solidarity with the people of Central America, they have showed us just how real and grace-filled that spirituality is—a spirituality that is manifested in the midst of brutal warfare and poverty. Perhaps the providence of God has introduced their spirit to us knowing that we too will now need to begin a lifelong, century-long undertaking of nonviolent resistance to the evil we face in our own government and military, at home and abroad.

We are spiritually dead as a nation, as Dr. King predicted, and it is too soon to tell if we can be revived. If the truth of our country's motivations was not clear many years ago, if the scales did not fall from our eyes during the Vietnam horror, then they have now—or they might never. We face a *kairos* moment, a moment of testing, when the very claims of our faith are at stake. Once and for all, we will have to decide if we believe in the God of peace, if we are going to be followers of the Nonviolent One.

No matter what the politicians and the generals say, I still claim adherence to the nonviolent Christ and his way of peacemaking, and I know many others do as well. I still agree with Pope Paul VI's plea to the United Nations in 1965: "No more war, war never again!" I concur with the words of Pope John Paul II at Coventry in 1982: "Today the scale and horror of modern warfare—whether nuclear or not—makes it totally unacceptable as a means of settling differences between nations. War should belong to the tragic past, to history; it should find no place on humanity's agenda for the future." May the churches heed these calls for peace, stand up and be counted as peacemakers, and resist all wars and injustices in our world from now on. In that nonviolent love, may we be a true sign of hope in a despairing age.

Meanwhile, I imagine Jesus this day—dead on the cross, his body, covered with blood, being lowered from the cross, the nails in his hands and feet being removed, the crown of thorns being carefully taken off his head, his body being carried away to an empty tomb. The bodies of over a hundred thousand Iraqis lie shattered in Kuwait City or on the highways going into Iraq. The dead are left in their tombs: bombed out tanks, destroyed trenches, blown up trucks.

I look in faith to the tomb of Jesus in hopeful expectation that his way of peace, as the poet Gerard Manley Hopkins wrote, will Easter in us. May we all look to that empty tomb and learn to banish every trace of war from our hearts as we hear anew the greeting of the Risen One: "Peace be with you."

Acknowledgments

Grateful acknowledgment is made to the following publications for permission to use previously published material:

"The Legacy of Horace McKenna," *America* (February 25, 1989); "Sheltering the Homeless," *New Oxford Review* (December 1989); "Christ Is with the Homeless," *Pax Christi* (Summer, 1989); "Putting the Gospel into Action," *Slow Miracles* (Fall, 1988); "Making Peace with the Homeless," *Slow Miracles* (Winter, 1989); "Stories from the Street," *Slow Miracles* (Spring, 1989); "Mondays at the Pentagon," *The Arlington Courier* (May 1989); "Disarming the Arms Bazaar," *Fellowship* (December 1988); "Our Kairos Moment is Now," *Desert Voices* (Winter, 1989-1990); "The Death and Life of Rutilio Grande," *The Catholic Worker* (March 1988); "Salvadoran Refugees Return Home Despite Great Risk," *The Catholic Worker* (October-November 1988); "Gethsemani Journal," *The Critic* (June 1990); "Salvadoran Martyrs, Raised, Carry On," *The National Catholic Reporter* (November 16, 1990); "Seventy Times Seven," *Sojourners* (August 1988); "The Joy of Peacemaking," *Pax Christi* (Spring, 1990); "Negros Islanders Thwart War with 'Zones of Peace,' " *The Catholic Voice* (July 30, 1990); "Silencing an Aquino Critic," *Christianity and Crisis* (September 10, 1990); "What Will It Take to Free the Philippines from U.S. Bases?" *Fellowship* (January-February 1991); "Thou Shalt Not Disable," *Harmony* (September-October 1990); "The Time Has Come to Begin the Journey of Loving Our Enemies," *The Oakland Tribune,* February 16, 1991; "Loving Our Enemies," *Harmony* (March 1991); "The Long Haul Keeps Looking Longer," *Fellowship* (December 1991).

Special thanks to Susan MacMurdy for her beautiful artwork on the cover, and to Bishop Thomas Gumbleton for his gracious foreword.